The Nature
of the
Early Ottoman State

SUNY series in the
Social and Economic History of the Middle East

Donald Quataert, editor

The Nature
of the
Early Ottoman State

HEATH W. LOWRY

STATE UNIVERSITY OF NEW YORK PRESS

Published by
State University of New York Press, Albany

For information, contact State University of New York Press, Albany, NY
www.sunypress.edu

Production by Kelli Williams
Marketing by Michael Campochiaro

Library of Congress Cataloging-in-Publication Data

Lowry, Heath W., 1942–
    The nature of the early Ottoman state / Heath W. Lowry.
        p. cm. — (SUNY series in the social and economic history of the Middle East)
    Includes bibliographical references and index.
    ISBN 0-7914-5635-8 (alk. paper) — ISBN 0-7914-5636-6 (pbk. : alk. paper)
        1. Turkey—Civilization. 2. Turkey—Social conditions. 3. Turkey—History. I. Title. II.
Series.

    DR432 .L69 2003
    956'.015—dc21
                                                                                    2002042648

10 9 8 7 6 5 4 3 2 1

Contents

List of Illustrations   vii

Acknowledgments   ix

Introduction   1

1   The Debate to Date   5

2   Wittek Revisited: His Utilization of
    Ahmedi's *İskendernâme*   15

3   Wittek Revisited: His Utilization of the 1337
    Bursa Inscription   33

4   What Could the Terms *Gaza* and *Gazi* Have Meant to the
    Early Ottomans?   45

5   Toward A New Explanation   55

6   Christian Peasant Life in the Fifteenth-Century
    Ottoman Empire   95

7   The Last Phase of Ottoman Syncretism—The Subsumption
    of Members of the Byzanto-Balkan Aristocracy into the
    Ottoman Ruling Elite   115

8   The Nature of the Early Ottoman State   131

Appendix 1   145

Appendix 2   147

Appendix 3   153

Appendix 4   155

Notes   159

Bibliography   177

Index   191

List of Illustrations

PLATES

PLATE 1   Orhan *Gazi*'s 1337 Inscription on Bursa's Şehadet Mosque   36

PLATE 2   Bayezid II's 1484 Summoning of the *Gazis* for His Moldavian Campaign   49

PLATE 3   1472 Order by Mehmed II for the Conscription of *Akıncıs*   53

PLATE 4   The 1417 Tombstone of *Gazi* Evrenos in Yenice Vardar   61

PLATE 5   1391 Imperial Order *(biti)* on Behalf of Mihalogli 'Ali Beg Issued by Bayezid I   62

PLATE 6   The 1324 Mekece *Vakfiye* of Orhan *Gazi*   75

PLATE 7   Titles Accorded Orhan *Gazi* in His 1360 İznik *Vakfiye*   84

PLATE 8   Titles Accorded Süleyman *Gazi* in Orhan *Gazi*'s 1360 İznik *Vakfiye*   85

PLATE 9   Titles Accorded Murad I in His 1365 Bursa *Vakfiye*   87

PLATE 10   List of Witnesses Signatory to Murad I's 1365 *Vakfiye*   88

TABLE

TABLE 7.1   Ottoman *Vezir-i A'zams* (Grand Vezirs), 1453–1516   120

Acknowledgments

In the course of its preparation this book has benefited from the input of a wide variety of colleagues, students, and friends. While thanking them all, I absolve each one from any responsibility for the final product; any shortcomings are mine and mine alone. At Princeton, my colleagues Michael Cook and Norman Itzkowitz read and commented on earlier drafts; while Hossein Modarressi and Negin Nabavi assisted with the reading, reconstruction, and translation of Orhan *Gazi*'s 1337 Mekece Endowment. Two of my students, Baki Tezcan and Nenad Filipovic also made useful suggestions.

Friends who read and commented on earlier drafts include Rifa'at 'Ali Abou El-Haj, Giles Constable, Oktay Ozel, Donald Quataert, and Kemal Silay. In particular, I received a number of valuable suggestions from two former teachers, Andreas Tietze and Halil İnalcık, both of whom were unstinting with their time and encyclopedic knowledge of all things Ottoman.

I take pleasure in acknowledging my appreciation to audiences at Columbia University, Indiana University, the Bosphorus University, and Bilkent University, who after listening to various segments of this work, forced me to rethink and reshape my approach with their often penetrating questions and comments.

Finally, as with any book, the author's family share in each and every stage of its development. My wife Demet, and more recently our granddaughter Alize, have inspired me by their support and love.

Introduction

With the appearance in 1995 of Cemal Kafadar's *Between Two Worlds: The Construction of the Ottoman State*,[1] the debate which has waxed on and off since the publication in 1938 of the late Paul Wittek's *Rise of the Ottoman Empire*,[2] was reignited. At issue is the pivotal question of what were the factors which led to the birth, growth, and ultimate transformation of the Ottoman *Beylik* (Principality) into the Ottoman Empire (ca. 1299–1923). What role, if any, did Islam play in the cultural or civilizational roots of the first Ottoman rulers and those who joined them? Or, stated differently, how did the early Ottomans manage to attract people to their banner? What was the role of local Bithynian Christians in the formation of the Ottoman polity? Did those who joined their cause do so by virtue of being conquered, or, alternatively, did they rather see themselves as joining a new movement? In short, given the dearth of contemporary fourteenth-century sources with which to assess these queries, is there any way in which we can project later accounts back in time in a justifiable manner?

Paul Wittek's response to these and related questions was the advancement of the "*Gazi* Thesis," an explanation which, in its simplest form, set forth the concept that the motivating explanatory force accounting for the fact that the Ottomans (alone of numerous contemporary Muslim Principalities in Anatolia), were ultimately able to build a powerful empire was religion. *Islam* was the magnet by which they attracted ever-increasing numbers to their war machine. Their primary goal in the formative period was the "*gaza,*" or Holy War. In his words, they were "a community of *Ghazis*, of champions of the Mohammeden religion, a community of Moslem march-warriors, devoted to the struggle with the infidels in their neighborhood."[3]

In several subsequent works, most particularly in two lectures he delivered at the Sorbonne in March 1938, which were published later in the same year as: "De la défaite d'Ankara à la prise de Constantinople," Wittek continued to stress the theme that the *gaza*, or Holy War, was the essential ingredient, even the raison d'être of the Ottoman state in the fourteenth century.[4]

Almost all Western students of Ottoman history have come of age with Wittek's "*Gazi* Thesis," and, if the corpus of debunking works produced in the past generation is any indication, many of my contemporaries (myself included) are troubled by the impact his *Rise of the Ottoman Empire* has had, and continues to have, in the still fledgling field of Ottoman studies. Somewhat paradoxically, Wittek's reputation and impact stem primarily from this work, which in style and content is atypical of his real contributions to the field. His forte was as a master philologist and yet, the work in question for which he is best remembered, is one in which he moved away from his strength of philological analysis into a broader and more speculative genre of historical synthesis and reinterpretation.

At the outset let me say that a survey of this growing corpus of responses to Wittek's *Rise of the Ottoman Empire* clearly shows that while most scholars are uncomfortable with his basic premise, no one has successfully managed to advance a viable alternative. This may well stem from the fact that most respondents have approached the problem within the parameters established by Wittek. To wit, they have implicitly accepted that Islam was indeed a key factor in explaining Ottoman growth. As the present study will attempt to illustrate, it is only by approaching the problem prospectively rather than retrospectively, that is, by ferreting out the earliest surviving contemporary fourteenth- and fifteenth-century sources and basing our understanding upon them, that we may possibly begin to shape the parameters of a new understanding of the formative stage of Ottoman growth.

In the opening pages of the present study, I have set myself the task of briefly reviewing the earlier stages of the debate, and then of addressing the only two pieces of evidence actually presented by Wittek in support of his argument that the Ottomans originated as a state whose motivating impetus was the *"Gaza,"* that is, to the expansion of Islam at the expense of their Christian neighbors. Namely, the Turkish text of a work by the early-fifteenth-century poet Ahmedi and a dated stone inscription from 1337, which is preserved in the first Ottoman capital, the city of Bursa. This is not a new approach. Indeed, a Greek scholar, the late George Arnakis questioned in a 1947 book Wittek's exclusive reliance on these two sources,[5] as did the late Ronald C. Jennings, in his "Some Thoughts on the *Gazi* Thesis."[6] Neither Arnakis nor Jennings (nor for that matter any of the other scholars who have addressed this subject) actually presented an analysis of what is problematic with Wittek's utilization of both the "epic" and the "inscription." Via a new contextual reading, the present study will attempt to show that both Wittek's utilization of these sources and the underlying assumptions with which he approached them were badly flawed.

Then, by focusing on the known surviving fourteenth-century Ottoman sources, and specifically upon those relating to one of the first important steps in the early history of the Ottomans, namely, the conquest of the city of Bursa in 1326, and its subsequent history in the first century of Ottoman rule (based on travelers' accounts, extant fourteenth- and fifteenth-century Ottoman documents, inscriptions, and Byzantine and early Ottoman chronicles), I will advance a new hypothesis to shed additional light on some of the factors which may help explain the emergence of this state.

Utilizing two case studies: a) an analysis of Christian peasant life in the fifteenth century; and, b) an examination of the manner in which members of the preexisting Byzantine and Balkan nobilities were subsumed into the Ottoman administrative apparatus, I will argue that we must replace the religious motivations advanced by Wittek with one which focuses on the interactive symbiotic, or syncretic nature of the early Ottomans. That is, one which highlights their role as a predatory confederacy open to all rather than as an Islamic-based one.

Finally, I will advance an alternative explanation to account for the origins and growth of the Ottoman polity during the first two hundred years of its existence.

ONE

The Debate to Date

Before embarking on such an analysis, it may be useful to review briefly the nature of the debate which preceded that sparked by Wittek and his thesis. For Wittek himself was not living in a vacuum, but rather responding to a still earlier debate which predated his own "*Gazi* Thesis" by some twenty years. The steps in this earlier discussion may be summarized as follows:

In 1916, with the publication of Herbert Gibbons' *The Foundation of the Ottoman Empire*, the first stone was cast. Gibbons set out (without benefit of a knowledge of Ottoman Turkish), to show that the Ottomans were in fact a new "race," one formed by the commingling of Greek and Balkan Slavic converts to Islam, together with Turkish peoples.[1] In the ensuing admixture the Christian element was by far the most important. He accounted for Ottoman growth by arguing that the formation of this new "race" ensured the continuity of Byzantine administrative practices under an Islamic guise. That is, since the Ottomans were in fact the inheritors of Byzantine traditions and administrative practices, they remained (until the conquest of the Arab world at the beginning of the sixteenth century) a kind of Islamic-Byzantine admixture. Implicit in his interpretation was his belief that the mighty Ottoman Empire could not have emerged from purely Turco-Muslim roots, hence its Byzantine-Christian origins. Further, he stressed that it was the religion of Islam which served to cement the new amalgam thus formed. Finally, he argued that in attempting to look at the reasons for Ottoman success one should first focus on the fact that they benefited from a variety of peripheral factors, such as Byzantine dynastic struggles, which led to frequent internecine wars. In short, they were bound to succeed because they were both a superior racial admixture blending "wild Asiatic blood" with "European stock," and, administratively, the lineal descendants of Byzantium.[2]

Within a few years of its publication, Gibbons' work drew both an indirect and a direct critique from two Ottomanists. First in 1922, the Turkish scholar M. Fuat Köprülü, authored a long study in which he rejected that portion of Gibbons' reasoning, positing a Byzantine origin for the Ottomans administrative apparatus.[3] In this work, which was actually addressing an earlier article by the German Ottomanist Franz Babinger,[4] he successfully demonstrated the extent to which early Ottoman institutional roots derived from Seljuk and Ilhanid precedents.[5] In so doing, he strongly rejected the idea that the Ottomans were not equipped culturally to create a state. Then, two years later, in 1924, the German scholar Friedrich Giese, in an important article responding to Gibbons' analysis of the origins of the Ottoman state, stressed the bridge role played by the *Akhi* federation of craftsmen and merchants in the towns of Anatolia in transferring the administrative infrastructure of earlier Anatolian Muslims states to the emerging Ottoman entity.[6]

Despite these reservations, many Western specialists in the next generation continued to accept the basic thrust of Gibbons' argument, namely, that the Ottoman state was formed by an amalgam of peoples which included a significant number of local western-Anatolian and Balkan-Christian converts to Islam. Specifically, prior to Paul Wittek, W. L. Langer and R. P. Blake, in a seminal 1932 essay, focused attention on the heterodox nature of Islam practiced by the Turks in Anatolia and argued that this helped to explain the ease with which Byzantine Christians converted. They also contributed the important observation that it was the geographical position of the Ottomans, namely, their location on the weakened Byzantine frontier, which helped account for their rapid expansion. They did however reject Gibbons' view that the administrative structure of the Ottomans was fully inherited from Byzantium, and argued persuasively (*à la* Giese) that the infrastructure provided by the *Akhi* federations in the towns of Anatolia provided the underpinnings of early Ottoman administrative practice, as well as serving as a "bridge" to bring the Bithynian peoples together.[7]

In 1934, Köprülü went one step further and, in a series of lectures delivered at the Sorbonne, advanced the thesis that the Ottoman state was purely Turkish in nature, that is, he responded to and categorically rejected Gibbons' argument that it was formed from a commingling of Byzantine, Slavic, and Turkish peoples; he averred that it was derived from an amalgamation of various Turkish groups (tribes) that lived in Anatolia. These groups were the inheritors of an administrative tradition which passed to them from Seljuk and Ilhanid roots.[8] Here, once again, he rejected Gibbon's premise that the early Ottomans were unequipped to create a state without the institutional framework inherited from the Byzantines.

This first phase of the debate culminated with the series of lectures given by Paul Wittek in London in May 1937, where he laid forth what has come to be known as the "*Gazi* Thesis," to wit, the idea that the early Ottomans were not a tribe, or people linked genealogically, but were rather groups of Anatolian Muslims bound by a common desire to fight the Christian infidels. They were, in his words, motivated by the "*ghazi ethos,*" which meant that they were "a community of *Ghazis,* of champions of the Mohammedan religion; a community of Moslem march-warriors, devoted to the struggle with the infidels in their neighborhood."[9] He saw their roots as emerging from the late Seljuk period, at which time the *gazi* frontier guards had grown in strength and ultimately produced a society of their own (the Ottomans) which grew in influence and in turn finally came to dominate the former Byzantine and Seljuk Frontier territories.

In one generation the explanation for the question of the identity of the early Ottomans had been transformed from one which styled them as an admixture of Islamicized Byzantines and Turks (Gibbons); to Turks who attracted a large number of Byzantine converts to their banner due primarily to the heterodox form of Islam they practiced (Langer/Blake); to an amalgam of Turkish tribes and groups whose administrative skills were inherited from earlier Turkish states in Anatolia, the Seljuks, and the Ilhanids (Köprülü); and finally, to a group of dedicated Muslim *gazis* who came together for the express purpose of fighting and converting the Christian infidels in the border marches of northwest Anatolia (Wittek).

It was this last explanation, the "*Gazi* Thesis" advanced by Wittek which came to dominate the thinking of Western scholars (it was generally ignored or rejected in Turkey) for the next forty years. Indeed, the *doyen* of Ottoman studies in this generation, Halil İnalcık, is the sole Turkish historian to accept and incorporate fully (albeit with one important difference) the Wittek thesis in his works. While accepting that the small frontier principality of Osman *Gazi* was "dedicated to a Holy War against Christian Byzantium,"[10] and wholeheartedly embracing Wittek's thesis that the "*gaza,*" or Holy War "was an important factor in the foundation and development of the Ottoman state,"[11] he has, like Köprülü and unlike Wittek, on occasion, also emphasized the tribal origins of the Ottomans.[12]

Somewhat paradoxically, while on one hand denouncing Gibbons' theory as "groundless speculation," İnalcık seemingly adopted its underlying argument in 1973, when he stressed (as had Wittek) that a common background tied together the Byzantine frontier troops with the Muslim *gazis* and that this led to assimilation. All this in turn shaped what he described as:

> a true "Frontier Empire," a cosmopolitan state, treating all creeds and races as one, which was to unite the Orthodox Christian Balkans and Muslim Anatolia in a single state.[13]

İnalcık leaves unanswered one key question: What were the factors in the early fourteenth century (prior to the advance into the Balkans) which had served to unite the Bithynian Christians and Muslims into a single state? While citing the role played by one Byzantine Greek, *Köse* Mihal, who joins forces with the Ottoman rulers Osman and Orhan "as a famous example of the process of assimilation,"[14] he states that this *Köse* (beardless) Mihal was a *"Gazi"* and "a Greek frontier lord who accepted Islam."[15] I have encountered no source which alleges that Mihal was a Muslim prior to the closing years of the reign of Osman (1299–1324).[16] Less clear are the reasons behind İnalcık's insistence on making *Köse* Mihal a Muslim, when in fact he mentions him in support of his contention that the Ottomans in this period were a "Frontier Empire," marked by its treatment of "all creeds and races as one." The key point here is that *Köse* Mihal was a *gazi* while still formally a Christian. Only when İnalcık posits that "Holy War and colonization were the dynamic elements in the Ottoman conquests," and that the administrative forms adopted in the newly conquered territories derived from earlier Seljuk (Turco-Islamic) models,[17] does he totally reject that aspect of Gibbons' work which argues for the non-Turkish nature of the Ottoman's institutional base.

In 1982, İnalcık published an article specifically addressing the "Question of the Emergence of the Ottoman State."[18] While stressing the importance of the migration of large numbers of Turcoman tribes into Anatolia, he also highlights the importance of a Holy War ideology as the unifying factor which prompted these *"ghazi* mercenary bands" to conquer and enslave the indigenous population.[19] In one sense, İnalcık's article may be viewed as an attempt to reconcile Köprülü's emphasis on the tribal origins of the Ottomans with Wittek's *gazi* thesis.

In a more recent general work, his important contribution to the 1994 volume he coedited with Donald Quataert: *An Economic and Social History of the Ottoman Empire, 1300–1914,* İnalcık is seemingly arguing more strongly for the *gazi* character of the early Ottoman state. His earlier depiction of the Ottomans as "a cosmopolitan state, treating all creeds and races as one," is watered down. In its place:

> The Ottoman state came into existence around 1300 as a small
> frontier principality which devoted itself to the *gaza*, Holy War, on the
> frontiers of the Seljukid Sultanate in Asia Minor and of the Byzantine
> Empire. Its initial *gazi* frontier character influenced the state's histori-
> cal existence for six centuries.[20]

İnalcık here has further modified Wittek's *Gazi* Thesis by emphasizing (in keeping with Köprülü) the basic Turkish origins of the state while
fully endorsing the premise that it was the *gaza* which provided the raison d'être for Ottoman growth and expansion. In 1994 (as in 1973) he
is still equating the *gaza* with Holy War, rather than as a term whose primary meaning was raiding and pillaging, that is, he is providing a clear
religious connotation for a term which may well have had a far more
secular meaning in the early fourteenth century. In so doing, he is de-
emphasizing the interactive symbiosis which typified the early
Ottomans. If, as we shall see, the early Ottoman forces included Christians (e.g., *Köse* Mihal) in their numbers, we are faced with the possibility that any reference to *gaza* and *gazis* in contemporary sources may
indeed reflect the literary meaning of these terms rather than the social-
cultural reality which actually existed in the formative years of the
Ottoman state. Alternatively, as will be highlighted in the ensuing analysis of Ahmedi's work, the *gaza* ethos may be a retrospective reading projected backwards in time for political and dynastic reasons.

With three exceptions the debate to date has been engaged in primarily by Ottomanists/Turcologists. However, the earliest book length critique
of the Wittek-Köprülü responses to Gibbons appeared in the aforementioned 1947 study by the Greek scholar, George Arnakis. This work, *Hoi
protoi othomanoi* has been largely ignored in the subsequent debate (modern Greek is a language not generally accessible to Ottomanists). However,
Arnakis touched on the major weaknesses of the Wittek thesis by emphasizing that the connotation of the title *gazi* in that context did not mean
that the early Ottomans were motivated by the goal of converting the
Bithynian Christians, but rather by amassing plunder, slaves, and booty.
He argued persuasively that in the conquest of Bithynia, which stretched
over half a century, there simply was no manifestation of Islamic fanati-
cism. To the contrary, he pointed out that the Ottomans initially encountered a peasantry which had been abused by their Byzantine rulers with a
resultant loss of morale. He stressed the lenient attitude of the Ottomans
which facilitated widespread conversion and subsequent assimilation.
Ultimately, Arnakis highlighted the fact that the physical growth and success of the early Ottoman state can be directly linked to its absorption of
the indigenous Greek population of Bithynia.[21]

The second such work (written by a non-Ottomanist), was a book devoted to the first two hundred years of Ottoman history by the East-German Marxist medievalist, Ernst Werner. Titled *Die Geburt Einer Grossmacht-Die Osmanen (1300–1481)*, it first appeared in 1966 (and was subsequently republished with significant revisions in 1972 and again in 1985 with yet further changes). Werner's work includes a pioneering critique of modern Turkish historiography, in which he highlights its chauvinistic tendencies. This book (in its various redactions), which has had almost no impact upon the thinking of later scholars, is limited by the author's adherence to a very rigid Marxist-Leninist interpretation of early Ottoman history.[22]

The third exception is the American Byzantinist, Speros Vryonis Jr., who in his landmark 1971 opus entitled: *The Decline of Medieval Hellenism in Asia Minor and the Process of Islamization from the Eleventh through the Fifteenth Century*, set out to synthesize a variety of Byzantine and Turco-Islamic cultural traditions. He underlined the fact that by the time of the emergence of the Ottomans, the process of Islamization followed by Turkification had been in progress in Anatolia for over two hundred years. Vryonis argued further that the seminomadic Turkish steppe life was ideally suited to the *gaza* (meaning, raiding), and that it was this fact rather than any particular zeal for Islam which motivated the early Ottoman conquests.[23]

In the course of the past two decades, a number of other scholars have joined the debate and addressed the *Gazi* Thesis. Among the works in this genre (discussed in order of appearance) are:

The 1979 article of the Hungarian Turcologist Gyula Kaldy-Nagy, who in essence argues that as the Ottomans in the first centuries were only nominally or "superficially" Muslims, neither their early conquests nor their growth can be seen as springing from a *gaza* ethos. Stated differently, for Kaldy-Nagy there simply was no struggle between Christianity and Islam in the early Ottoman period.[24]

In a 1983 book, the American Ottomanist Rudi Lindner argued (using the tools and methodology of the cultural anthropologist) for the tribal, that is, inclusive, nature of the early Ottoman state. It should be noted that his wholesale adoption of the vocabulary of the anthropologists was not supported by a full exploration of the hard data on the Ottoman side of the equation. His critique of Wittek stressed a few examples of Christians who actually participated in the Ottoman conquests. Most tellingly he argued that later chroniclers, who depicted the early Ottomans as having been motivated by the *gaza* ethos, were in reality projecting their own contemporary views back in time.[25]

In 1984, Pal Fodor, a Hungarian Turcologist, opened a fresh pa;
the debate with an important article in which he convincingly demonstrated that the ideas of *gaza* and *gazi* in the work of Ahmedi (Wittek's
most important source), were a literary device, whereby "Ahmedi pre-
sents the Ottoman rulers as *gazis* in a manner that served well-definable
political objectives."[26] Fodor's article is in many ways the most original
contribution to the renewed debate on Ottoman origins, for it textually
challenges one of the pieces of evidence put forth by Wittek in support
of his thesis.[27]

In a 1986 article, the late American Ottomanist Ronald C. Jennings
became the next scholar (following Arnakis and Fodor) specifically to
criticize Wittek's selection of passages from the early-fifteenth-century
epic poem by Ahmedi and the 1337 dedicatory inscription on a mosque
Bursa. In so doing, he stressed that as the conquest of the Balkans was
clearly the result of a shared endeavor by both Muslim and Christian
Ottoman commanders and forces, Wittek's insistence on the *gaza* ethos
simply didn't work.[28]

The English Turcologist Colin Heywood (himself a former Wittek
student), in two insightful articles published in 1988 and 1989 respectively, approached Wittek as a demon who must be exorcised (or rather,
explained as a piece of cultural history), and correctly suggested that the
notion of a *gazi* hero as some kind of idealized figure tells us a lot more
about Wittek's upbringing and education in the late Hapsburg capital
Vienna, than it does about early Ottoman history.[29]

A second English Turcologist, Colin Imber, in a series of three articles
published in 1986, 1987, and 1993 respectively, argued that the fourteenth
century is basically a "black hole" which should be accepted as such, that
is, that we simply do not have a sufficient number of contemporary sources
to allow us to recreate that era of Ottoman history. Further, he argued that
scholars who attempt to reconstruct the history of this period are doing
exactly what their predecessors the sixteenth- and seventeenth-century
Ottoman chroniclers did. Namely, they are projecting the contemporary
views and concerns of their own period backwards in time.[30]

In 1993, the Turkish philologist, Şinasi Tekin, published two articles
in which he tried (unsuccessfully, as will be demonstrated later in this
study), to show that the 1337 Bursa inscription (the second key piece of
evidence for Wittek's thesis), was in fact a late-nineteenth century
forgery. He argued (correctly) that the inscription's current location on
a gateway of the Şehadet Mosque could not have been its original provenance. However, his attempts to argue (on the basis of script and language) that the inscription itself should be dated to the late nineteenth
century are unconvincing.[31]

In 1995, responding to Lindner, Jennings, Imber, and Tekin, the İstanbul University Ottomanist, Feridun Emecen, thoughtfully examined fourteenth-century Anatolian sources dealing with *gaza* and *gazis,* and provided an insightful critique of both Tekin and others of the abovementioned works produced by Western scholars in the 1980s. He highlighted the extent to which the title of *gazi* and the concept of *gaza* appear in a wide variety of texts and inscriptions which have survived from other Anatolian Turkish states in the fourteenth and fifteenth century, and therefore argued against the uniqueness of the appearance of these terms in Ottoman usage.[32]

The most important recent book length study attempting to reexamine the emergence and growth of the Ottomans, is Cemal Kafadar's 1995 work: *Between Two Worlds: The Construction of the Ottoman State.* Kafadar, a Turkish born and North American trained Ottomanist, tries to look at the fourteenth-century *gazis* as just one element in the patchwork of groups identifiable in Anatolia at that period. Were Kafadar to define what he feels the most salient aspect of early Ottoman frontier culture to have been, he would likely use the expression: "liquidity and fluidity of culture."[33] His view of Islam and Christianity alike emphasizes the "inclusivism" of these two dominant cultures.[34] In the harshest criticism yet bestowed on Kafadar's book, the English scholar Imber dismisses it as a

> defence of Wittek's famous "*gazi*-thesis," or more precisely, a defence of İnalcık's modification of the "*gazi*-thesis" to accommodate it to the traditional view of the tribal origins of the Ottomans.[35]

Imber, whose criticism of this work reflects as much a defense of his own revisionist "black hole theory" as it does a critique of Kafadar,[36] seems to be right on one basic point: Kafadar has not succeeded in advancing the overall debate beyond the point at which İnalcık in 1982 made the accommodation between Wittek's "*Gazi* Thesis" and Köprülü's insistence on the basic Turkish tribal origins of the Ottomans.[37] This fact does not negate the real value of the study, which stems from its bringing together in a new form a great deal of useful information and some interesting new insights on the period it addresses.

Since the appearance of Kafadar's study, two additional works by nonspecialists on the origins of the Ottomans have also appeared. First, a Greek scholar, Dimitri Kitsikis, argues (without benefit of reference to a single one of the aforecited works) that the Ottoman Empire was in reality a "Turkish-Greek Empire."[38] Second, Turkish social scientist, Sencer Divitçioğlu, while fully citing both the published texts and the extant secondary literature, discusses the founding of the Ottoman Principality in a theoretical framework and in a vocabulary which are largely unintelligible to the specialist (or any other reader for that matter).[39]

In short, half a century of scholarly attention has not succeeded in replacing Wittek's "*Gazi* Thesis," with a more convincing and nuanced explanation for the emergence and expansion of the Ottoman dynasty. While there has been, and continues to be, a great deal of nipping at his heels, his work remains at the center of the debate.

Indeed, as we enter the twenty-first century, *The Rise of the Ottoman Empire* (which was in print from 1938–1970), is about to reappear in an edition prepared by the English Turcologist Colin Heywood. This will ensure that the next generation of students are likewise exposed to its *Gazi* Thesis.

TWO

Wittek Revisited

His Utilization of
Ahmedi's İskendernâme

In the ensuing pages, we will reexamine the sources advanced by Wittek in support of his thesis, in an attempt to determine whether or not the emphasis he placed on religious zeal as a primary factor in Ottoman growth was justified. As noted earlier, there are basically two sources cited by Wittek to prove that the early Ottoman rulers viewed themselves as *Gazis,* meaning Holy Warriors. First, and by far most important, is his utilization of the early-fifteenth-century epic verse poem, the *İskendernâme* written by Tacüddin İbrahim bin Hidr, better known by his pen name Ahmedi. More specifically, Wittek cites the appendix to this work which Ahmedi titled: *Destân-i Tevârîh-i Mülûk-i âl-i 'Osmân* (The Epic Chronicles of the Ottoman Rulers), a postscript of 334 couplets appended to his *mesnevi* (poem in rhymed couplets),[1] as proof for his *Gazi* Thesis.

At the outset it should be noted that Wittek's utilization of Ahmedi's work was highly selective. A careful reading uncovers the fact that he confined himself to citing passages from the introductory section, that is, to only thirteen of the three hundred thirty-four couplets (less than 4 percent of the actual text devoted to the early Ottoman rulers). Specifically, the references he makes to Ahmedi are taken only from *beyts* (couplets) 14–20 and 25–30.[2] As will be demonstrated in the following pages, had he made use of the entire three hundred thirty-four couplets devoted to the dynasty, it is unlikely that he would have come to the conclusions set forth in his London lectures and subsequent book.

Moreover, even Wittek's interpretation of the passages he extracted from Ahmedi seems to be contradicted by the full text of his source, which (as the ensuing discussion will illustrate) in no way supports the view that the early Ottomans saw themselves as servants of God whose role was to purify the Earth from the filth of polytheism. Ahmedi, as we shall see, was not writing history. On the contrary, he was writing a "mirror for princes" type work designed to serve as a model for his intended patrons, who were initially the Ottoman ruler Bayezid (1389–1402), and, following his death, his son Süleyman Çelebi (d. 1411).[3] As for his description of Ottoman origins, it was written well over a century after the events he describes.

Wittek sets forth his understanding of Ahmedi's aims in the following passage:

> The chapter which Aḥmedī devotes in his *Iskender-nāme* to the history of the Ottoman sultans, the ancestors of his protector Sulayman Tshelebi, son of Bayezid, begins with an introduction in which the poet solemnly declares his intention of writing a *Ghazawāt-nāme*, a book about the Holy war of the *Ghāzīs*. He poses the question: "Why have the *Ghāzīs* appeared at the last?" And he answers: "Because the best always comes at the end. Just as the definitive prophet Mohammed came after the others, just as the Koran came down from heaven after the Torah, the Psalms and the Gospels, so also the *Ghāzīs* appeared in the world at the last," those *Ghāzīs* the reign of whom is that of the Ottomans. The poet continues with the question: "Who is a *Ghāzī?*" And he explains: "A *Ghāzī* is the instrument of the religion of Allah, a servant of God who purifies the earth from the filth of polytheism (remember that Islam regards the Trinity of the Christian as polytheism); the *Ghāzī* is the sword of God, he is the protector and the refuge of the believers. If he becomes a martyr in the ways of God, do not believe that he has died—he lives in beatitude with Allah, he has eternal life."[4]

This passage leaves no doubt in the reader's mind that in his view the *Iskendernâme*'s postscript on the Ottomans is clear in defining the state as one whose primary function was the spread of Islam. The following analysis represents the first effort to examine Ahmedi's full text on the early Ottoman rulers in an attempt to establish his probable purpose in appending it to his larger work. As such, its conclusions must be viewed as a preliminary effort to open a dialogue on the value of this important source. Such an approach is greatly assisted by the recent appearance of Kemal Sılay's critical edition of Ahmedi's *Tevârîh-i Mülûk-i âl-i 'Osmân*.[5] While the earliest redactions of this work all label it a *destân* (epic),[6] that used by Sılay does not. Complete with a facsimile of the text, a transliteration, an English translation, and a detailed glossary of words appearing in the text, Sılay's edition facilitates the following examination of Ahmedi's treatment of the *"gaza/gazi"* and "justice" themes which dominate his work.

Ahmedi's epic, which Wittek characterizes as a "versified chronicle,"[7] might better be viewed either as the earliest Ottoman prototype of the popular genre known as the Mirror for Princes,[8] or as the first known example of a *destân* (epic) used as a work of advice, that is, a *nasihatname*, or a book of advice for rulers. Begun during the reign of Sultan Bayezid (1389–1402), it was continued after his death in 1403 for Ahmedi's new intended patron Prince Süleyman (between the years 1403 and 1411),[9] that is, in the immediate aftermath of the Timurid invasion, which had led to the capture and death of his father Bayezid. A careful reading of the full text establishes that Ahmedi had initially envisaged the work for Bayezid,[10] as an attempt to warn him away from the errors (his wars against his fellow Muslim rulers in Anatolia) which were ultimately (while the work was still in progress) to lead to his downfall. With the death of Bayezid, Ahmedi's focus shifted and he began to remold the final segment of his work with the objective of shaping the mind of his new intended patron Prince Süleyman. Stated differently, he was intent on guiding him away from the errors that had led to his father's downfall. Ahmedi is attempting to convince first Bayezid and then Prince Süleyman that the true role of the Ottomans was to fight against Christians, not (as had Bayezid) to turn their armies against their fellow Muslim rulers in Anatolia and the Arab world. Before his work was finished, Prince Süleyman too had died, leaving Ahmedi with a work of advice the intended patrons of which were both deceased. A second motif, and one more in keeping with the traditional Ottoman *nasihatname*, is the emphasis which Ahmedi places on justice as a key attribute of the good ruler. This interpretation is supported by the manner in which Ahmedi's leitmotif of the *gaza* and the Ottoman rulers as *gazis* and just rulers is handled throughout his work. Indeed, these dual themes are underlined in the introductory segment of Ahmedi's work where he characterized the Ottoman Begs in the following couplet:

> Let us tell of those Begs, from the first to the last who were not only Muslim but also just rulers *[Analum ol begleri kim serteser/hem Müsülmân idiler hem dâdger].*[11]

In the opening segment on the Ottomans, entitled: "History of the Rulers of the House of Osman and Their Campaigns Against the Infidel" [couplets: 1–15], Ahmedi contrasts rulers such as the Mongols (known for their injustice) with the early Ottomans (hailed for their justice). It is within this context that he introduces the theme that it was the

Mongol attacks on Muslims which accorded them their reputation for injustice, whereas it was the Ottoman's adherence to the duty of fighting against the infidels which establishes them as just. It is under this rubric that Ahmedi announces his intention of writing a *Gazavatname*, an epic of exploits in verse outlining the heroic deeds of the early Ottoman rulers. In so doing he sets forth the theme of the *gaza*, and the *gazis* who pursue it, as a literary topos, that is, the recurring theme that our subsequent examination will show separates those Ottoman rulers who were *gazis* fighting against the infidels (Osman, Orhan, Murad) from Bayezid who turned his back on the *gaza* (and paid for it with his life). He does not as Wittek has led us to believe pretend to be writing a "versified chronicle" of the first century Ottoman state. Wittek's reading is anachronistic and overlooks the fact that Ahmedi was writing his polemic a century after many of the events he was describing had actually occurred.[12]

The next section of Ahmedi's work, entitled: "An Apology for the Delay in *Gazi* Affairs" [couplets: 16–24], provides the author an opportunity to reiterate the topos announced above, to wit that God has saved the best for last, that is, in the same way that he sent the Prophet Mohammed after the Jewish and Christian prophets, so, too, he has sent the *gazis* (Ottoman rulers) after earlier Muslim dynasties who did not have a lasting legacy as the Prophet Mohammed did.[13]

Ahmedi's third subsection, the "Beginning of the Story" [couplets: 25–56], is devoted to setting forth a definition of the ideal *gazi* and illustrating the manner in which the thirteenth-century Seljuk ruler, Sultan 'Ala'eddin, met these criteria. The definition he provides includes the following elements:

- The *gazi* is the instrument of the true religion (Islam).
- The *gazi* is the servant of God, who purifies the world from the filth of polytheism.
- The *gazi* is surely the sword of God.
- He (the *gazi*) is the protector and the refuge of the true believers.

Having defined his terms, Ahmedi then sets out to show how the Seljuk ruler 'Ala'eddin fit the role of *gazi* thus projected. First, due to his desire to be known as a *gazi,* 'Ala'eddin summons his troops, who included Gündüz Alp and Ertuğrul (the father of the first Ottoman ruler Osman), in addition to Gök Alp and other unnamed members of the Oguz tribe. In the course of the ensuing battles, Ertuğrul distinguished himself by "attacking cities endlessly" and by the taking of "booty and captives." Conquest, booty, and captives are here introduced as the practical benefits of the *gaza*. The question raised by this passage is: Does this emphasis on attacking cities for the purpose of obtaining booty and slaves, actually reflect the *gaza* tradition, or does it reflect the pre-Islamic Turco-Mongol tribal tradition of conquest and plunder now transplanted into western Anatolia?

It is at this point [couplet 41] that Ahmedi inserts the first of several implied messages for his intended patrons, Bayezid (and later Prince Süleyman). When he writes that "the Tatars were at peace with him ('Ala'eddin) when they heard that he was going against the infidels," he sounds the first indirect warning about the dangers of turning away from the fight against the infidels *(gaza)* and the potential danger from the Tatars should one succumb to it. Given the fact that Bayezid was ultimately to turn against the Tatars (Timur) and lose his life as a result of similarly deserting the *gaza* in favor of fighting against his fellow Muslims, Ahmedi's warning seems prophetic.

This section ends with the Tatars having broken their pledges and attacking 'Ala'eddin, a fact that caused him to turn away from the *gaza*, in an attempt to protect his capital city of Konya. In his place on the frontier, he left Ertuğrul (the father of Osman), who conquered the region of Söğüt in northwestern Anatolia and died shortly thereafter.[14]

In the following segment, entitled: "The Emirate of Osman, the Attributes of His Service and His Character" [couplets: 51–56], Ahmedi bestows the title of *gazi* on Osman the real founder of the dynasty, describing him as having "attack[ed] the cities and kill[ed] the infidels," and having "annihilated the infidel," that is, having fulfilled Ahmedi's definition of what a good *gazi* was.[15] What he conveniently overlooks is the fact that some of Osman's earliest battles were fought against the Turkish Beylik of the Germiyans, his neighbor to the south and east.[16] As will be repeatedly stressed, Ahmedi's silence in this regard may well have stemmed from his desire to depict the early Ottoman rulers (in contrast to Bayezid) as having been exclusively concerned with the *gaza*.

In his next segment, which Ahmedi titles: "The *Padişahi* (Reign) of Orhan, the Son of Osman" [couplets: 57–93], the author makes it clear that it is the model of Orhan which he is setting forth for his patrons. Over and again he reiterates the extent to which Orhan busied himself with the *gaza*. In numerous passages he not only underlines the importance of this role but repeatedly emphasizes the material blessings that accrued to Orhan as a result of his never deviating from it:

- He [Orhan] plundered the infidels day and night.
- [He] crushed the rest, old and young.
- They drove the infidel out from their own land.

- Since then [the time of Orhan] *gaza* has become a sacred obligation.
- The great *gazi* conquered five or six forts.
- [He] took villages, cities and countries.
- Wherever he sent an army, they burned the infidel.
- Much silver and gold came to him from everywhere.
- [He gained many] beautiful servants and fair-breasted concubines.
- The flag of blasphemy fell down. They exhausted the infidel.

In short, Orhan is described by Ahmedi as the *gazi* par excellence, as a leader whose attention was never diverted from the primary objective of the *gaza,* the expansion of Islam at the expense of the infidel. He also concentrates on the material benefits which such activity brought to practitioners of the *gaza*: plunder, slaves, silver, gold, and concubines are enumerated among the rewards which accrue to the *gazis*.[17]

Ignoring totally Ahmedi's actual depiction of both the role of the *gazis* and the *gaza,* Colin Imber in a recent article has advanced the untenable theory (following Kortantamer,[18] that Ahmedi viewed Holy War *(gaza)* solely as an act of worship, rather than as a means of gaining wealth from pillage and plunder.[19] As the foregoing discussion amply illustrates this is not the position generally taken by Ahmedi, who, to the contrary, repeatedly emphasized the material rewards which accrued to the *gazis* as a result of their activities. While for religious zealots, certain of the justness of their cause, war plundering can certainly be justified as fulfilling God's will (*fi sebili-llah,* in Allah's path), Imber's suggestion that the *gaza* was purely "an act of worship" implies a highly sophisticated and religiously orthodox Ottoman society at the beginning of the fourteenth century. As a thorough reading of Ahmedi establishes, this was not the case. The material benefits clearly equalled if not outweighed the spiritual ones in his account.

Ahmedi's next subsection is devoted to the topic of: "Orhan's Sending of Süleyman *Paşa* to the Opposite Shore [Thrace] in Order to Fight on Behalf of Islam" [couplets: 94–135]. At first glance the forty-one couplets he devotes to this Ottoman prince (versus the six couplets for Osman, and the thirty-six couplets he accords Orhan), are difficult to comprehend. However, when one realizes that he is describing the individual who took the *gaza* to southeastern Europe (the home of Christianity), and doing so in terms that leave no doubt but that he is setting him forth as a model prince and as an ideal *gazi,* the reasons become clearer. Ahmedi is once again providing a subliminal example for his own patrons. When he describes Süleyman *Paşa* in the following words, he is describing his model of the ideal Prince for his intended patrons to follow:

Whatever he found in the region of the infidel, he would destroy, [and] he would burn their homes. He would kill those who did not accept [Islam] at his invitation, and would make the army of Islam victorious. By the order of God and his father's judgment, he arrived in the region of the infidels with his army. There, he made several *gazas* for the faith [and] his name became suitable to be a *gazi*.[20]

In portraying Süleyman *Paşa* as the ultimate warrior for the faith, one whose prowess resulted ultimately in "Mohammed being thought of where Jesus used to be worshipped,"[21] he is setting forth an ideal for his own patrons, one which he clearly hopes will be emulated. In turn, by stressing that the title of *gazi* is an earned one, which results from leading the *gaza*, he is laying the groundwork for the contrasting portrait he is later to draw of Bayezid. Not surprisingly, Ahmedi is totally silent on the career of Süleyman *Paşa* prior to his assuming the role of leader of the *gaza* in southeastern Europe. For this was the period in which this Prince led the Ottoman forces against their Muslim neighbors, most particularly the Turkish Beylik of Karası.

Ahmedi's insistence that the true *gazi*'s role was the destruction of all those unbelievers (Christians) who refused to accept Islam is not unique to this author. Şükrullah, the mid-fifteenth-century Ottoman chronicler, describes Orhan's decision to spread the *gaza* into the Balkans in the following terms:

One day [Orhan], while sitting quietly alone, was thinking about how to destroy the unbelievers at their roots. Suddenly it came to him. He should cross the sea and summon that country's unbelievers to accept the true faith. If they failed to accept he would destroy them in the name of God."[22]

Here, too, the gap between rhetoric and reality was large. While beginning with Ahmedi and Şükrullah (and carefully followed by later Ottoman chroniclers), the *gaza* topos claimed that the sole role of the good *gazi* was to spread Islam by confronting the unbelievers with the choice of conversion or death, in point of fact there is simply no indication that such a policy was ever followed by the Ottomans.

While Ahmedi had no real trouble portraying Osman, Orhan, and Süleyman *Paşa* as prototypes of his ideal *gazi* by simply ignoring any fighting they had engaged in against their fellow Muslims, the same was not true for the next Ottoman ruler Murad, who, while leading the *gaza*, also fought against the fellow Anatolian Turkish state of the Karamanids. That this caused Ahmedi some problems may be inferred from the manner in which he treats the reign of this ruler.

Rather than following his normal procedure of devoting one section to each figure, he breaks down the reign of Murad into no less than five separate segments, the first of which is titled: "The *Pâdişâhî* (Reign) of Murad Beg *Gazi* Which Lasted Thirty Years" [couplets: 136–157]. In this segment, he portrays Murad as the ultimate just leader, one who warranted the title *Gazi* Murad, because he "devoted himself to fighting on behalf of Islam forever." Ahmedi ends this section of his work by noting that it was Murad "who first extended his hand to Rum (Anatolia)," that is, who first fought against fellow Muslim states.[23]

The tone of the ensuing segment, titled: "The Battle of the Karamans with Murad Beg and the Crushing Defeat of the Army of Karaman" [couplets: 158–171], is set by Ahmedi in the first line: "The Shah of Karaman fought with him [Murad]." He is implying by this passage that the responsibility for this conflict rests with the Karamanid ruler 'Ala'eddin (Murad's son-in-law), and that it is not the Ottoman ruler who is unjustly attacking a Muslim state. There are at least two problems with Ahmedi's account: *a)* he places this event at the beginning of Murad's reign, when in fact it occurred in 1387, fully twenty-seven years into it; and, *b)* it was Murad who marched on Konya, not 'Ala'eddin who attacked the Ottomans, although arguably Murad's action was precipitated by the Karamanid leader's occupation of Ottoman territories while he had been campaigning in the Balkans.[24] What is strange is Ahmedi's juxtaposing of the order of events, that is, placing those which occurred in 1387 ahead of his account of Murad's role as a *gazi* famed for his conquests in the Balkans (all of which predated his war with the Karamanids). Is it possible that he did so intentionally? By mentioning something which was surely too well-remembered to be overlooked in such a manner that it would be followed by lengthy accounts of the *gaza* and Murad's role as a paramount leader of the *gazis,* was he hoping not to detract from the real message his work was designed to provide his intended patron Bayezid? While this will have to remain in the realm of conjecture, the fact that he makes such a distortion of events which had occurred during his own lifetime (he was born in the mid-1330s) raises the possibility that his motive in so doing was to make sharper the contrast between Murad and Bayezid. This collapsing of chronology is quite in keeping with epic or wisdom literature, the primary aim of which is argument, not fact.[25]

In the following segment which Ahmedi titles: "The Departure of Murad Beg *Gazi* to the Opposite Shore on Behalf of the *Gaza* and the Conquest of Countries" [couplets: 172–182], he reestablishes Murad's reputation as the *gazi* par excellence, one whose sole motivation is the service of God. In a series of passages this theme is driven home. Murad is described as having "had no expectations from fighting except to obtain God's pleasure," and the reader is informed that:

> He who has thought about worldly desires has not found anything useful. Destroy the desires for the world in your heart, so that your affairs will go well. Strive, take everything ungodly from the heart, if you don't want your affairs to be inauspicious.[26]

Here, too, without much subtlety, Ahmedi is lecturing his intended patron Sultan Bayezid. The message reads: do not be a victim of your own desires, rather, follow the path of your father Murad I and focus your efforts not on worldly gains, but on seeking to please God by pursuing the *gaza* rather than by attacking your Muslim neighbors.[27]

This interpretation is strengthened by the next section of Ahmedi's work which is called: "The Story About the Inauspiciousness of Deficient Belief" [couplets: 183–237]. In this, the longest segment of the work ostensibly devoted to the Ottomans, Ahmedi is simply lecturing his patron on the righteousness of Murad, whom he contrasts with the Koranic account of the biblical story, regarding the manner in which, as a result of a "deficit" in their belief, the Jews who believed and drank only a handful of water were strengthened in their fight against Imlik, whereas those with little faith drank too much and became ill.[28] Against this example of "deficient belief," he cites the Ottomans, who: "because [their] sincere belief became distinguished, they found a special attachment in the presence of God." Again, Murad is depicted as the just ruler who was "a true and devout believer," who, due to the efforts he expanded in constructing poorhouses, mosques, and tombs (for his ancestors), "prepared himself for the next world."[29]

Ahmedi's description of Murad's reign ends with a segment, entitled: "The Battle of the Auspicious Sultan Murad Beg with the Laz Unbelievers, His Martyrdom and the Defeat of the Infidels" [couplets: 238–253]. Here, in discussing events which occurred in 1389, for the first time Ahmedi refers to an Ottoman ruler by the title: "Sultan," a designation our subsequent discussion will show is historically correct. In describing the death of Murad on the battlefield, he refers to Murad as "the Auspicious Sultan—who was a *gazi*—[and] certainly became a martyr." In short, Ahmedi has portrayed the first three rulers of the Ottoman dynasty as God-fearing men who fought as *gazis* against the unbelieving Christians.[30]

With this as background, we turn to Ahmedi's description of his intended patron Bayezid. Even his heading: "The *Pâdişâhî* (Reign) of the Auspicious Sultan Bayezid, the Son of Murad *Gazi*" [couplets: 254–278], suggests that the ensuing discussion is going to distinguish between the mundane preoccupations of "Sultan" Bayezid and the religious goals of his father, Murad, the *"Gazi"* leader. Not once in the total of forty-three couplets does Ahmedi confer the title of *gazi* on Bayezid, or use the term *gaza* to describe his military exploits. This is in marked contrast to his treatment of earlier Ottoman rulers each of whom had been extolled as *gazis* leading the *gaza* (this is true of Osman, Orhan, Süleyman *Paşa*, and Murad, although only the latter two were consistently referred to as Süleyman *Gazi* and Murad *Gazi*).

This failure is brought into sharp focus by virtue of the fact that Ahmedi does indeed praise Bayezid as a just ruler.

> He arrived in the country and established his authority. He greatly constituted, in the state, justice and equity. Because the people obtained justice from him, they were all, children and adults, prospering. There was not any place in all of Rum which did not prosper due to his justice. In the country there was no desert or mountain left which was not turned into either a sown field, a garden, or an orchard.[31]

Not only does Ahmedi fail to use the title *Gazi* in reference to Bayezid, he goes as far as expunging any reference in his work to campaigns led by Bayezid against Byzantium or other Christian rulers in the Balkans, activities which should be termed *"gaza."* When noted by earlier scholars,[32] this was explained in terms of flaws in Ahmedi's knowledge of contemporary history. Indeed, only Paul Wittek and Pal Fodor seem to have realized that the failure of Ahmedi to bestow the appellation *gazi* on Bayezid may have stemmed from other reasons.[33] Wittek takes Ahmedi's silence as an indication that the *gazi* idea had become insignificant by the reign of Bayezid,[34] whereas Fodor argues a bit more persuasively that Ahmedi was actually writing this section following the death of Bayezid, and may have been concerned that it would hardly sound appropriate to have a *gazi* defeated by Timur at the Battle of Ankara in a work whose object was now to stress the importance of the *gaza* to his new patron Prince Süleyman.[35]

Neither of these arguments is particularly convincing. It seems clear that Ahmedi's failure to mention either Bayezid's campaign at Nicopolis or his siege of Constantinople stems from the fact that had he done so he would indeed have had to bestow upon him the title of *gazi*. This he would not do for the simple reason that his work, which was initially intended to serve as a guide for Sultan Bayezid, had been overtaken by events. With the death of Bayezid his focus necessarily shifted and he now sought to influence Prince Süleyman, whom he wanted to see return to the path of his grandfather, not that followed by his late father with such disastrous results. Stated differently, Ahmedi throughout his work on the Ottoman dynasty is purposely trying to distinguish between those members who followed the *gaza* (Osman, Orhan, Süleyman *Paşa* and Murad) by focusing their campaigns on their Christian neighbors to the west, and Bayezid who had turned his might against his fellow Muslim rulers in Anatolia. As long as Bayezid was alive, this message was intended for him as a subtle warning to correct his ways. Once he is dead, it is his path which Ahmedi is obliquely warning his new intended patron, Prince Süleyman, to avoid. He does so with caution for he can hardly appear to be criticizing the recently deceased father of his patron. This is the real political purpose behind Ahmedi's elaborate topos of the *gaza*, that is, he seems to have assigned himself the task of making his patrons (initially Bayezid and later Süleyman) look West, hence the focus on the *gaza* against the Christians, rather than dividing their attention between East (the home of other Muslim states) and West (the site of the *gaza*). Whether Ahmedi's purpose stemmed from his own self interest (he was born and raised in the state of Germiyan and actually joined the Ottomans only in the 1380s),[36] or from an actual concern for the well-being of his new patron remains unclear. We may assume that both he and Prince Süleyman were well aware that during the Battle of Ankara, those Ottoman forces consisting of Anatolian cavalrymen had deserted Bayezid to join up with their former princes who were fighting under the banner of Timur.[37] Ultimately, Bayezid was defended only by the Christian vassal-troops supplied by his Serbian brother-in-law Prince Stefan Lazarević and his own Janissary contingent who were no match for Timur.

From Ahmedi's description of the exploits of Bayezid (clearly compiled after his death and designed to serve as a warning for Prince Süleyman), the portrait which emerges of the fourth Ottoman ruler is one of a man driven to conquest. As for his commitment to the religion of Islam, Ahmedi damns him with faint praise: "He looked favorably on those who were religious."[38] This statement is in stark contrast to the plethora of superlatives with which he described the devotion to religion (read: *gaza*) of each of his predecessors. Even in his description of Bayezid's successes against his Muslim Turkish neighbors, one detects more than a hint of displeasure. According to Ahmedi:

> He took Sivas and Tokat from the Rum. Conquering Canik he arrived in Samsun. Since that one was also conquered by him, he returned to his country. That Sultan conquered all the cities and regions as far as the frontiers of Antaliye. He also took Alaşar, Saruhan, Aydin, Menteşe and Germiyan. Even Kastamoniye was

conquered by him. . . . Because he arrived in the cities of Karaman, he took Konya and Larenda, too. There was no city or land in that region which he did not take.[39]

Because he appends to this litany a rationale: "because that is the way state affairs should be, according to him," one senses a not too well concealed tone of disapproval. Ahmedi's earlier passages have endlessly reiterated the message that the real role of the Ottoman rulers was to press the *gaza* against their Christian neighbors to the west.

Even in one of the rare passages which might be construed as praise of the late ruler:

> For some time, he was openly ascetic; his [only] action was to worship night and day. He never handled a glass of wine; he listened to neither harp nor flute.[40]

One can not help but wonder if Ahmedi is not simply mouthing known falsehoods in an effort to remind Prince Süleyman that it was his father's addiction to drink and debauchery which had (along with his betrayal of the *gaza*) led to his downfall. Alternatively, may it be that his use of the phrase "for some time he was openly ascetic" is a subtle way of referring to the fact that Bayezid had not always been a debauched drunkard focused exclusively on his own entertainment?

Given the fact that Prince Süleyman himself was, by all contemporary accounts, a true son of his father in terms of his addiction to drink and debauchery, a character trait which ultimately cost him his life in 1411 (when his army and his people abandoned him to the less than tender mercies of his rivals),[41] it is possible that Ahmedi's reminder that Bayezid had not always been a debauched drunkard is intended as a warning to Prince Süleyman to mend his ways. Ahmedi is simply lecturing his new intended patron as to what his end will be if he does not turn his back upon the life-style which cost his late father his life and return to the path of his ancestors, all of whom (with the exception of Bayezid), had been both just rulers and good Muslims.

In support of this interpretation is the picture drawn of Bayezid that survives in later chronicle accounts which is at complete variance with the characterization of him as a God-fearing abstentious ascetic. Even the official historian of the Turkish Republic, the twentieth-century chronicler, İsmail Hakkı Uzunçarşılı (basing his assessment on the Ottoman chronicle accounts) argues that Bayezid's *"addiction to alcohol had destroyed his nerves."*[42]

His lack of dedication to religion is also supported by Mükrimin Halil Yınanç in his *İslam Ansiklopedisi* article on "Bayezid," where he reports that he had been corrupted by his Serbian wife and his Vizier Ali *Paşa,* and adds the story that Şemseddin Muhammed [Molla] Fenari, the *Kadı* (religious judge) of Bursa refused to accept Bayezid as a witness in a court case on the grounds that he had given up the practice of public prayer.[43]

By far the most damning account of Bayezid's irreligiosity is the widely known story concerning a warning given him by his saintly son-in-law Emir Sultan. Reportedly, before embarking on his Nicopolis campaign in 1396, Bayezid vowed that should his endeavor succeed he would build twenty mosques. Following his victory he had instead constructed the Ulu Cami in Bursa with its twenty domes. As he, accompanied by Emir Sultan, went to examine the completed construction, he asked: "If anything were missing?" Emir Sultan replied: "No my Sultan, everything is all right. There is however one thing missing, if you complete it, it will reflect well on your Sultanate." Bayezid asked: "What is it?" The reply was: "If you were to construct four *meyhanes* (saloons) in the four corners of the mosque, it would give you a reason to come to the mosque and it would make a great place for you to drink with your friends." Bayezid, shocked by his statement, replied: "Would it be proper to have *meyhanes* in a mosque?" Completely undaunted, Emir Sultan replied: "My sultan, one's heart is similar to a house of God; for one to drink forbidden wine turns it into a *meyhane,* and one's body into a temple of idolatry. This is the same as constructing a *meyhane* inside a mosque."[44] There is no question but that the reputation Bayezid enjoyed among his contemporaries was hardly that of a religious ascetic.

This reputation is recorded in the anonymous fifteenth-century Ottoman chronicle *Tevârîh-i âl-i 'Osmân,* as stemming from the influence of Bayezid's Serbian wife:

> Until Vulkoğlu's daughter came to him, Yıldırım Khan (Bayezid) did not know what drinking parties were. He did not drink and held no carouses. In the times of Osman, Orhan and *Ghazi* Murad, wine was not drunk.[45]

The Byzantine chronicler Doukas is even less circumspect in detailing Bayezid's debauchery. In describing the aftermath of the Nicopolis campaign (1396):

> In Prusa [Brusa/Bursa] Bayazid enjoyed the many fruits of good fortune and reveled in the daily homage of many nations. He lacked nothing that was beautiful from the coffers of the nations. . . . Boys and girls, selected for their unblemished bodies and beauty of countenance, were there—young and tender youths, and girls who outshone the sun.

> From where did they come? Romans, Serbs, Vlachs, Albanians, Hungarians, Saxons, Bulgarians and Latins, each speaking his own language and all there against their will. And Bayazid, living idly and wantonly, never ceased from lascivious sexual acts, indulging in licentious behavior with boys and girls.[46]

Doukas, a contemporary of Bayezid, is generally fair in his assessment of this ruler. His inclusion of the above description may not be dismissed as some kind of anti-Ottoman invective. Rather, it must be seen as reflecting the reputation which Bayezid had acquired in the closing years of his reign.

The impression that Ahmedi, by stating that Bayezid "for some time" had lived as an ascetic and never drank or even listened to the harp and the flute, is referring to the period prior to his having become ruler (born in 1354, he became ruler at the age of thirty-five in 1389), is heightened by a passage in the work of the Byzantine ruler Manuel II Palaeologus, who as vassal of Bayezid accompanied him on his Anatolian campaigns in 1391 (shortly after he had assumed the throne). In his *Dialogue with a Muslim,* Manuel II complains about the rigors of campaigning with Bayezid in December of that year:

> Above and beyond all this, should we not mention the daily hunting, the dissipation at meals and afterwards, the throngs of mimes, the flocks of flute players, the choruses of singers, the tribes of dancers, the clang of cymbals, and the senseless laughter after the strong wine? Is it possible for those who suffer through all this not to have their minds dulled?[47]

In the course of the same campaign (against the Turkish rulers of Sinope and Kastamonu) in late 1391, Manuel II also addressed a letter to his tutor Cydones (the recipient of most of his correspondence). This letter, which provides a detailed description of the deserted and devastated nature of the Anatolian landscape, which Manuel ascribes to the fear of Bayezid that exists among the local Muslim inhabitants who are repeatedly plundered by both the Ottoman soldiery and Bayezid's Balkan Christian vassals (and thereby undermines Ahmedi's depiction of Bayezid as a just ruler), ends with the following passage:

> This is just what I am doing as I bring this letter to a close. For already, I can all but make out the messengers inviting us to go off to the ruler [Bayezid]. I suppose he again wants to drink a few toasts before dinner and to force us to fill ourselves with wine from his varied collection of golden bowls and cups. He thinks that these

will assuage the depression caused by what we have been writing about, while, even if I were in good spirits, they would only fill me with sadness.[48]

Given the fact that Bayezid married the Serbian princess Olivera only following the Battle of Kosovo (June 15, 1389) in 1392,[49] it seems certain (based on this contemporary testimony of Manuel II), that the Ottoman ruler must have had more than a passing familiarity with the fruit of the vine, prior to coming under his new spouse's influence.[50]

The idea, set forth by Colin Imber, that all such references to Bayezid's corruption and drinking, are the result of interpolations by late-fifteenth-century Ottoman chroniclers who were attempting to find a cause for Bayezid's ignominious defeat at the hands of Timur (in 1402), is difficult to sustain in light of Manuel II's eyewitness account of events in December of 1391.[51]

In the next to last segment of his work, entitled: "The Announcement of Sultan Berkuk's Death to Bayezid Beg" [couplets: 279–297], Ahmedi's tone changes and he adopts a critical attitude toward Bayezid's decision to take advantage of the death of the Mamluke Sultan of Egypt, Berkuk, and to attempt to conquer Syria and Egypt. Specifically, he criticizes Bayezid for not accepting Berkuk's death as a reminder of his own mortality and instead attempting to take unfair advantage of the situation. He then immediately proceeds to the following couplets regarding Bayezid's own death:

> In the meantime, Timur marched towards Rum. The state became full of instigation, fear, and languor. Because Timur did not have any justice, necessarily, he had a lot of cruelty and oppression. It was certainly such a savageness, that, even to mention it is a kind of wildness; the only solution is not to talk about it! The Sovereign passed away amid this languor. Many cities and countries were annihilated and burned.[52]

This entire section must have been written after the death of Bayezid. While Ahmedi does not openly express his feeling that Bayezid got his just deserts, that message is implicit in the manner he subtly equates Bayezid's unjust attempt to conquer Syria and Egypt, with the equally unjust havoc wrought in Anatolia by Timur.

Ahmedi's negative portrait of Bayezid, albeit understated in keeping with the sensitivities of his new intended patron, was one designed to provide a sharp contrast in the mind of Prince Süleyman, between the saintliness of his ancestors (Osman, Orhan, Süleyman *Paşa*, and Murad), each of whom had faithfully followed the path of the *gaza*, and that of his own father (Bayezid), the debauched pleasure seeker, who had turned from the idealized role of *gazi* and waged war on his Muslim neighbors.

Ahmedi ends his work with a segment, entitled: "The *Pâdişâhî* (Reign) of the Auspicious Martyr Sultan Emir Süleyman—May God Glorify His Tomb"—[couplets: 298–334]. By virtue of this title it is apparent that before Ahmedi was able to complete his self-appointed task of providing guidance to his intended patron (Prince Süleyman), he, like the earlier intended target of his *nasihat* (Bayezid), had died. Clearly, Ahmedi has been deprived of the raison d'être for his poem, not to mention the financial reward he must have anticipated were his *mesnevi* to have been actually presented to a patron. While he goes through the motions of praising the late Prince Süleyman, he can hardly praise him as a *gazi* (given the fact that the only fighting he did was against his own brothers), and therefore ends his work as he began it by noting that God always saves the best for last. In the same manner that this served as his initial way of introducing the Ottoman dynasty, it now becomes the motif with which he ends his work.

As such, it illustrates the basic polemical-literary, rather than historical nature of his work and, in so doing, highlights the reasons that it is more fruitful to view Ahmedi's work as a *nasihatname* rather than as history. As this critique has demonstrated, Ahmedi was concerned with delivering a message to his intended patrons, rather than with providing later generations a history of the Ottomans in the fourteenth century. In the words of the Hungarian scholar Fodor:

> For Ahmedi history was not something to explore, but much rather a thesaurus of examples from which one must draw the events and facts that most snugly fit the portrayal of the ideal types embodied by his characters. As the historical events are in this way reduced to mere illustration, their choice is random and arbitrary, devoid of their real significance. What Ahmedi describes is at most a sketchy outline of Ottoman history studded with an array of legends. This, in turn, provides the important conclusion that no matter [that] the facts selected by Ahmedi may well be true, his reticence on certain subjects can by no means be regarded as authoritative.[53]

Wittek's attempt to construct his "*Gazi* Thesis" on a few lines from the introduction of Ahmedi's section on the Ottoman dynasty is simply untenable when one reads the full text of the work in question. Contra Wittek, Ahmedi's work was not intended to be a "versified chronicle." Rather, it resembles a *nasihatname* (book of advice for rulers), in that it is designed to encourage his intended patrons (first Bayezid and then

Prince Süleyman) to look westward. As such the *gaza* topos is just that, a literary convention within which he guardedly proffers his thinly veiled warning that the fall of Bayezid had been caused by his turning the force of arms against his Muslim neighbors in Anatolia and the Mamluke world, rather than by concentrating on the continued westward expansion of the state. His use of the concepts of *gaza* and *gazi* is nothing more than a literary device designed to contrast the successful past with the questionable future. Bearing in mind that Ahmedi was writing this section of his work during the interregnum (1403–1413), that is, at a point in time when the future of the Ottoman dynasty was far from clear, his idealized view of a more perfect time was one in which the Ottomans had been just and directed their conquests against their Western Christian neighbors rather than upon their eastern Muslim compatriots.

THREE

Wittek Revisited

His Utilization of the 1337 Bursa Inscription

Wittek saw the introductory verses in Ahmedi, in which he introduced the concept of the *gaza* and *gazis,* as a description of actual events. When he wrote: "It is under the aspect developed in these introductory verses that the whole of Ottoman history is treated by the author,"[1] Wittek is standing firmly behind his belief that Ahmedi's work was a "versified chronicle." Realizing that all of his readers might not share his views in this regard, he continued: "One might ask the question: 'But is this not once more a mere literary form introduced by the author?'" He then proceeds to introduce his second (and only other) piece of evidence in support of his *gazi* Thesis:

> A glance at the oldest epigraphic document we have from an Ottoman ruler will dissipate all such doubt. In this inscription from 1337, dealing with the erection of a mosque in Bursa eleven years after the conquest of the city, the Ottoman ruler gives himself the following titles: "SULṬĀN, SON OF THE SULṬĀN OF THE GHĀZĪS, GHĀZĪ, SON OF GHĀZĪ, MARQUIS OF THE HORIZONS, HERO OF THE WORLD," an ensemble of titles absolutely unique in the Ottoman protocol, where generally the classical and quite different formulas of the Seljuk period are used. We can therefore be sure that this strange formula is the expression of an historical reality, of the same reality which dominates the chapter of Ahmedi.[2]

Normally when the historian is confronted with "an ensemble of titles absolutely unique in the Ottoman protocol," the first reaction should be to question their provenance. Particularly when, as we shall

33

see, a key title given by Wittek is not among those recorded in the 1337 inscription. Not so for Wittek, who embraced his flawed reading of the 1337 *kitabe* as the ultimate proof for his contention that Ahmedi's work is indeed a "versified chronicle" and for his belief that the primary factor in Ottoman growth and expansion was the *gaza*.

A careful examination of the inscription in question only adds to our contention that Ahmedi's use of the concepts of *gaza* and *gazis* was nothing more than a literary topos. Leaving aside for the moment the use of the title *gazi*, there are a number of other problems related to the 1337 inscription. These include the following:

Wittek does not name the mosque in Bursa which contains the 1337 inscription, nor does he provide the full text of the *kitabe* (dedicatory inscription) from which he has excerpted the lines he cites. Nor does he inform us exactly who built the monument in question. His failure in this regard is not accidental. For had he attempted to answer these queries, his certitude of the "historical reality" he attributes to the inscription would have been cast in some doubt.

The dedicatory inscription (written in Arabic) which is cited by Wittek is located above the eastern door of the Şehadet Mosque built in memory of Sultan Murad Hüdavendigar who died in 1389, some fifty-two years after the 1337 *kitabe* was initially erected. As the inscription is dated h. 738 (1337), and specifically mentions that it was set up by Orhan the son of Osman, there is no way that its present site could have been its original location. Nor, as most scholars have assumed, did it originally come from the Orhan Cami. For that monument contains its own dated restoration inscription which clearly states that it was erected in h. 820 (1417) by Mehmed the son of Bayezid in the course of repairs to the original structure which had been built in h. 740 (1339) by Orhan Bey the son of Osman Bey and then destroyed by the Karamanids in their sack of Bursa in 1413.[3] The question of the provenance of Wittek's inscription is thus in doubt. We have no idea what it may have originally adorned, or when it was moved to its present location. A. Memduh Turgut Koyunluoğlu's suggestion (later adopted by Mantran) that the 1337 inscription originally adorned the mosque built two years later in 1339 is seemingly impossible,[4] as the wording of the full text of the inscription establishes that it originally adorned a *mescid* (chapel mosque), as distinct from the Orhan Cami, which is a Friday mosque (a site where Friday noon prayers are held).

As noted earlier Şinasi Tekin has recently tried to demonstrate that the 1337 Bursa inscription is actually a late-nineteenth-century forgery. His effort in this regard is unconvincing. He adduces two lines of argumentation in support of his contention, both of which are unsustainable.

First, he argues that the *"yazı üslubu"* (style of writing) found on the inscription does not conform to that seen on the 1417 inscription on the city's Orhan Bey mosque.[5] Nor should it. The 1417 *kitabe* was erected eighty years after that of 1337. What is important is the extent to which the 1337 *kitabe* conforms to other contemporary fourteenth-century inscriptions. Had Tekin examined the 1927 and 1929 works of Uzunçarşılı in which he surveyed extant fourteenth-century Anatolian inscriptions,[6] as well as the numerous other published works which provide photographs of thirteenth- and fourteenth-century inscriptions in Anatolia, for example, Rudolf M. Riefstahl and Paul Wittek, "Turkish Architecture in Southwestern Anatolia"; F. Taeschner, "Beitrage zur frühosmanischen Epigraphik und Archaologie"; A. Memduh Turgut Koyunluoğlu, *İznik ve Bursa Tarihi;* Halim Baki Kunter, "Kitabelerimiz"; Kâzim Baykal, *Bursa ve Anitlari;* Robert Mantran, "Les Inscriptions Arabes de Brousse"; and Ekrem Hakki Ayverdi, *Osmanli Mimarisinin İlk Devri,* it would have been readily apparent that the "style of writing" preserved in the 1337 Bursa inscription is fully in keeping with contemporary examples erected in a number of other Anatolian Beyliks in that period. Second, Tekin tries to argue that the *unvanlar* (titles) used in the 1337 inscription were not in fact used by the Ottomans until the sixteenth century.[7] This, as our subsequent examination will demonstrate, is incorrect. All of the titles given to Orhan in 1337 are found in other fourteenth- and early-fifteenth-century Ottoman inscriptions. The inscription is authentic, albeit the question of how and when it got to where it is today (above the east doorway of the Şehadet Mosque) is open to question.

Turning back to Wittek, the relevant portion of the text of the inscription dated 1337, which he bases his *"Gazi* Thesis" on, reads:

> [Line 2] . . . *al-amīr al-kabīr al-mu'azzam al mujāhid (fi sabêl Allāh)*
> [Line 3] *sultān al ghuzāt, ghāzi ibn al-ghāzi, shujā' al-dawla wa'l-dīn wa-l āfāk*
> [Line 4] *pahlavān al-zamān* [?] *Urkhān bin 'Uthmān*
> [The Exalted Great Emir, Warrior on Behalf of God, Sultan of the *Gazis, Gazi* son of the *Gazi,* Champion of the State and Religion, and of the Horizons, Hero of the Age, Orhan, son of Osman]. (See plate 1.)

Wittek, in contrast, misread the same list of titles Orhan accorded himself as:

> *Sultān ibn sultān al-ghuzāt, ghāzī ibn al-ghāzī, Shujā' ad-daula wa 'd-dīn, marzbān al-āfāq, bahlavān-i jihān, Orkhān ibn 'Othmān* (which he translated as: Sultan, son of the Sultan of the *Ghazis, Ghazi,* son of *Ghazi,* marquis of the horizons, hero of the world.[8]

PLATE 1
Orhan *Gazi*'s 1337 Inscription on Bursa's Şehadet Mosque

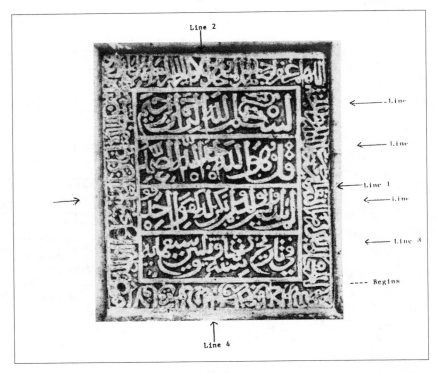

TRANSCRIPTION: *[Line 1] "'Umrahu al-masjid al-mubārak li-ridā' Allāh ta'ālā [man banā masjidan li'llāh banā Allāh lahu baytan fi'l-janna] [Line 2] Allāhumma aghfir li-sāhib hādha'l-masjid wa huwa al-amīr al-kabīr al-mu'az-zam al-mujāhid fi sabīl Allāh [Line 3] sultān al-ghuzāt, ghāzī ibn al-ghāzī, shujā' al-dawla wa'l-dīn [muttafaq?] [Line 4] pahlavān al-zamān[?] Urkhān bin 'Uthmān—adām Allāh 'umrahu [Line 5] [emphasis is mine] "Bism Allāh al-rah-man al-rahīm [Line 6] qul huwa Allāh ahad, Allāh al-samad lam yalid wa [Line 7] lam yūlad wa lam yakun la-hu kufuwan ahad. [Line 8] Fi ta'rīkh sanat thamān wa thalāthīn wa sab'a-mi'a (h.738).*

SOURCE: Ayverdi, *1966*, p. 59.

In so doing, Wittek created a number of ambiguities. In particular, his conferring of the title: "Sultan" among the list of honorifics supposedly accorded Orhan in 1337 is unjustified. This is not what the 1337 inscription says, rather it names Orhan as "The Exalted Great Emir, Warrior on behalf of God" (all of which is ignored by Wittek who renders these titles as "Sultan"). The title of "Sultan" is first attested to have been used on an Ottoman inscription nearly half a century later. Specifically, it was at the end of the reign of Murad I (1362–1389) that this honorific is first used in reference to a member of the Ottoman dynasty, when on a dated (1388) dedicatory *kitabe* of the *imaret* of Nilüfer Hatun (the wife of Orhan) in İznik, we see Murad I referred to as "Sultan, son of Sultan Orhan."[9] Interestingly, as seen in our earlier discussion of Ahmedi, he too first applied this title to Murad I in 1389.

It is Wittek himself, in a later section of his work, who provides us a clue as to the meaning of the title: "Sultan of the *Gazis*" (which does appear in the inscription), when, citing Eflaki, he mentions that one of the Emirs of the Principality of Aydin had been designated "Sultan of the *Gazis*" by a Mevlevi dervish sheikh.[10] Not only was this form of title not unique to the Ottomans, as Wittek himself illustrates, it was already in common usage among the leaders of other Turkish principalities in western Anatolia in the fourteenth century.

Returning to Wittek's addition of the nonexistent "Sultan" among the titularies listed for Orhan, as will be subsequently demonstrated, this is an error which when rectified serves to cast doubt on his theory for the uniqueness of the titles found in the inscription. As such, it undermines his assertion that the titles contained in the 1337 inscription are a reflection of historical reality.

My own reading of the 1337 inscription (based on risking my neck by climbing onto the roof of the porch in front of the East doorway of the Şehadet mosque and removing the row of tiles which, following a recent renovation, obscure the bottom line of the inscription, and on the earlier photographs provided by Kunter, Baykal, and Ayverdi, and the text as recorded by Kunter, Koyunluoğlu and Mantran)[11] varies significantly from that provided by Wittek. First, as noted above, his "Sultan, son of the" does not actually appear on the inscription, that is, that portion of the title begins with: "Sultan of the *Gazis, Ghazi,* son of the *Ghazi. . . .*" What this corrected reading establishes is that the title of "*Sultan*" per se was not in fact claimed by Orhan, rather that he was simply terming himself: "Sultan of the *Gazis.*" The real title of "The Exalted Great Emir, Warrior on behalf of God," which the inscription lists for Orhan, is ignored by Wittek. Further, his readings of the remaining titles accorded this ruler are questionable.

Given the fact that Wittek's work provides no indication as to what he based his reading on, it is impossible to determine the reasons for his errors in this regard. Did he actually visit Bursa between the years 1927–1932, while he was working at the German Archeological Institute in Istanbul,[12] and record his reading at that time? Did someone else provide him their reading? Or, did he rely upon the only published text of the inscription available at the time, that of Ahmed Tevhid, which had appeared in 1912?[13] The latter explanation seems unlikely, for while in his work Wittek cites Tevhid "as having made a first attempt to read this inscription,"[14] in an earlier study (his 1934 *Das Fürstentum Mentesche*), he had categorically stated that Tevhid "unquestionably misread" the Bursa *kitabe*.[15] However, Tevhid's reading is in most respects superior to that provided by Wittek. Tevhid, for example, clearly titles Orhan as "The Exalted Great Emir" not "Sultan." Likewise, Tevhid does not give Orhan the titles *"marzban al-afaq"* (marquis of the horizons) and *"bahlavan-i jihan"* (hero of the world), which Wittek ascribes to him. Here it must be noted that the last line of the *kitabe* is partially obliterated and Wittek's educated guess at reconstructing what he reads as *bahlavan-i jihan* is a possible rendering, though (in my view) harder to justify than *pahlavan al-zaman*. As for his reading of the preceding phrase, as *marzban al-afaq*, it too is hard to sustain. What is more perplexing are those titles ignored or overlooked by Wittek, which Tevhid, Kunter, Ayverdi, and so forth all read correctly. Whatever the reasons, Wittek's reading of the 1337 inscription differs in several significant aspects from the actual text. Strangely, in his 1934 *Das Fürstentum Mentesche* book, Wittek implies that he had published (or was about to publish?), both a photograph and detailed description of the 1337 inscription in his *Rumtürkische Studien I*.[16] As Wittek never published such a work the questions stemming from his misreading of the *kitabe* remain unanswerable.

Furthermore, Wittek's contention that the ensemble of titles accorded the Ottoman ruler in the 1337 inscription is "absolutely unique" in Ottoman protocol, "where generally the classical and quite different formulas of the Seljuk period are used,"[17] does not appear to be in keeping with the preserved record. As will be demonstrated shortly it is this 1337 inscription which uses "classical" Seljuk formulations (e.g., *al-amīr al-kabīr al-mu'azzam al-mujāhid . . . shujā' al-dawla wa'l-dīn*, etc.), in stark contrast to all other extant fourteenth- and fifteenth-century Ottoman *kitabes* preserved in Bursa. The fact that Wittek chose to ignore these titles in his discussion does not make them disappear, it does however mitigate his argument as to the uniqueness of the 1337 Bursa inscription. Appendix 1, which compares Wittek's reading of the 1337 *kitabe* with the corrected version provided here, illustrates the extent to which he not only misread the inscription, but also based his ensuing interpretations upon this misreading.

Even a survey of the earliest surviving inscriptions in the first Ottoman capital of Bursa, far from substantiating Wittek's claim (or that advanced in 1993 by Şinasi Tekin), shows that the Ottomans used a variety of titles in this period (none of which resemble Seljuk models to the extent that of 1337 does) and one of which made fanciful claims that in no way reflect the historical reality. As illustrated by the following breakdown, it is difficult to make any kind of definitive statement about how the Ottoman rulers viewed themselves in the fourteenth and fifteenth century based on the titles preserved in their dedicatory inscriptions.

The actual inscription on the Mosque of Orhan built in 1339 (that placed there at the time of major repairs undertaken in 1417–1418), bears the following titles: "Sultan of the *Gazis* and of the Fighters *(mücahidin)*, Orhan Beg son of Osman Beg."[18] Whether or not this *kitabe* actually reproduces the original inscription, that of 1339 when the mosque was built, is beyond determination. It is clear that the use of the title "Sultan of the *Gazis*" for Orhan, the second Ottoman ruler, is not, contra Wittek (and Tekin), unique to his reading of the 1337 inscription.

Further, on the city's Great Mosque (Ulu Cami), constructed in 1399 by Bayezid I, he is simply titled: "The Great Sultan Bayezid Han son of Murad."[19] Here, too, there is no indication that in the fourteenth century the Ottoman rulers were using the "classical and quite different formulas of the Seljuk period," as Wittek contended. This is hardly an elaborate title.

The next oldest surviving inscription is on the tomb of Bayezid I which was built by his son in 1406. The honorifics it accords Bayezid include the following: "Bayezid Han the son of Murad Han, the Great Sultan, the Master of the Kings of the Arabs and Persians" (equals other peoples).[20] To say the least, even bearing in mind the grief of a son for a father who had recently been humiliated by Timur and who had ultimately taken his own life, it takes a real stretch of the imagination to claim (as this inscription does) that Bayezid I was the "Master of the Kings of the Arabs and the Persians." What this *kitabe* does illustrate is the gap between reality and the flowery titles which sometimes appeared on Ottoman inscriptions in the first hundred years of that state's existence. It further suggests that if by 1406 Prince Süleyman was still engrossed in a grandiose vision of himself as the son of the "Master of the Kings of the Arabs and Persians," our earlier argument that Ahmedi was writing his *destân* (epic) with the intent of guiding his patron Prince Süleyman away from the follies of his father is strengthened. If only three years after his father's suicide, Prince Süleyman is still embracing his dream of worldwide Islamic Empire, rather than worrying about his own survival, this was indeed a young man in need of guidance.

Finally, a restoration inscription from 1418 which once adorned the entrance to the Bursa castle (now preserved in the Bursa Museum), suggests that the titles accorded Bayezid by his son Prince Süleyman represented nothing more than a temporary aberration. Mehmed I refers to himself by the more familiar: "Sultan, son of Sultans, Sultan Mehmed the son of Bayezid Han."[21]

That the use of the title *gazi* was not unique to the fourteenth and fifteenth centuries is further illustrated by yet another dedicatory inscription from Bursa, a restoration *kitabe* dated 1904 and located on the Mosque of Murad I. The title of its restorer is given as: "Sultan, son of Sultan, Sultan, the *Gazi,* Abdülhamid Han."[22] At the risk of being facetious one can not help but wonder what kind of thesis would have emerged if Wittek's only surviving inscriptions from the Ottoman period were those from the reign of Abdülhamid II (1876–1909), who used the title *"gazi"* in numerous dedicatory *kitabes* throughout the empire?[23] Not unlike his ancestor Orhan, Abdülhamid II also had a political objective in claiming this title for himself. It is unlikely to be a coincidence that in 1886–87 when Abdülhamid II undertook the refurbishing of the tombs of Ertuğrul, his wife and son Savcı in the town of Söğüt, two of the inscriptions he erected refer to both his ancestor Ertuğrul and himself as *gazis*.[24] Both Orhan and Abdülhamid II sought to give an Islamic justification to their activities. Neither, however, engaged in the forceful expansion of Islam at the expense of their Christian neighbors in keeping with Ahmedi's definition of the *gaza*.

It becomes obvious that none of the scholars who have questioned the *"Gazi* Thesis" have heretofore actually reexamined Wittek's use of Ahmedi, or his reading of the 1337 Bursa inscription. R. Jennings, who found incongruity in the title "Sultan" being applied to Orhan in 1337, had not read Ayverdi (the source he cites), as even a cursory examination of the photograph and reading provided by that author shows no such title.[25] The same is the case with Colin Imber, who in his 1987 article based his discussion of the titles in the 1337 inscription on the aforementioned reading by Ahmed Tevhid, which appeared in 1912 (and, in so doing ignored the important photographs published in 1942 by Halim Baki Kunter and in 1966 by Ekrem Hakkı Ayverdi).[26] While there can be dissent on the order in which the lines of the 1337 inscription are intended to be read (this due to the fact that it consists of four lines surrounded by a square made up of four additional lines), there is little doubt about the titles it actually accords its builder. Perhaps it is the survival of what we might term the Wittekian mystique that accounts for the fact that even when later scholars are uncomfortable with his thesis, they are still so awed by his reputation as a philologist that they only pick at the edges, rather than challenge his utilization (indeed readings) of his sources.

This tendency is most apparent in Cemal Kafadar's *Between Two Worlds*. In this, the most serious reexamination of Wittek to date, the author does not even appear to have looked at the work of Ahmedi or to have actually read the 1337 Bursa inscription. Despite frequent references to the *İskendername*, a close reading shows that all of Kafadar's quotes are taken from the secondary works of Wittek, Arnakis and Ménage. Indeed, there is not a single reference to any of the edition's of Ahmedi's work in either Kafadar's voluminous Footnotes[27] or Bibliography.[28] Similarly, Kafadar's work contains numerous references to the 1337 Bursa inscription, all of which are also taken from the secondary literature. Here, too, neither his Footnotes nor his Bibliography refer to the extensive epigraphic literature on this inscription. One can not help but wonder if Kafadar would have been as sanguine about his wholesale adoption of Wittek's thesis (as modified by İnalcık) had he actually reexamined the work of Ahmedi and the 1337 Bursa inscription which are the key evidentiary elements underlying Wittek's assumptions.

Finally, the titles listed as uniquely Ottoman by Wittek in the 1337 inscription also had precedents in those used by the Seljuks and other Anatolian Begs in the thirteenth and fourteenth century. There are numerous formularies which appear on the 1337 Bursa *kitabe* that are also found in the inscriptions of earlier Turkish states in Anatolia.

In the Kütahya village of Karaca Viran, there is a *kitabe* dated 1270 on the wall of a *tekke* (dervish lodge), which gives the Seljuk ruler Hüsrev son of Kılıç Arslan, titles such as "the Great Sultan *(al-sultan al-mu'azzam),*" "Helper of the World and of Religion" *(ghiyath al-dunya wa'l-dīn).*[29]

There is an undated inscription from the reign of the Seljuk Sultan Alaettin Keykubat (1219–1236), from the Afyonkarahisar castle, which titles him the: "the Great Sultan" *(al-sultan al-mu'azzam)* and "Exaltation of the World and Religion" *('ala' al-dunya wa'l-dīn).*[30]

There is an inscription on a fountain built by the Seljuk ruler İzzetin Keykavus in Afyonkarahisar's Camii Kebir quarter in 1250, where the titles he is accorded include: *al-sultan al-mu'azzam 'izz al-dunya wa'l-din abu'l-fath* (the Great Sultan, the Glory of the World and Religion, The Conqueror).[31]

From the period of the Germiyan Beylik (1324), there is an inscription on the castle of Afyonkarahisar, in which the ruler

(Hüsamettin Yakup son of Umur Beg) is titled: "The Great Emir" *(al-amir al-mu'azzam)*.[32]

Far from being the only Anatolian rulers to take the title *gazi* in this period, the Ottomans were only one of many. In short, contra Wittek's claim of uniqueness, the title *ghazi* is found in a wide variety of four-teenth-century Anatolian Beylik inscriptions. There are other four-teenth-century examples found on extant dedicatory inscriptions.

A dated inscription (1378) on the Ulu Cami in Manisa, titles the Saruhanid ruler İshak Han son of İlyas, son of Saruhan: *al-sultān al-a'zam, nāsir al-ghuzāt wa'l-mujāhidīn* (The Great Sultan, Champion of the *Gazis*, and Fighters for Islam).[33]

A dated inscription from 1312 of the Aydınoğlu's in the western Ana-tolian town of Birgi, refers to its builder Aydın Oğlu Mehmed Beg as: *mawlana, al-amir al-kabir, al-ghazi* (Our Lord, the Great Emir, the *Gazi*).[34]

In the Menteşe town of Milas, there is a 1378 inscription on the Ahmed Gazi Cami in the Hoca Bedrettin quarter, whose builder is given the titles: *sultan muluk al-'arab wa'l-'ajam, ghazi Ahmad Beg* (Sultan of the Kings of the Arabs and the Persians, *Gazi* Ahmet Beg), a fact which can hardly have been unknown to Wittek who had published a mono-graph on this principality in 1934.[35] There are other extant inscriptions from the reign of this ruler, each of which accords him the title *Gazi*, in a *medrese* (school) he constructed in Peçin in 1375 and on his tomb in the same town.[36]

In short, the only seemingly novel thing about the 1337 Bursa inscrip-tion in comparison to other contemporary Anatolian *kitabes* is the curi-ous reading accorded it by Wittek, and the fact that it includes the title: "Sultan of the *Gazis*." This is plausibly explained as an attempt on the part of the Emir Orhan to stake his claim for primacy among other lead-ers of Turkish emirates who so titled themselves. That he was not the only Anatolian ruler to do so is clear from a 1333 inscription which adorns the tomb of Mehmed Beg of Aydın. Erected just four years prior to Orhan's Bursa inscription, it too styles Mehmed Beg as: *Sultan al-ghuzat* (Sultan of the Gazis).[37] The rest of the formularies Orhan accorded himself in the 1337 inscription are all likewise titles used by a variety of Seljuk Sultans and by other contemporary Turkish Beys in Anatolia. As this brief survey of extant fourteenth-century inscriptions in western Anatolia has demon-strated, even Emir Süleyman's attempt in 1406 to title his late father Bayezid I as "Master of the Kings of the Arabs and Persians," was noth-ing new. Twenty-eight years earlier the Menteşe ruler, *Gazi* Ahmet Bey had (with no more claim to legitimacy) so styled himself.

While technically correct (in 1938) in claiming that the 1337 inscription is the "oldest epigraphic document" we have from the

Ottoman era, Wittek must have become aware shortly after the appearance of his work that the *kitabe* was not the oldest source we have for titles used by the fourteenth-century rulers of the dynasty. Rather, as will be discussed hereafter, we have a *vakfiye* (religious foundation document), dated 1324 from Orhan's reign (first published in 1941), which predates the inscription by fifteen years and several other inscriptions and documents from the reign of this ruler as well. Not only do several of these not include the title *gazi* for this ruler, none of them use the title of Sultan.[38] Nor do the earliest Ottoman coins which survive from the reigns of Osman and Orhan preserve either the title *gazi* or that of sultan for the first two Ottoman rulers.[39]

This review of the only two Ottoman sources produced by Wittek in support of what came to be known as the "*Gazi* Thesis," has established that the specific evidential underpinnings upon which it rests were both misrepresented by him. Not only does a close reading of Ahmedi's epic poem provide a far different meaning than it was accorded by Wittek, even the actual language found on the 1337 Bursa inscription, which he hails as his final proof, when correctly read, produces meanings significantly at variance with those he accorded to it. Without the support provided by Ahmedi, Wittek's interpretation rests solely on the title "Sultan of the *gazis, gazi* son of the *gazi*" which is accorded to Orhan in the 1337 Bursa inscription. As we have seen several other local rulers in thirteenth- and fourteenth-century Anatolia referred to themselves in similar fashion, even some who shared no borders whatsoever with any Christian state. Wittek, who was clearly aware of this fact, attempted to buttress his carefully edited selection of passages from Ahmedi, with his equally edited and vetted readings and interpretations of the meanings of the 1337 inscription, an exercise the present study has demonstrated was not supported by his sources. As a result, his attempt to argue that it was the Ottoman's *gazi* role, coupled with their unique geographical position, which provided their raison d'être and accounted for their growth and ultimate success is undermined. As will be demonstrated in the following section of this work, the Ottomans were not primarily a state dedicated to the concept of *gaza* (Holy War), nor were its *gazis,* many of whom were not even Muslims, primarily motivated by a desire to spread Islam. Their goal was booty, plunder, and slaves, no matter the rhetoric used by their rulers in their dedicatory inscriptions.

Appendix 2, which provides an overview of all the titles used by the Ottoman rulers in the fourteenth and early fifteenth century, clearly establishes that they did not generally refer to themselves as *gazis* in their inscriptions, chancery documents, or coinage. Further, Wittek's assertions to the contrary notwithstanding, there is nothing unique about the titles they did employ, all of which were equally used by the leaders of other Turkish principalities in Anatolia in that period. That language reflected the political vocabulary of fourteenth-century Anatolia, not the historical reality of the early Ottoman period. Later writers (beginning with Ahmedi and including subsequent chroniclers), defined the terms *gaza* and *gazi* in keeping with their traditional Islamic meanings. These meanings were in turn projected backward in time and applied to a far different fourteenth-century Ottoman reality.

Read retrospectively it appears that the evidentiary underpinnings for Wittek's "*Gazi* Thesis" rest solely on what seems to have been a conscious attempt on his part to make his sources say what he wanted to hear. Neither Ahmedi nor the 1337 Bursa inscription—when correctly read in context—support his interpretation of their contents. This is readily apparent from the translation he provides for the Bursa inscription,[40] where he leaves out those titles which argue against the uniqueness he proclaims for the titularies it preserves. Far from reflecting some kind of unique early Ottoman historical reality, the 1337 inscription (in terms of style, titularies, etc.), fully establishes the extent to which even by that date the Ottomans were strongly influenced by the Seljuk-Ilhanid traditions which preceded them. They were already surrounded by calligraphers well-versed in Arabic and had (contradicting Wittek) fully adopted the "classical . . . formulas of the Seljuk period." Stated bluntly: neither of the two sources presented by Wittek in support of his *Gazi* Thesis actually provide the evidentiary underpinning he ascribed to them.

Wittek died in 1978. He did so without ever having modified his by then forty year old *Gazi* Thesis. In the generation following his death a wide variety of scholars have focused attention on his thesis without ever examining the sources upon which it was based. This is despite the fact that both a readable photograph of the 1337 Bursa inscription and a critical edition of Ahmedi's *İskendernâme*, were published within four years of the initial appearance of *The Rise of the Ottoman Empire*.[41] Even accounting for the fact that the field of Ottoman studies is still in its infancy, the failure of scholars who have addressed the issue to move beyond the flawed parameters established by Wittek is difficult to comprehend.

FOUR

What Could the Terms *Gaza* and *Gazi* Have Meant to the Early Ottomans?

Our attempt to come to grips with this query is focused not on the theoretical handbooks on *gaza* and *cihad,* which were produced in Islamic scholarly circles,[1] but rather upon the testimony of Ottoman sources and documents which reflect the practices associated with these concepts. Our effort in this regard is facilitated by the fact that Ahmedi's versified epic contains one *beyt* (couplet) which points us clearly in the direction of determining just what it was the early Ottomans meant when they used the terms *gaza* and *gazis.* When describing the reign of Orhan, and after regaling his readers with tales of how this ruler "plundered the infidel day and night," he adds the following couplet:

> "*Kāfir üzre akdılar a'vān-ı dīn*
> *Andan itdiler gazā adın akın*[2]

> The helpers of religion flowed [over]
> the unbelievers and that's why they
> called "*gaza*" (Holy War) "*akın*" (raid).[3]

As Colin Imber has pointed out in a recent article, Ahmedi in this couplet makes it clear that it was not *gaza/gazi* but rather *akın/akıncı* (from the Turkish verb *akmak* meaning to flow) that he was the most familiar with in daily usage. Given the intended purpose of his *destân* (epic) it is Ahmedi who emphasizes the religious *(gaza/gazi)* over the *Realpolitik/*secular *(akın/akıncı).* Imber argues persuasively that the Arabic *gazi* found in Ahmedi and other early Ottoman texts is in fact nothing more than a calque on the Turkish *akıncı.*[4] It is this definition which appears to best fit the actual activities Ahmedi describes the

Ottoman *gazis* as being engaged in. That is, rather than fired by religious zeal to convert the Christians of Bithynia and the Balkans, they were stimulated by a desire to gain booty and slaves. They were in fact a plundering confederacy which focused upon "flowing over" their enemies, rather than a religious brotherhood intent upon "converting" them to Islam. As such, we may infer that the terms *gaza/gazi* were in fourteenth- and fifteenth-century Ottoman usage synonymous with *akın/akıncı*.

This interpretation is further substantiated by the titularies used for *Köse* Mihal and *Gazi* Evrenos (and their descendants), who were the hereditary leaders of the *akıncı* forces in the Balkans from the mid-fourteenth century forward. As will be discussed in further detail in the ensuing chapter, these *akıncı* rulers styled themselves (and were so styled by the Ottoman Sultans) as *Malik al-ghuzat* (Lord or King of the *Gazis*), thereby illustrating the synonymous nature of the terms *gazi* and *akıncı* in Ottoman usage.[5]

That this is how they were seen by their foes is clear from a passage in the work of [Michael] Doukas, a Byzantine chronicler, whose account covers the first half of the fifteenth century. Doukas, who served variously as an emissary to the Ottoman rulers Murad II and Mehmed II (on behalf of the Genoese rulers of Yeni Foça and the island of Mytelene), had more than a passing familiarity with Ottoman practices in the fifteenth century. He described the typical Ottoman plan of conquest in the following terms:

> If they [the Turks] hear the herald's voice summoning them to the attack—which in their language is called *aqin*—they descend like a flooding river, uninvited, the majority without purse and food pouch and without spears and swords. Countless others come running, swelling the number of troops, the majority of them carrying nothing but a club in their hands. They rush against the Christians and seize them like sheep.[6]

Not only was Doukas familiar with the word *akın* as the common term used to describe Ottoman attacks, his likening of its affect to that of a "flooding river," also suggests that he knew it derived from the Turkish verb meaning to flow. As such he seemingly confirms Ahmedi's quotation that *gaza* was known by the early Ottomans as *akın*. His account of what the *akıncıs* did to their Christian foes closely parallels that provided by Ahmedi for his prototypical *gazis*.

Nor is Doukas the only fifteenth-century observer to indicate that these two terms were used interchangeably by the Ottomans. Konstantin Mihailovic, who served as an Ottoman Janissary in the mid-fifteenth century, uses terms similar to those employed by Doukas to describe the Ottoman raiders:

> The Turkish raiders are called in their language *akandye* [sic. *akıncı*] which means "those who flow," and they are like torrential rains that fall from the clouds. From these storms come great floods until the streams leave their banks and overflow, and everything this water strikes, it takes, carries away, and moreover, destroys, so that in some places they cannot quickly make repairs. But such sudden downpours do not last long. Thus also the Turkish raiders, or "those who flow," like rainstorms, do not linger long, but whatever they strike they burn, plunder, kill and destroy everything so that for many years the cock will not crow there.[7]

Finally, the late-fifteenth-century Byzanto-Italian chronicler, Spandugnino (whose work will be discussed in detail in the following chapter), also describes the Ottoman *akıncıs* in terms which are synonymous with those used by Ahmedi for the *gazis*. In his account of the various types of servants of the Ottoman Sultans: "the *achinzi* [sic. *akıncı*] or auxiliary cavalry, [are] especially committed to the slaughter of Christians as a passage to Paradise."[8] In so doing, he is echoing Ahmedi's earlier definition of what a good *gazi* was.

The works of the Ottoman Ahmedi, the Byzantine Doukas, the Serbian Mihailovic and the Italian Spandugnino are united in making it clear that to the contemporary fifteenth-century observers the term most commonly used to describe the Ottoman attacks against their neighbors was *akın*. It is only Ahmedi (writing for an intended Muslim audience) who uses the terms *gazi* and *akın* interchangeably. Even there (as a close reading of his text suggests), it was raiding and pillaging for slaves and booty which he was really describing, rather than an attempt to spread the message of Islam to the nonbelievers. This interpretation is further strengthened when one surveys the remainder of the extant corpus of fourteenth- and fifteenth-century Byzantine authors who provide the bulk of the contemporary descriptions of early Ottoman history. In addition to Doukas, writers such as Nikephoros Gregoras, Georges Pachymeres, George Sphrantzes, and Laonikos Chalcocondyles, make no mention whatsoever of the terms *gazi* or *gaza*.[9] This *ex silencio* argument, when coupled with the number of contemporary writers who do use variants of *akın* to describe the early Ottoman's military organization, points to the likelihood that this was the term actually used in the fourteenth century.

Indeed, if Ahmedi's work is taken at its face value, that is, as history as alleged by Wittek, there simply would have been no Christians left alive as such in Bithynia or southeastern Europe by the end of Murad I's reign (1389). They either would have been converted to Islam, or put to the sword. For Ahmedi's epic makes it clear that the role of the Ottoman *gazi* was to be "the servant of God, to purify the world from the filth of polytheism,"[10] to "kill the unbelievers," to "demolish all their churches," and ultimately "to kill all those who did not accept Islam at [their] invitation."[11] As will be demonstrated in the following chapter this was in fact the exact opposite of the policy followed by the early Ottoman rulers.

If, as our analysis of both the relevant passages from Ahmedi and the 1337 Bursa inscription has shown, *gaza/akın* was not viewed by the Ottomans and their followers as a religious obligation, what did it mean in the fourteenth and fifteenth century? Our answer to this query is facilitated by the survival of an imperial order issued by Sultan Bayezid II in 1484. This edict (written in Ottoman Turkish), which preserves the earliest surviving indication of how *gazas* were actually planned and organized by the Ottoman rulers, may be summarized as:

> Edict of the Sultan to all Kadıs (religious judges and governors of kazas): To defenders of the right path for Muslims and Islam, you are ordered to communicate in your respective districts the decree for the campaign I have ordered for all those wishing to comply with the obligation of *gaza*. All those wishing to join in the sacred conquest, engage in the pleasure of *gaza* and *cihad*, [all those] desiring booty and plunder, [all those] brave comrades who gain their bread by the sword, and all those wishing to receive a *timar* by comradeship, are requested to join me with their weapons and accessories in this blessed *gaza* and for a share in the rewards of this *gaza* and *cihad*. And all those who gain booty and comradeship will enjoy my kindness and assistance. And those seeking *timars* will have my help in obtaining *timars* and *dirliks,* and as this year there will be no *pençik* [the fifth, i.e., the 20 percent normally accruing to the Sultan], taken from anyone's booty, they should perform accordingly. Issued in the beginning of May 1484 in Kabaağaç.[12]

This edict, issued prior to the date at which the Ottoman court chronicles describing *gaza* as Holy War were compiled, provides a number of important clues as to the actual meaning of this term in the late fifteenth century. First and foremost is its relative silence on the subject of the participants engaging in any kind of religious observance, the killing of infidels, and so forth. To the contrary, Bayezid II is appealing solely to the ephemeral and temporal concerns of his potential *gazis*. Rather than discussing the rewards of paradise which will result for those falling in the cause of Islam, he holds forth not only the promise

PLATE 2

Bayezid II's 1484 Summoning of the *Gazis* for His Moldavian Campaign

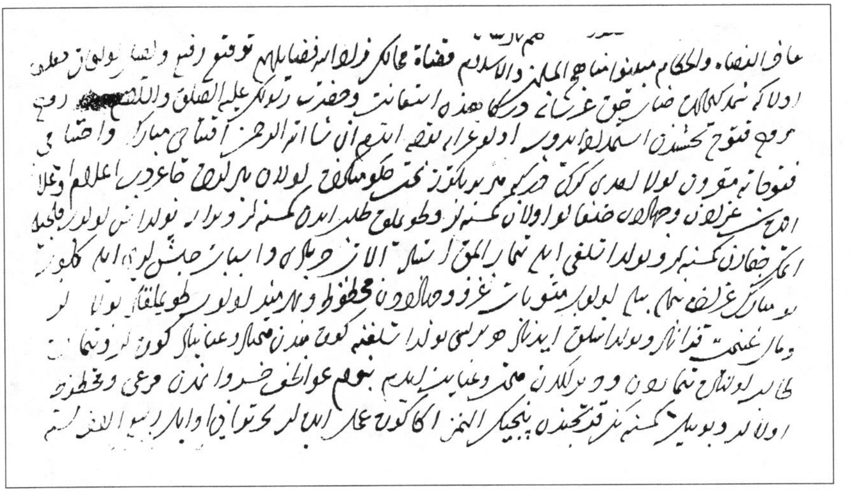

TRANSCRIPTION: *Süret-i hükm-i Padişah: Mafakhir al-qudat wa'l hukkam, mübayyinu manahij al-müslimin wa'l-islam, qudat mamalik [al-mahrusa], -zada Allah fada'ilahum. tevki'-i refi' vasıl olıcak ma'lum ola-ki şimdiki-halde Cenab-i Hakk ['azza shanahu] dergahından isti'anet ve Hazret-i Resul'ün—'aleyhi al-salat wa'l-salamin—ruh-ı muravvah-i futuh-bahşından istimdad idüb eda'-i gazaya teveccüh etdüm—inşa' Allah al-Rahman—iftitahı mübarek ve ihtitamı fütuhata makrun ola imdi gerekdür-ki her birinüz taht-i hükumetünüzde olan yerlerde çagırub i'lam u i'lan idesiz: gazadan ve cihaddan safalu olan kimesneler ve doyumlık taleb iden kimesneler ve yarar yoldaş olur kılıc-ıyla etmek çıkaran kimesneler ve yoldaşlıgı-ile timar almak istiyenler alat-i harbları ve esbab-i ceyşleri-ile gelüb bu mübarek gazada benümle bile olub mesubat-ı gazv u cihaddan mahzuz ve behremend olub doyumlıklar bulalar ve mal-i ganimet kazanalar ve yoldaşlık idenler her-birisi yoldaşlıgına göre benden himmetler ve 'inayetler göreler ve timara talib olanlara timardan ve dirlikden himmet ve 'inayet idüm; benüm 'avatıf-ı hüsrevanemden mer'i ve mahzuz olalar ve bu yıl kimesnenün kazancından pencik alınmaz ana göre 'amel ideler. tahriren fi awa'il Rabi' al-akhir li-seneti tis'a wa semanine wa semanimi'ete. Bi-yurt-i Devletlü Kaba Agaç*

SOURCE: İnalcik, *"Osmanlı İdare"* (1981), pp. 16–17.

of booty and plunder, but also that of *timars* (military fiefs) and *dirliks* (revenue sources granted as income), for those who respond to his invitation to participate in the 1484 campaign. Then, as if to sweeten the pot, he provides an added incentive by informing would be participants that contrary to the normal practice whereby 20 percent of all booty acquired on such campaigns went to the ruler, in this instance the *gazis* will be allowed to keep everything they acquire in the way of plunder, slaves, and booty.

We can only conjecture that the added incentive of being allowed to keep all the booty was necessitated by virtue of the fact that there were not hordes of fighters waiting in line for a summons to participate in the spread of Islam. As this edict was issued in Kabaağaç, a village in European Thrace, while Bayezid was already en route to Moldavia, it may well reflect a shortage of manpower and an attempt on his part to ensure an adequate force of combatants. The promise of *timars* and *dirliks* as a reward for those responding to his call may be viewed as an indication that it was not Wittek's *"gazi ethos,"* but rather the hope of financial gain which served to create *gazis*. Nor should we overlook that this document emanated from the chancery of Bayezid II, the Ottoman ruler most venerated for his pious observance of Islam. Referred to in the Ottoman sources as *"Veli"* (Friend of God), it is Bayezid II we would normally expect to have paid the closest attention to the religious aspects of *gaza* and *cihad*. Instead, we see him summoning his *gazis* in 1484 by appealing primarily to their desire for material gain.

Bayezid II's 1484 campaign which assembled in Edirne in early May was indeed directed against a Christian enemy, the Prince of Moldavia (Boğdan),[13] and as such fits the classic definition of a *gaza*. However, as the edict he issued to potential combatants clearly illustrates, it was the hope of booty and plunder rather than religious zeal which he used to stimulate the interest of his potential soldiery.

As this decree contains reference both to *gaza* and *cihad*, it seems possible that these two terms may have been used with distinct meanings by the Ottomans in this period. Could it be that *gaza* here has the meaning of raid, which is specifically appealing to the *akıncıs* (who were not necessarily Muslims), whereas the term *cihad*, or Holy War, is addressed to his Muslim subjects? This hypothesis is suggested by virtue of the fact that this *hükm* (decree) is not specifically limited to Muslims, but instead uses the religiously neutral term *"yoldaş"* (comrade or companion) in addressing its intended audience. Indeed, it summons all those desiring *yoldaşlık* (comradeship), booty and *timars* or *dirliks* to join the 1484 Moldavian campaign.

Here then was the probable meaning of *gaza* in the political vocabulary of the early Ottomans and their followers. As Ahmedi's work suggested *gaza* was but a calque for *akın* (a pillaging raid). The potential *gazis* addressed in Bayezid's edict are not his *timar*iot forces, that is, those *sipahis* (military fief holders) who are required to join him on campaign in return for their fiefs, rather this edict is seemingly issued to peasant irregulars or *akıncıs* (raiders), whom he terms *gazis*. Presumably his feudal *sipahi* cavalry forces, together with his standing Janissary army had already joined him at Kabaağaç (a village to the east of Edirne), which was the staging point for the 1484 campaign. It was only when he realized that he did not have a sufficient number of pillagers and raiders, that is, *akıncıs* (whom he calls "*gazis*"), that he was forced to take the extraordinary steps of renouncing his claim to a percentage of the booty and proffering the promise of *timars* and *dirliks* in an attempt to attract the Christian and Muslim irregulars who traditionally led the Ottoman advance. This would explain Ahmedi's statement that already by the beginning of the fifteenth century the Ottomans referred to "*gaza*" as "*akın.*"

To anyone familiar with the standard explanations of the nature of the Ottoman armies in the fourteenth and fifteenth century, the obvious question at this stage would be: on what do you base your assumption that the Ottoman auxiliary force known as the *akıncıs* was in fact formed of Muslims and Christians? After all, standard works on this force usually state that the *akıncıs* were a Muslim body of mounted irregulars who led the Ottoman advances.[14] To answer this query we must turn to an important document which is preserved in an *Akıncı Defter* (Register of the *Akıncıs*), housed in the National Library in Sofia, Bulgaria. Published a generation ago by the Bulgarian scholar Boris Nedkov, this document has been heretofore ignored by scholars working on early Ottoman history. It is dated December 1472, during the reign of Mehmed II, and relates to the levying of *akıncıs*, who are to serve in the Sultan's upcoming 1473 campaign against Uzun Hasan, the ruler of the White Sheep confederation in eastern Anatolia. The document itself is an imperial order issued by Mehmed and addressed to a number of *kadıs* (judges) in the Balkans. It provides not only detailed instructions on the manner by which *akıncıs* are to be registered, conscripted, and have their expenses met, but also specifically states that:

> From every thirty households of unbelievers and Muslims you are to conscript one mounted *akıncı*.
>
> *Kafirden ve Müsülmanlardan otuz eve bir atlü akıncı vaz' edesiz.*[15]

Bearing in mind that the Balkans in this period were overwhelmingly Christian in population, this order allows us to infer that in the late fifteenth century the forces of the *akıncıs* not only contained Christians, but that this body was primarily comprised of non-Muslims. We may illustrate this interpretation with a case study from the region of Çirmen (one of the provinces to which Mehmed's order was sent in 1472). A generation later, at the beginning of the sixteenth century, this province had a total of 12,684 Christian households *(hanes)* and 1,578 Muslim ones.[16] At that point in time, applying Mehmed's 1472 decree solely to the population of this one Balkan province would have resulted in the mustering of 423 Christian *akıncıs* and just 53 Muslim ones. Stated differently, over 85 percent of the *akıncıs* so summoned would have been Christians.

Mehmed II's order leaves no doubt but that the above interpretation is correct, for in a second passage (as if to reiterate the fact that he is primarily interested in Christian *akıncıs*), he instructs his *kadıs* as follows:

> When there are persons among the Unbelievers (Christians) who are able to serve as *akıncıs* they are to be registered [first], and only if it is not possible to find such persons among them are you to register Muslims [as *akıncıs*].
>
> *Kafirlerden içlerinden akıncılığa kabil bulunur ise yazalar ve eger bulınmaz ise Müslümanlardan yazalar.*"[17]

Clearly, Christians were not only serving as *akıncıs,* but it appears that during the period we are discussing preference was given to non-Muslims for service in the corps of mounted irregulars who traditionally led the Ottoman army's advance (even in campaigns such as this one which was directed against a Muslim ruler of the White Sheep confederation).

Thus, when a decade later Bayezid II sends out his decree promising a variety of financial rewards to those who will join him on the 1484 Moldavian campaign, we may infer that his use of the religiously neutral term *"yoldaş"* did in fact mean that he was summoning both Muslims and Christians to join in his endeavor. The *gazis/akıncıs* who responded to his invitation may be assumed to be following in the footsteps of several generations of earlier recruits. There simply is no reason to assume that the mounted auxiliaries who pillaged ahead of the Ottoman armies in the fourteenth century had not been comprised of a similar admixture of Muslims and Christians. Here we are faced with a late-fifteenth-century example of what must have been a far older practice, one whose roots stretch back to the formative years of the state.

To the early Ottomans, and indeed throughout the fifteenth century, the term *gaza/akın* seems to have had the meaning of raiding. Its aim was

PLATE 3
1472 Order by Mehmed II for the Conscription of *Akıncıs*

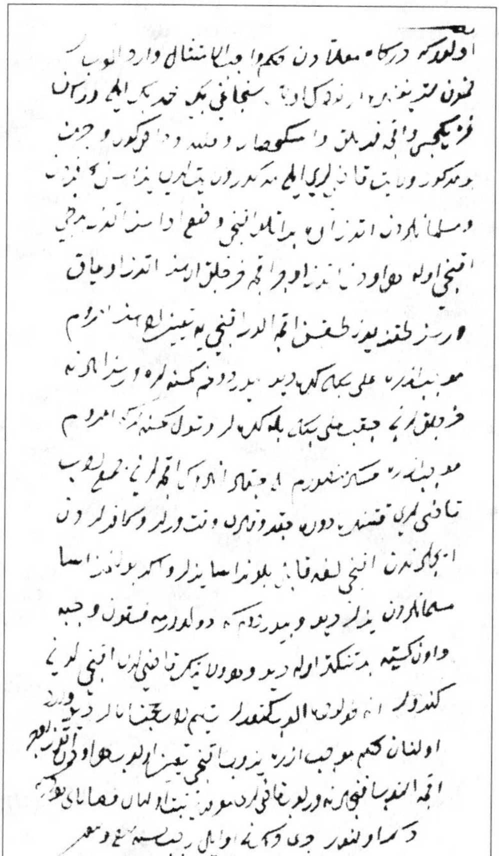

TRANSCRIPTION: *[Line 1] Mufassal* // *[2] oldur-ki Dergāh-i Mu`allā'dan hükm-i vācibü-l-imtisāl vārid olub* // *[3] mazmün-i şerīfinde Arvavud' ün evvelki Sancagi Begi Mehemmed Beg-ile varsın* // *[4] Zagra Yenice ve Akçe Kazanlık ve Eskihisār ve Filibe ve Hās Köy ve Çirmen* // *[5] bu mezkür Vilāyet Kādıları-ile mezkür Vilāyetleri yazasız Kāfirden* // *[6] ve Müsülmānlardan otuz eve bir atlü akıncı vaz' edesiz otuz birinci* // *[7] akıncı ola her evden otuz üçer akçe harclık alasiz otuz ev yamak* // *[8] versiz tokuz yüz toksan akçe alub akıncıya ta'yīn edesiz emrüm* // *[9] mücib üzre 'Alī Beg'e gide deyü buyurduğum kimesnelere versiz ellerine* // *[10] harclıklarını çıkub 'Ali Beg-le bile gideler ve şol kimesneler ki emrüm* // *[11] mücib üzre 'asker-i mansürum [sic!]-ile çıkmaz anlarün akçelerin cem' edüb* // *[12] Kādıları katında devre çıkdukları vakıt var[a]lar ve Kāfirlerden* // *[13] içlerinden akıncılığa kābili bulunur ise*

yaz[a]lar ve eger bulınmaz ise // *[14] Müslümanlardan yaz[a]lar deyü ve buyurdum-ki doldurma fiston ve cebe* // *[15] ve on kişiye bir tenktar ola deyü ve her Vilayetün Kadıları akıncıların* // *[16] gendüler Anatolu'da alub gönder[e]ler teslīm edüb hüccet alalar deyü vārid* // *[17] olınan hükm mücib üzre yazub akıncı ta'yīn olub her evden otuz üç* // *[18] akçe alınub akıncılarına verilüb Kadıları ma'rifet-le sebt olınan kazāyāyı budur-ki* // *[19] zikr olınur cerā zālike fi evāyili recebi li-sene seb'a ve seb'īn* // *[20] ve semāne-mi'e hicriye.*

(continued on next page)

PLATE 3 *(continued)*

SUMMARY TRANSLATION: Detailed [The Beginning of the Detailed Register]: From my elevated post the order which is in need of being fulfilled. And in his noble text it is written: you should come from the former Sancak Bey of Albania Mehemmed Bey and both of you have to register together with the *Kadıs* of the Vilayets (Provinces) of Zagra Yenice, Akçe Kazanlik, Eskihisar, Filibe, Has Köy and Çirmen. *You should register from each thirty houses of unbelievers and Muslims one mounted* akıncı and he should be the thirty-first from among them [?]. From every house you should assess 33 *akçes* as expenditures, and the *Yamaks* of thirty houses must be provided and then you should take 990 *akçes* and apportion it to the *akıncıs*. In conformity with my order you should give to the persons whom I ordered to go to Ali Beg their expenses, and they should go together with ʿAli Beg and those persons who in keeping with my orders will not accompany my victorious army. From them you should collect their *akçes,* and when it is their turn to go [on campaign] they should appear before the *Kadıs* who will pay their expenses. *If there are persons who are able to engage in* akın *among the* kafirs *(unbelievers) you should register them [first], and only if it is not possible to find such persons among them are you then to register* akıncıs *among the Muslims.* [emphasis is mine] I order that they come with weapons, garments, light coats of mail and for each ten persons there must be a tent. And the *Kadıs* of each province should gather the *akıncıs* and personally bring them to Anatolia and deliver them. They should take the *Hüccet* (court order) and register them in accordance with it, and they should provide them with everything they need. They should take from each house 33 *akçe* and give that money to the *akıncıs*. My decisions are those which are registered under the control of the *kadıs* and this is here registered as it happened in December of 1472.

SOURCE: Nedkov, *Osmano-turska diplomatika* (1972), p. 321.

less the conversion of infidels who refused to accept the true faith, than it was the amassing of booty, slaves, and plunder for its practitioners. The Ottoman *gazis/akıncıs* included both Muslims and non-Muslims united in the singleminded aim of material betterment. Participating in a *gaza/akın* gave nonmembers of the ruling elite the opportunity of upward social mobility on the basis of their contribution. It was this, rather than religious zeal, which attracted ever-growing bodies of warriors to the Ottoman banner. By becoming an Ottoman the doors of opportunity were opened. The frontier represented the possibility of wealth, security, and advancement, factors which worked like a magnet to attract men of ambition. The resulting Ottoman juggernaut rolled through Bithynia and into the Balkans, fueled not by the zeal of a religious brotherhood, but by the greed and ambition of a predatory confederacy.

FIVE

Toward a New Explanation

Now in the time of Michael Paleologo [Michael VIII, 1261–1282], the first of his house to reign as Emperor in Constantinople, there were four lords of the Turks in the vicinity. One was called Michauli, the second was Turachan, the third Evrenes, the fourth Ottomano. Each was no more than a petty chieftain. They knew that the Emperor Michael had left their frontier. But as they were, they were too divided and scattered to attack their enemies as was their wont; rather they thought of defending themselves. They saw that the power of the Christians was too great for them to resist it singly, and they soon decided to look not to their own self-interest but to their common good; and they did something generous and memorable. . . . One day they assembled together to elect one lord from among them. Each of these present had his own say but all were agreed that none could match Ottomano in authority, courage and strength of character. They found it hard to decide, for by common consent they would rather have had a brother than a sovereign lord. But they elected Ottomano as such; and he became the first Emperor of the Turks.

—Nicol, *Theodore Spandounes*

If, as we have seen, the "*Gazi* Thesis" fails adequately to explain the forces which account for the fact that Osman and his followers planted the seeds for what in the following century was to grow into the mighty Ottoman Empire, we are left with the need to advance an alternative theory based on a reexamination of the surviving evidence. The starting point for such an endeavor is the above passage from Spandugnino's *On the Origin of the Ottoman Emperors,* which provides us several clues as to the impetus which led to the formation of the early Ottoman polity.

It is by comparing its version with the earliest Ottoman chronicle accounts detailing the conquest of the city of Bursa in 1326, that we begin to see the outline of who the Ottomans actually were at that point in their historical development. In this regard, the work of the fifteenth-century chronicler Aşıkpaşazade is particularly important. While written down several generations after the emergence of the Ottomans, its description of the origins of the state relies on an authentic fourteenth-century narrative.[1] By carefully weeding out those polemical passages which İnalcık has shown reflect the conflicts between the state and traditional ruling elite during the reign of Mehmet II, and focusing our attention on the earliest history of the Ottomans as Aşıkpaşazade related it to the dervishes who were his intended audience,[2] we may gain valuable insights into the heroic deeds *(menakıb)* of the founders of the Ottoman state prior to the time at which they were sanitized by the sixteenth-century imperial chroniclers.

Aşıkpaşazade provides a detailed account of the conquest of Bursa based on earlier oral traditions, which supplies the basis for the following interpretation: Bearing in mind that the actual surrender of the city was accomplished by *Köse* (the beardless) Mihal, a newly converted Muslim, who a few years earlier had been a Greek-Christian fighting alongside Osman, and that he negotiated the terms with the Byzantine ruler's chief minister Saroz (another Greek who opted to remain with the Ottomans rather than take a ship to Constantinople with the governor and his entourage), Aşıkpaşazade's account of the ensuing purported conversation between Saroz and Orhan is particularly illuminating. Orhan is clearly interested in the reasons which led to the city's surrender in April 1326. After all, Bursa had withstood an Ottoman siege for over ten years. When he questions Saroz as to the factors which finally prompted the surrender, he also queries him as to why upon entering the castle his men had found stacks of dead bodies. Saroz replies:

> We surrendered for a variety of reasons. For one thing your state is growing bigger and bigger every day. Ours [in contrast] has turned. This we were well aware of. For another, your father struck against us and then left. His state took our villages. They submitted to you. We understood that they were comfortable. We realized that they didn't miss us. We, too, desired that comfort. [As for the dead bodies] they died of starvation.[3]

It appears clear that the expansion of the Ottomans in this period was directly linked to the fact that their banner brought together peoples of various ethnic and religious backgrounds (Bithynian Greeks, Armenians, and Jews, together with Turks), whose leaders were united by the common goals of plunder and wealth. In this sense, it was a classic example of what we might term a "Predatory Confederacy," a commingling of frontier peoples, which served to bring together Muslim and Christian warriors in Bithynia. At the bottom of the social pyramid, Aşıkpaşazade suggests it was the security provided by the new state thus formed (coupled with a reasonable tax load), which ensured the loyalty of the largely Christian peasant population to the enterprise.

The Greek Minister Saroz negotiates the surrender of the city with *Köse* Mihal, a newly converted Muslim (who happens to be an important Ottoman commander), and then opts to become an Ottoman himself, rather than be repatriated to Constantinople. Whether or not he did so before or after converting to Islam is unclear from Aşıkpaşazade's account. The clue he provides for his reasoning is important and must have played a role in numerous such shifts in allegiance. He states it openly: "For one thing your state is growing bigger and bigger every day. Ours [in contrast] has turned." Nothing succeeds like success, and with the example of numerous Greek Ottomans like *Köse* Mihal in front of them, the option of switching to the winning team must have been particularly attractive to the local Greek rulers of the castles and towns of Bithynia. For their subjects it was simply a matter of accepting the reality on the ground. Even there, Saroz makes it apparent that he realized that their loyalties had shifted. They were "comfortable" under the new order and did not miss their former rulers.

Herbert A. Gibbons, citing the fourteenth-century Byzantine chronicler, Nicephorus Gregoras, names the aforementioned "Saros" as "Evrenos," who, following his becoming an Ottoman, was to emerge as one of the conquerors of the Balkans. He and his descendants were to become one of the most important "noble" families of the Ottomans.[4] Gibbon's identification (which I am unable to confirm in Gregoras?) in this regard follows Hammer, who citing the Ottoman chroniclers Idris and Sadeddin states that "Ewrenosbeg was originally the Greek commander of Bursa, who joined Orhan and became a Muslim."[5] This interpretation is likewise accepted by the Turkish scholar İsmail Hami Danişmend (albeit without benefit of source), who in describing the fall of Bursa on April 6, 1326 names the Byzantine ruler's negotiator as "Evrenos,"[6] and İsmail Hakkı Uzunçarşılı, who quoting Gibbons states that the defender of the Bursa castle, Evrenuz, entered Ottoman service as a Muslim.[7] Despite this seeming identification, in a later article on Evrenos, Uzunçarşılı described him as a Karasi warrior who joins the Ottomans following their absorption of that neighboring principality.[8]

Neither Irene Melikoff nor İsmail Hakkı Uzunçarşılı, the two scholars who have provided the standard encyclopedia articles on *Gazi*

Evrenos,[9] discuss the fact that the name "Evrenos" is derived neither from Arabic, Persian, or Turkish, that is, that it is not a Muslim name, a fact which points strongly to a Christian origin for this individual. Nor do they discuss the chronicle tradition which links Evrenos to Bursa. Rather, they both identify him as a leading Karasi warrior who passed into Ottoman service following the annexation of that neighboring Beylik (neither provide a source in support of their identifications). Indeed, the earliest reference I have found to Evrenos in an Ottoman source is Aşıkpaşazade's naming of a *Gazi* Evrenos, who in 1357 was playing a role in the Ottoman expansion into the Balkans.[10] The first compiler of the Ottoman chronicle tradition, the sixteenth-century translator Johannes Leunclavius, in his *Pandectes Historiae Turcicae,* provides the Greek name "Evrenosides" as the origin of "Evrenos," while also identifying him as a Turk.[11] Claude Cahen has posited a Balkan origin for the name, suggesting that it may recall a temporarily Hellenized form of the toponym Varna/Evren[12]

As to the still unanswered question of the origins of *Gazi* Evrenos the son of 'İsa Beg, an alternative explanation is inferable from the fact that Uzunçarşılı, citing Ö. L. Barkan, states that Evrenos' father was known by the nickname "Franki" (which is later preserved as "Prangi" or "Pirangi" [*Frengi* meaning European])[13] 'İsa (Jesus) Beg. This raises the possibility that he was a Frank (European), allowing us to posit an Aragonese or Catalan origin for this family. In the opening decade of the fourteenth century, numerous such Spanish mercenaries fought both for and against the Byzantines in western Anatolia and the Balkans. Indeed, the contemporary Catalan chronicler Muntaner relates that at one point their forces were augmented by some eight hundred Turkish cavalry (supported by two thousand infantry), under the leadership of one Ximelich (Melik?),[14] who had originally been mercenaries in the service of the Byzantine emperor. He stresses the close relationship that bound these Turks and the Aragonese/Catalan mercenaries who fought for and against various Byzantine claimants to the Imperial throne in the opening years of the fourteenth century. Based on the fact that the contemporary Byzantine chronicler Pachymeres clearly states that in 1305 a detachment of Catalans joined the Ottomans,[15] it seems well within the realm of possibility to postulate that 'İsa the Frank and his son Evrenos were Catalans who either went into Byzantine, Karasi, or Ottoman service. This would account for the nickname "Franki" (Frenk meaning European) or Frengi meaning European, by which Evrenos' father 'İsa (Jesus) Beg was known, while at the same time explaining the origin of the non-Muslim name Evrenos. For the Catalans were called by the Greeks "Franks," and indeed they used this epithet as their battle cry when fighting both Byzantine and Genoese Christians and Muslims.[16] As these were indeed the first Franks encountered by the Muslims of Bithynia, the use of this epithet for 'İsa (Jesus) Beg, the father of Evrenos, would suggest the possibility of his having been one of these European mercenaries who entered Turkish service. As late as 1408, the seal of the Aragonese/Catalans which the chronicler Muntaner possessed at Gallipoli, read: "Seal of the Host of the *Franks* who are Ruling the Kingdom of Macedonia."[17]

While this suggestion clearly needs to be subjected to further study, both the non-Arabic, Turkish, or Persian origin of the name Evrenos, coupled with the fact that the 1417 Yenice Vardar inscription from the tomb of *Gazi* Evrenos clearly states that he had made the pilgrimage to Mecca (a common practice in this period for new converts to Islam), point to the possibility that he could have been the son of an Aragonese or Catalan mercenary, Isa (Jesus) the Frank, who stayed on in Bithynia in the service of the Karasi Principality and later joined the Ottomans.

Regardless of which hypothesis regarding the origin of Evrenos prevails, it appears that at least two of the three great Ottoman warrior families of the fourteenth and fifteenth centuries may have been founded by converted Byzantine Christians and/or Spanish mercenaries (those of the Mihaloğulları and Evrenosoğulları respectively). We know little in regard to the origins of the other family, the Turahanoğulları,[18] except for the fact that unlike Evrenos and Mihal the earliest reference we have to a member of this family is at the end of the first quarter of the fifteenth century in 1423.[19] This raises the possibility that in the fourteenth century there were *three* great warrior families in Bithynia, not four as stated by Spandugnino. One of these was Muslim (Osman) and two were Christian in origin (Mihal and Evrenos).

As even this short sketch illustrates, the actual origins of Evrenos are clouded in the same kind of confusion that covers all aspects of the early-fourteenth-century history of the rise of the Ottomans. What is clear however is that by the second half of the fourteenth century both a *Gazi* Evrenos and a *Gazi* 'Ali Beg, the son of *Köse* Mihal, were leading the *gaza/akın* in the Balkans. This was soon to become a hereditary role for these families and their descendants, who throughout the course of the following two centuries served as the leaders of the *akıncis/gazis,* or the "raiders" who preceded the Ottoman armies on their campaigns.

While a close perusal of the sources cited by Hammer in support of his contention that Evrenos was the Saros who surrendered the city of Bursa to Orhan's forces in 1326 shows no textual basis for his identification, and a careful reading of İsmail Hakki Uzunçarşılı and Irene

Melikoff uncovers no source for their contention regarding his Karasi roots, a more recent publication by the Greek scholar Vasilis Demetriades (one which appeared after the articles by Uzunçarşılı and Melikoff), provides us valuable new insight into both the chronology and importance of this individual.[20]

In 1974 while visiting the former Ottoman town of Yenice Vardar (Yenitsa), thirty miles to the west of Thessalonica, Demetriades discovered the previously unrecorded *kitabe* (dedicatory inscription) in the tomb of the original *Gazi* Evrenos Beg. This inscription provides the information that he died on Wednesday, November 17, 1417. This information removes any likelihood that he was the Saros mentioned by Aşıkpaşazade as the Byzantine official who negotiated the surrender of Bursa in 1326.[21] It further clearly states that he was a *hacı* (hadji, i.e., one who had made the pilgrimage to Mecca), and names him as Evrenos, the son of 'Isa. Moreover, it accords him the high-sounding title of: *malik al-ghuzat* (Lord or King of the *gazis*), a title strangely reminiscent of that used by Orhan in the 1337 Bursa inscription, where he had termed himself *sultan al-ghuzat* (Sultan of the *gazis*) This latter title likewise appears (Wittek's assertion to the contrary notwithstanding) in several later Ottoman inscriptions, including that of a *hamam* (bath house) built by Murad II in 1440–41 in the city of Edirne.[22] The actual text of the titles accorded Evrenos on his 1417 tomb reads:

Malik al-ghuzat wa'l-mujahidin, qâtıl al-kafara wa'l-mushrikin.[23]

Lord/King of the *Gazis* and the Fighters for the Faith, Slayer of the infidels and polytheists.

Here we have nothing less than the founder of the Evrenosoğulları line described in terms heretofore seen only for members of the Ottoman dynasty. A comparison of the titles thus ascribed to Evrenos with those previously discussed as used by the Ottomans in the fourteenth and fifteenth century,[24] shows parallels which suggest that in the opening century of Ottoman rule at least one of the great families did not hesitate from viewing themselves as near equal to the dynasty.

Nor was this tendency limited to the Evrenosoğulları. We have a similar series of titles conferred on *Gazi* Ali Beg, a son of *Köse* Mihal, who in a *berat* (patent of appointment) from 1390, is accorded (by no one less than the Ottoman Sultan Bayezid I himself), the titles of:

al-amir al-kabir . . . malik al-ghuzat wa'l-mujahidin.[25]

The Great Emir . . . Lord/King of the *Gazis* and the Fighters for the Faith.[26]

PLATE 4
The 1417 Tombstone of *Gazi* Evrenos in Yenice Vardar

TRANSCRIPTION: *[Line 1] Qad mata wa nuqila min Dari l-fana ila Dar-i l-baqa al-marhum // [2] al-maghfur al-sa'id al-shahid Maliku l-guzat wa-l—mujahidin // [3] Qatilu l-kafara wa-l-mushrikin al-za'ir Beyta-llahi l-haram // [4] al ta'if bayna-l-rukn wa-l-maqam Haci Awranuz bin 'Isa // [5] nawwara-llahu qabrahu wa taba tharahu ila rahmati-llahi ta'ala // [6] wa ridwanihi fi-l-yawmi l-arbi'ā al-sabi'min // [7] shahri Shawwali li-sanati 'ishrina waa thamanimi'ata hijriyya."*

TRANSLATION: He died and has been transferred from the abode of Transience to the Abode of Permanence, the recipient of mercy and forgiveness, the felicitous, the martyr, King/Lord of the *Gazis* and the fighters of the *Jihad,* slayer of the infidels and the polytheists, he who has visited the sacred house of God [Mecca], he who has performed the circumambulation between the corner and the station, Haji Evrenoz, son of 'Isa, may God illumine his grave and may his dust be fragrant, to the mercy of Almighty God and his approbation, on Wednesday the seventh of the month of *Shawwal* in the year 820 of the *Hijra.*

SOURCE: Demetriades, "The Tomb of *Gazi* Evrenos" (1976), pp. 330–332.

In this instance, Bayezid I is himself describing the son of *Köse* Mihal in terms which pointedly suggest that he, too, viewed *Gazi* Ali *Beg* as a near equal, or at least as a ruler in his own right. This brings to mind the description of the origins of the Ottomans provided by Spandugnino (with which this chapter began), in which he alleged that the state had initially been formed by a group of Bithynian Muslim (Ottomano and Turahan) and Christian warriors (Mihauli and Evrenes), who joined together under the leadership of Osman to press their fight against the weakened Byzantine frontier.

PLATE 5
1391 Imperial Order *(biti)* on Behalf of Mihalogli 'Ali Beg Issued by Bayezid II

TRANSCRIPTION: *[Line 1] Tevqi'-i ref-i Hümayunum hukmi oldur-ki: Mer-hum ve Maghfur lehü // [2] babam Khudavendigar'un shehid vaqi' oldığı jeng-i 'azimde // [3] işbu Emirü l-kebir Müftekhirü l-ümer'i l-'izam Melikü l-guzat ve l-müjahidin // [4] Qahirī l-kefere ve l-mushrikin Mikhalbeg-ogli 'Ali Beg—dame // [5] ülü-khidmetlerinün külli erligi ve yoldashligi zuhura // [6] gelmegin emr eledüm-ki evladlarına batnen ba'de // [7] badninve garnen ba'de garnin Sanjaq verilüb min ba'du // [8] mu'zul olmamaq içün be Bitiyi virdüm ve buyurdum-ki benüm // [9] evladumdan ve intisabumdan her-kime Haqq janibinden Devlet müyesser // [10] olur ise bu Bitiye maqbul tutub Ghazi 'Ali Beg // [11] evladumun evladlarına Sanjaq Beg-ligi virüb ve min ba'du // [12] ma'zul eylemeyüb ri'ayet ü himayet ideler her kim bu Bitiyi // [13] maqbul tut-miya—'Kama qalahu Subhanahu wa Ta'ala fa-man badala-hu ba'da ma // [14] sam'iaha fa-innama athimahu 'ala-lladhina yubaddiluna inna[ll]aha sami'un 'alim wa la'natu[ll]ahi // [15] wa-l-mala'ikata wa-u-nasi ajma'in—üzerine olsun bu Bitiye // [16] muqar-rer u muhaqqaq bitüb i'timad u i'tiqad qılalar tahriren fi eva'ili // [17] Muharremi l-harami min sene tha-lathina wa tis'ina wa saba-mi'a // [18] Bi-maqami Edirne el-Mahruse.*

[19] Şahid bi-zalike Qasim Beg // [20] Şahid bi-zalike Hamza Beg El-Menavi // [21] Şahid bi-zalike Menla Hafızeddin bin-i Mehemmed // [22]

(continued on next page

PLATE 5 *(continued)*

Şahid [bi-zalike] Şah Melek Paşa Lala Paşa // [23] Şahid bi-zalike Menla Mah-mud Eş-şohret Qoca Efendi // [24] Şahid bi-zalike Ümür Beg bin-i Efendi // [25] Şahid bi-zalike Qara Muqbil Lala // [26] Şahid bi-zalike Timurtaş Beg // [27] Şahid bi-zalike Menla Şemseddin bin-i Mehemmed // [28] Şahid bi-zalike Hasan El-Kuttab fi khidmeti s-Sultan // [29] Şahid bi-zalike Menla Celaleddin bin-i Mehemmed Efendi El-Hakim bi Memaliki s-Sultaniye // [30] Şahid bi-zalike Sulü Beg bin-i Aghzar [?] Şahin // [31] Şahid bi-zalike Es-şehir Ghasrakal [?] Mütev-elli // [32] Şahid bi-zalike Mufzilü l-fuzilat El-Haim Paşa // [33] Şahid bi-zalike diğer Qasim Beg // [34] Şahid bi-zalike Mahmud Beg bin-i _____ [?] // [35] Şahid bi-zalike İlyas Beg bin al-Haydarānī [?] // [36] Şahid bi-zalike Mevlahulu [?].

TRANSLATION: The order of my ruling is as follows: Because, in the great battle when my father Hüdavendigar died as a martyr, *this great Emir, of the Proud and Great Emirs, the Lord/King of Holy warriors and fighters, the destroyer of infidels and idolators, Mihal Beg's son 'Ali Beg* [emphasis mine]—may his exultation last—due to the great courage and comradeship of his service I order that the Sancak be given to the children of his children, from generation to generation, I gave this Order that they should not be dismissed from this position, and I ordered: that this Order be observed by whichever of my children and descendants are assisted by the Truthful One, and the children of my children should ensure that the Sancak be given to the children of the children of *Gazi* 'Ali Beg, and that they should not be removed from this post and they [the Sultan's children] should protect and respect this Order, let it be like God—Glory be to him the Elevated one—said: "And whosoever changeth [the will] after he hath heard it, the sin thereof is only upon those who change it. Lo! Allah hears and knows all," may they be cursed by God, His angels and mankind and having this Order corroborated and ascertained, they should rely on it. The first decade of the sacred month of Muharrem in the year 793 [1390].

SOURCE: Mehmed Nüzhet, *Ahval-i Mihal Gazi* (1897), p. 45–47. The where-abouts of the original of this document, reproduced by M. Nüzhet in his 1897 book, are unknown. However, its language, list of witnesses, and the similarity of the titles it accords *Gazi* 'Ali Beg with those found on the tombstone of *Gazi* Evrenos, all attest to its authenticity.

Aided by Appendix 2, it is possible to trace the usage of the title *"Malik"* (Lord/King) in the surviving fourteenth- and early-fifteenth-century sources for Ottoman history, that is, in accounts by travelers, documents, inscriptions, and coins. The profile which emerges (listed chronologically) provides the following examples:

In ca. 1333, the North African traveler İbn Battuta, who visits Orhan in İznik, refers to him as "the greatest of the Lords/Kings *(Malik)* of the Turkmens."[27]

In a 1360 *vakıfname* established by Orhan, he refers to himself by the titles: *mâlik riqab al-umam* ('possessor of the necks' meaning of peoples and nations) and *mâlik muluk al-umara' fi'l-'alam* (Lord/King of the kings of princes of the world).[28]

In a 1385 copy of a *vakıfname* drawn up for Murad I, he is referred to by the title: *melik-i mülük al-arab wa'l-acem* (Lord/King of the lords/kings of the Arabs and Persians meaning other peoples).[29]

In a 1388 inscription on the *imaret* of Nilüfer Hatun in İznik, which was erected by her son Murad I, he is titled: *al-malik al-mu'azzam* (the Exalted Lord/ King).[30]

In the aforementioned *berat* (patent) issued by Bayezid I to *Gazi* Ali Beg, the son of *Köse* Mihal, he is referred to as: *malik al-ghuzat wa'l-mujahidin* (Lord/King of the *gazis* and the fighters for the faith).[31]

On a copper coin minted in 1410, Mehmed I is titled: *al-malik al-a'zam* (the Greatest Lord/King).[32]

Finally in 1417, the tombstone of Evrenos in Yenice Vardar accords him the title: *malik ul-ghuzat wa'l-mujahidin* (Lord/King of the *gazis* and fighters for the faith).[33]

A preliminary survey of the surviving sources from the first one hundred and fifty years of Ottoman history establishes no other usages of the title *"Malik"* (King/Lord). What we have here is a title which was uniquely applied in Ottoman usage (with two exceptions) to members of the Ottoman dynasty. The fact that the only two nonmembers of the Ottoman family to be so addressed were from the lines of Evrenos and *Köse* Mihal can hardly be ascribed to coincidence given that Spandugnino names these two individuals as cofounders of the Ottoman state with Osman. Seemingly, as late as the early fifteenth century their role in this regard was still acknowledged by the titles accorded them and/or their Muslim-born offspring. That their preeminence is not so clearly affirmed in the later Ottoman chronicle tradition reflects that this historiography emerges in the late fifteenth and sixteenth century, at a time when the line of Osman has once and for all established its primacy. By the time these accounts were composed the descendants of the original Christian Princes were thoroughly Ottoman Muslims.

Returning to the passage from Spandugnino with which this chapter began, namely, his account of how originally there were four families, those of the Michauli (Mihaloğulları), Turachan (Turahanoğulları), Evrenes (Evrenosoğulları) and Ottomano (Osman), each of whom were petty chieftains in late-thirteenth-century Bithynia, we begin to see a possible explanation for the origins of the Ottoman state. He claimed that it was in order to strengthen themselves in their ongoing fight with

Byzantium that they came together and elected Ottomano (Osman) as their leader on the grounds that he was the most able among them. If true, it would then appear that the Ottoman state was cofounded by a Muslim and two Christian (or ex-Christian) warriors, who joined forces in pursuit of the twin goals of booty and slaves.[34] This account, while not actually written down until the opening years of the sixteenth century, is reminiscent of the Turco-Mongol practice of the *Khuriltay,* the assemblies where leaders were traditionally chosen/elected in such societies on the basis of their ability.[35] Unanswered in this passage from Spandugnino is the intriguing question as to what it was about Osman which made his fellow warriors decide that he was superior in terms of "authority, courage and strength of character?"[36] Could it have been that he was the only Muslim-Turcoman (?) chieftain among them who could appeal to the Muslim warriors flocking to the frontier? Stated differently, may it have been that he was the only one of the cofounders with the ability to attract a steady stream of new manpower to the war zone frontier region of northwestern Anatolia?

The fact that the families of Evrenos and Mihal are attested in 1390 and 1417 respectively to have been using the title "Lord/King of the *Gazis,*" and that in the case of the son of *Köse* Mihal (*Gazi* 'Ali Beg) this title is conferred by the Ottoman Sultan Bayezid I himself, seemingly strengthens the underlying truth of Spandugnino's account and thereby lends credence to the possibility that in the fourteenth and early fifteenth century, the Ottomans really were the first among equals. While Spandugnino may well have been misinformed in placing the origins of all these families back in time to the 1260s, his account of the manner in which Osman was elected by his fellow Bithynian leaders may well reflect what was still a current tradition among his contacts in the ruling elite in İstanbul at the end of the fifteenth century. The very fact that his work predates all but the very earliest Ottoman chronicles warrants its serious consideration.

Theodore Spandounes (Spandugnino), a descendent of the Byzantine family of Cantacuzene, was no stranger to things Ottoman. In the late fifteenth and early sixteenth centuries, he lived for extended periods in both Ottoman Serres in the Balkans and in İstanbul (Constantinople). More importantly, he was related to a number of high-ranking Ottomans. One such was his great aunt Mara/Maria, a Serbian princess who had been the wife of Sultan Murad II. Following the death of Murad, she had been settled on a large estate near the city of Serres in Macedonia, by her stepson, Mehmed II. In the 1490s, Spandugnino joined his great-aunt's retinue as her ward, and presumably began his study of both the Ottoman language and history.[37] Subsequently, he spent time in the Ottoman capital, ca. 1500, and it was there that he determined to write a history of the Ottomans. He describes his undertaking in the following terms:

> I made myself investigate with all studiousness and care everything that I could learn about the origins and the deeds of the house of the Ottomans, to see how such people had ascended to such heights and grandeur. *I felt qualified by the fact that I had long experience of the country and that I was able to consult two of the nobility who were on most intimate terms with the Emperor of the Turks; they were among my closest friends and my relations, men of rare talent with a great knowledge of these matters.*[38]

Almost certainly the two relatives referred to by Spandugnino were indeed very well placed to be described as *"on most intimate terms with the Emperor of the Turks,"* for they were no less than: *a)* Hersekzade Ahmed *Paşa* (a relative by marriage who was the son of the Duke of St. Sava in Bosnia), who had joined the court of Mehmed II, converted to Islam, married the daughter of Bayezid II, and ultimately rose to the positions of *Beylerbey* (Governor-General) of Anatolia and Grand *Vezir* (on five separate occasions); and, *b)* Mesih *Paşa*, a Palaiologos, and brother of Spandugnino's grandmother, who served under Bayezid II as variously *Beylerbey* of Rumelia and Grand *Vezir*.[39] Both had started their lives as Christians and were to end them as Muslims at the very apex of the early-sixteenth-century Ottoman administrative elite. As such, they may be viewed as the fifteenth-sixteenth century equivalent of the fourteenth-century Bithynian *Köse* Mihal and numerous other Byzantine officials who became Ottomans. This fact would account for Spandugnino's ready acceptance of the story that in the early fourteenth century the founders of the state had included Turks named "Michauli" and "Evrenes," for the experience of his own family members amply illustrated the manner in which individuals born as Christians, became Turks, that is, Muslims, and rose to the pinnacles of power in the Ottoman world.

One thing is clear: *Köse* Mihal, Evrenos, and other local Byzantine petty rulers of Bithynian towns and castles did not opt for pledging loyalty to the new Ottoman suzerainty due to their zealous desire to be a part of the spread of Islam. Indeed, if the *gazi* system was a factor it was the prospect of sharing in the spoils of conquest, rather than facilitating the growth of Islam which logically must have influenced the non-Muslims who joined the Ottoman banner. It is likely no coincidence that both *Köse* Mihal and Evrenos and their descendants became the hereditary commanders of the *akıncıs/gazis* in the Balkans, the special corps of Ottoman light cavalry whose duty was to pillage (not convert) the enemy.[40]

It is as if the behavior of *Köse* Mihal and others, several hundred years prior to the Treaty of Augsburg, exemplified the classic justification for the maxim *"cuius regio eius religio,"* as over time an increasing number of local Christians came to realize that sharing the religion of the ruler brought (or allowed one to retain) certain advantages. The predatory joint venture they were already engaged in made their decisions to adopt their new ruler's faith easier. By 1326 local Bithynian Christian rulers had come to accept the gathering speed of the growing Ottoman juggernaut and determined that their best course of action was to assist in pulling it rather than getting caught beneath its wheels.

Religious conversion was (together with a steady influx of immigrants), a primary source of Ottoman manpower in the early fourteenth century. Indeed, the phenomenon was so widespread that in 1338, and again in 1340, the Patriarch of Constantinople felt compelled to write to the Christians of the newly conquered Nicaea (İznik), urging them not to abjure their Christian faith. He even went so far as to tell those who had already converted that he was willing to take them back into the church, even if they did not renounce their new allegiance to Islam:

> [The Church] will heal and cure and number among the side of the Christians again those taking up the true belief in God and [those] removing [themselves] from the evil of the Muslims into which they fell. . . . As many as wish to live in secret practicing and keeping in their heart the Christian way, because of the fear of punishments against them, these also shall attain salvation. Only, they shall try as much as possible to keep the commands of God. And this present letter of the church of God became an assurance concerning this.[41]

Undoubtedly the Patriarch adopted this tactic of actually encouraging Crypto-Christianity in what was to be a futile effort to reverse the growing course of conversions which were decimating his Bithynian flock and consequently depleting his own financial base. He (and his congregation) saw faith in a far different light than is accepted today. The religion of the new rulers was Islam and increasingly it spread among the Bithynian Christian population as well. The end result was the disappearance of both the local Christian nobility and their subject peasant populace. In their place was formed a new symbiosis: the Muslim Ottomans. Nor was this process in anyway limited to Christians. When in the mid-fourteenth century, the Metropolitan of Thessalonica, Gregory Palamas, visited the Bithynian city of Iznik as a captive of the Ottomans, the ruler Orhan arranged for him to debate the respective virtues of Islam and Christianity. The Muslim side was represented by a group of Islamicized Jews.[42]

That the decisions of such converts were facilitated by what we might term the early Ottoman methods of "conquest" is clear from a close reading of Aşıkpaşazade. This fifteenth-century writer, drawing on the oral traditions passed down from the days of Osman and Orhan,[43] spends no small amount of time describing the philosophy of "conquest" followed by the founders of the state. The theme that runs like a leitmotif throughout the opening chapters of his work, is that Osman clearly favored the "carrot" over the "stick" in dealing with the indigenous inhabitants of Bithynia. Termed by İnalcık *istimâlet,* or the "gaining of goodwill," this process typified the manner by which the early Ottoman rulers ensured the support of their Bithynian Christian neighbors.[44] Even when towns such as Bursa and İznik chose to withstand Ottoman sieges for several years, when they ultimately surrended their inhabitants were not subjected to enslavement. This is in keeping with the Islamic concept of *aman* (guaranteed safety of persons and possessions), whereby those who respond positively to a call for surrender are treated differently than those who choose to fight and are conquered by force of arms.[45] The extent to which Osman sought to co-opt rather than to conquer his neighbors is amply illustrated by the following examples which serve to outline the features of the *istimâlet* process.

In Aşıkpaşazade's opening passage dealing with Osman *Gazi,* we are told that: "upon taking his father's place (in Söğüt), he began to get along well with those unbelievers who were his close neighbors."[46] His earliest enemies, according to Aşıkpaşazade were not the local Christians but rather his fellow Muslim neighbors, the Germiyans who viewed him as an upstart threat. This is followed by the well-known account of how, upon migrating to the mountains for the summer pasturage, Osman left the moveable goods he did not need in the secure hands of another of his Christian neighbors, the ruler of Bilecik.[47]

In discussing plans for future military actions with his brother Gündüz, Osman solicits his advice on where they should strike next. When Gündüz replied that they should attack the Christian towns in the immediate vicinity, Osman replied: "This is a bad idea. If we do this the city of Kara Hisar's [Osman's town] prosperity will be destroyed. What is necessary is for us to get along well with and make friends with our neighbors."[48] Clearly, Osman wanted to maintain good relations with the Bithynian Christians. This was a self-conscious state policy from the outset. This is illustrated by Aşıkpaşazade's account of the taking of Harmankaya (the hometown of Osman's Christian companion, *Köse* Mihal), where we are told: "They took no slaves. This they did in order to bind the local people to them."[49] When queried as to why he was so respectful of the Christians of Bilecik, Osman replied: "They are our neighbors. When we first came to this area they treated us well. Now it is fitting that we show them respect."[50]

That this policy worked is illustrated by Aşikpaşazade's description of the aftermath of Osman's conquest of the town of Yar Hisar: "All the villagers came back and settled in their places. Their state was better than it had been in the time of the unbelievers. When word spread of the comfort enjoyed by these unbelievers, people began to come from other places as well."[51]

These, and numerous other examples, illustrate what can only be termed a policy of allurement on the part of the first Ottoman ruler. Namely, his attempt not to coerce the indigenous local Christians into accepting Islam, but rather to gain their confidence through a policy of accommodation. The success of this endeavor is certainly reflected in the aforementioned passage where Saroz, the minister to the ruler of Bursa, woefully explained: "They [the peasants] submitted to you. We understood that they were comfortable. We realized that they didn't miss us."[52] As word of the treatment one could expect at the hands of Osman spread, it takes no great imagination to realize that more and more indigenous Bithynians (most of whom were Christians) chose to join the new endeavor. Being an Ottoman subject did not entail giving up one's religion. It did, however, ensure that one was attached to the winning team and thereby positioned to share in the relative peace and security its growing chain of victories afforded.

It is almost as if Aşikpaşazade is trying to justify and rationalize a fourteenth-century policy which must have been confusing to his fifteenth-century dervish audience, accustomed as they were to a far less tolerant attitude towards unconverted Christians. For by the time of his writing, while converts still found ready acceptance into the Ottoman ruling class (e.g., Hersekzade Ahmed *Paşa* and Mesih *Paşa* discussed above), the same was not true for unassimilated Christians.

Though referring to Osman and Orhan as *gazis*, Aşikpaşazade clearly saw nothing incongruous in providing these and similar accounts of their behavior in the opening decades of the fourteenth century. They fought when necessary, with the aim of gaining booty and slaves, not with the vigor of the proselytizing zealot. Clearly, the aim of the *gaza/akin* was not as much to spread Islam as it was to gain the material advantages of conquest. Stated differently, the emerging Ottoman polity was more of a "predatory brotherhood" united for conquest and booty, than a "religious brotherhood" designed to spread Islam among its Christian neighbors. Bearing in mind the extent to which Christians or newly converted Muslims played key roles in the period of Ottoman emergence, it was most likely the hope of material gain rather than faith which served to unite the early Ottomans.

Indeed, as was illustrated in the analysis of Ahmedi's epic, the motivation behind what he terms the *gaza* focused primarily on the *Realpolitik* aim of accruing wealth, and, in particular, slaves. While this was accompanied by a great deal of rhetoric about killing the infidels, the emphasis on acquiring wealth and slaves was obviously far more important in fourteenth-century Bithynia than were attempts to conquer Christians and give them the choice of accepting Islam or death (as Ahmedi repeatedly stressed the early Ottoman rulers had done). Even following what must have been a rather frustrating ten year siege of the city, when Bursa finally capitulated, Orhan does not appear to have hesitated in trading off the freedom of its ruler and his entourage for the sum of thirty thousand gold florins. When Orhan sends *Köse* Mihal to demand the surrender, its ruler asks for an escort of guards so that he and the inhabitants of the castle will not be harmed by the Turkish soldiers. In the ensuing bargaining, a deal is struck for thirty thousand gold florins and after paying this sum, the ruler and his entourage depart under escort for the coastal town of Gemlik.[53] When a decade later in the 1337 Bursa inscription Orhan termed himself the "Sultan of the *gazis*," he clearly did not think that his earlier action in accepting thirty thousand gold florins rather than converting or killing the infidels of the Bursa castle had in anyway deprived him of this title.

Turning now to an examination of the history of Bursa and the Bithynian countryside in the ensuing century, it is possible to illustrate a number of factors which relate directly to our reexamination of the "*Gazi* Thesis." This exercise in arguing from context is facilitated by the survival of the accounts penned by three fourteenth-century travelers who visited the city. The first such was the North African traveler Ibn Battuta, who visited Bursa in September of 1331, only five years after the city's conquest.

This traveler's account of the first Ottoman capital is not one of a bustling frontier town swarming with wild-eyed *gazis*. To the contrary, he terms it "a great and important city with fine bazaars and wide streets,"[54] thereby presumably reflecting the fact that its surrender had not resulted in the displacement of the indigenous population. Nor is its ruler, Orhan Beg, discussed in language which suggests he was some kind of country ruffian. Ibn Battuta describes Orhan whom he met in the town of İznik:

> This sultan is the greatest of the kings of the Turkmens and richest in wealth, lands and military forces. Of fortresses he possesses

nearly a hundred, and for most of his time he is continually engaged in making the round of them, staying in each fortress for some days to put it into good order and examine its condition. It is said that he never stays for a whole month in any one town. He also fights with the infidels continually and keeps them under siege. . . . It was there [İznik] that I met him and he sent me a large sum of money.[55]

Noticeably lacking in this description is any reference to Orhan as a *gazi*. Even when he states that Orhan "fights with the infidels continually and keeps them under siege," he does not use the term *gazi* for Orhan, or *gaza* for the activity he is engaged in. On the contrary, what impresses Ibn Battuta is the extent of the territories (the many fortresses) ruled by Orhan and the wealth which he had accrued as a result. He does bestow on him both the titles *"Sultan"* and *"Malik"* (King/Lord) of the Turkmens, and, in so doing, is presumably reflecting the manner in which he heard others refer to Orhan (or alternatively, his own political vocabulary). That the term *gazi* was not unknown to him is clear from the fact that he does use the title for the Emir of Kastamonu, whom he titles *Gazi* Çelebi.[56] While this does not prove that Orhan may not also have been called *gazi* by his contemporaries, it does suggest that it was not this aspect of his political persona which most impressed Ibn Battuta.

In another passage, Ibn Battuta establishes that within five years of its occupation by the Ottomans, the city of Bursa was home to a thriving branch of the *akhi* brotherhood, the groups of craftsmen who provided an infrastructural network throughout the towns of Anatolia in this period. Ibn Battuta, who was in Bursa on the tenth of *Muharram*, the voluntary fast day of *Ashura*, reports that he was a guest of the city's *Akhi* hospice and one of its leaders, Shams al-Din. From the fact that on the evening of that day, Shams al-Din hosted a great feast which was attended by the "principal officers of the army and leading citizens,"[57] it is clear that the *Akhi*'s were already an established part of the city's elite. Upon leaving Bursa Ibn Battuta went to the newly conquered İznik (1331), which is one of the few towns he visited in Anatolia where he was not hosted by the local *Akhis*.[58] This, too, is logical given the fact that this town had only been an Ottoman possession for a few months. While scholars have long speculated about the important role played by the *Akhi* associations in the aftermath of the Seljuk collapse, Bursa is the one case where we see their presence in a city which has only just become home to its first Muslim population. Within the short span of half a decade the *akhis* have established themselves in the new Ottoman capital to such an extent that their hosting of an *Ashura* dinner attracts the leading administrators and civilians of the city.

Another sign of the rapidity with which Bursa had assumed its new Muslim identity may be found in Ibn Battuta's detailed description of the *Ashura* dinner he attended. He specifically mentions that the entertainment consisted of "Qur'an readers reciting with beautiful voices," as well as the presence of the jurist and preacher Majd al-Din [al-Qunawi/Konyavi (?)], who "delivered an eloquent homily and exhortation."[59] While unstated, this sermon must have been in Arabic, as Ibn Battuta makes it clear he did not know Turkish. Finally Ibn Battuta notes how while in Bursa he met another Muslim traveler "the pious sheikh 'Abdallah al-Misri," who had traveled throughout the world (but not to all the places visited by the narrator).

The clear impression gained from Ibn Battuta's account (dating from six years prior to the erection of the 1337 *kitabe*), is that Bursa was less of a bustling *gazi* frontier town and more of a well-established Islamic city, one which was already attracting fairly well-known scholars and jurists. If Ibn Battuta's account actually reflects the status quo at the time of his visit, Bursa hardly resembles a newly conquered city, for he suggests that there was no discernible disruption of the fabric of urban social and economic life.

This sense that even within the first generation of their existence the Ottomans already had a developed state apparatus in place is heightened by the earliest known original surviving Ottoman document, a *vakfiye* (endowment charter), drawn up in Persian for Orhan in 1324, two years prior to the conquest of Bursa. Given its date and, as our subsequent examination will establish, the importance of its contents, we may even view it as a kind of "birth certificate" for the early Ottoman state. Unique, as the only document originating from the first half of the fourteenth century which is accepted by all scholars working on the period as unquestionably authentic, this *vakfiye* has strangely not been accorded the attention its contents clearly warrant.[60]

First published over half a century ago by the late İsmail Hakkı Uzunçarşılı, it is not even cited in much of the subsequent literature dealing with the origins of the Ottomans. Even the few works which have used it have failed to analyze fully its importance.[61] This charter document, originating in a period when the Ottoman state structure is generally described as having been carried on the back of the ruler's horse, is particularly important due to the fact that it is composed in Persian with the terminology and the *nesih* script of the late Seljuk bureaucracy. Though some of the first six lines of its text is missing, it is still clear that its endower called himself *Şücâeddîn* (Champion of Religion) Orhan Beg son of *Fahreddîn* (Glory of the Faith) O[sman].[62] As we have seen, these titles are fully in keeping with those which earlier Seljuk rulers, and other contemporary Turkish Beys in Anatolia were using in the thirteenth and fourteenth centuries. This charter raises the likelihood that even prior to the conquest of Bursa, the Ottoman ruler Orhan was already surrounded by representatives of what we might term the "more formal urbanized Islamic tradition."

By this endowment, Orhan was establishing a *hânegâh* (hospice), in the Bithynian town of Mekece, to feed and house the *faqīran* (traveling poor), *gharī`bān* (strangers), *miskīnān* (the mendicants), *darwīshān* (dervishes), and *tālibān-i 'ilm* (searchers after knowledge). As the administrator of the foundation he names his freed slave, the Eunuch *(Tavâşî)* Şerefeddîn Mukbil and orders that from that time forward he will be succeeded by the most capable of the sons of the slaves of the *hânegâh*.[63] As if acknowledging the strange nature of this bequest he then goes on to state: "no single one of my children or any of my heirs have any claim whatsoever [on this property]."[64] While phraseology of this nature is standard in endowment documents of the Hanefi School of Islamic Law to which the Ottomans adhered, no other surviving Ottoman *vakfiye* goes as far as listing all the members of the donor's family as witnesses to the endowment. Here, as if to guarantee that none of his descendants ever attempt to advance such a claim, Orhan attaches a large number of his children and heirs as witnesses to the transaction. These include his brothers (Çoban bin Osman, Melik bin Osman, Hamid bin Osman, and Pazarlu bin Osman), his sister (Fatma bint-i Osman), his mother[?] (Mal Hatun bint-i Ömer Beg) and two other unidentified women (Efendi bint-i Akbaşlu and Melik bint al-Melek). While each of the above witnesses are named at the foot of the document, there is a second list of witnesses whose names are added in the margin. They include three of Orhan's own sons (Sultan bin Orhan, Süleyman bin Orhan, and İbrahim bin Orhan), and four unidentified officials.[65] Finally, to further strengthen his bequest, he states that the curses of God and his Prophet will fall on anyone who attempts to alter his naming the ablest of the sons of the slaves of the *hânegâh* as the perpetual administrators of the foundation.[66]

As our subsequent examination will establish, it is no coincidence that the earliest surviving Ottoman document mentions a freed eunuch by name as being entrusted with the administration of what may have been the very first religious foundation *(vakıf)* established by an Ottoman ruler.

The first question which comes to mind in light of this document is: What is Orhan Bey doing in 1324 with a eunuch in his entourage? Indeed, a eunuch who has been in his family's service long enough to have been manumitted? And one who has attained such a level of confidence and trust that Orhan is alienating property on his behalf in such a fashion that even his own heirs will have no future claim to it? Almost certainly Şerefeddin Mukbil had been a slave in the service of Orhan's father Osman (whose death presumably predates the time this document was drawn up). It may well be that Orhan was acting on his late father's behalf in naming his freed eunuch as the administrator of the foundation. The presence of eunuchs in the court of an Islamic ruler in this period suggests a level of political savvy and sophistication far in advance of that generally attributed to the House of Osman in the opening decades of the fourteenth century. By the same token the drawing up of documents in Persian, which are written in the style of the Seljuk court chancery, suggests that the first Ottoman rulers may well have benefited from a classical Islamic education in the Seljuk tradition, or, at the very least that they were surrounded by individuals who had. What we are faced with here is an entity in the early stages of its development which appears to have already obtained the accoutrements of an established Islamic court modeled on those of earlier Anatolian Turkish states and principalities.

Nor is this the only reference we have to slaves serving as administrators during Osman's reign. The chronicler Aşıkpaşazade names yet another former Christian, this one a slave *(kul)*, one Balabancik, who played a key role in the conquest of Bursa. Specifically, he is named as the commander of one of the two forts Osman had constructed as part of his effort to starve the city into surrender. Aşıkpaşazade informs us that this *kul* (slave) was a great hero.[67] Bearing in mind that we are discussing an era almost half a century prior to the appearance of the Ottoman standing slave army (the Janissary Corps), what we are faced with here is almost certainly the word *kul* as a calque on the Arabic/Persian *gulam,* that is, with the term being used for slave administrators and military officers. From the work of Speros Vryonis Jr., we know that the *gulam* corps of the Seljuk rulers was copied by other Turkish Begs in Anatolia.[68] This individual may even be the Balaban (Palapanis) who resurfaces thirty years later in March of 1354 when the Metropolitan of Thessalonica, Gregory Palamas, engages in a debate in İznik with a group of Islamicized Jews. These new converts were less than overjoyed at the prospect of confronting the Greek Orthodox theologian, and only did so after Orhan had agreed not to attend the session. In his place he was represented by several of his notables, one of whom was named Balaban.[69]

Both the manumitted eunuch Şerefeddin Mukbil and the slave military commander, Balabancik, present clear testimony to the fact that the Ottomans cannot have been simple farmers and/or nomads. The fact that they, like the Seljuks and other Anatolian Begs, were already using slave administrators in the opening decades of the fourteenth century,

PLATE 6
The 1324 Mekece *Vakfiye* of Orhan *Gazi*

TRANSCRIPTION: *[Line 1] Urkhān bin-i 'Uthmān //
[2] Man-ki Shujā'al-dīn Urkhān bin-i Fakhr al-
dīn 'U[thmānam dar 'ayn-i] // [3] sihhat [u] rizā
tamāmī   nāhiye'-i   Makaja-rā   bā-hudud-i
[mushakhkhasa-i ma-rifa (or: ma'luma) waqf
kardam] // [4] khālisan mukhlisan li-wajhi-illāhi
Ta'ālā jw=?[. . .] // [5] tāwāshī Sharaf al-dīn
Muqbīl-ki mu'taq-i man ast barā-yi s[arf bar
masālih-i] // [6] darwīshān u miskīnān u gharībān
u faqīrān āyanda wu rawanda [wu tālibān-i] //
[7] 'ilm [kī] dar-ān khānqāh muqīm shawand
har-ān-chi wazīfa-'i waqf ast [bar-masālih-i
ānān] // [8] sarf shawad u har-kas-ki ahl-i waqf u
mustahaqq nabāshad . . . [. . .] // [9] mutala'a-i
kunandagān chunīn dānand-ki tawliyat-i Makaj-
rā ba-farzandān-i bandāgān-i īn khānqāh // [10]
har-ki aslah bāshad dādam bā-īn Sharaf-al-dīn
Muqbīl tawliyat-i madhkūr-rā ba'd. . . . // [11]
tafwīz kardam-ki khidmat namāyad az asl-i
ghallāt   wa   ghayrihā   bi-masraf-i   nās   //   [12]
āyanda wu rawanda sarf gardad bi-was'-i tāqat
khidmat namāyad wa jihat-i amr-i // [13] khid-
mat-i tawliyat az jam'-i hāsil-i 'ushrīn satānad
hīch āfrīda kā'inan man kāna ba-farzandān //
[14] wa wārithān-i man istihqāq . . . nadārad (?)
īn tawliyat [ba-]farzandān-i bandagān-i // [15]
khānqāh har-ki asl bāshad naslan ba'da naslin
wa batnan ba'da batnin wa qarnan // [16] ba'da
qarnin rasad [har]-ki dar-īn bāb nizā' aghāzat
(sic. = aghāzad) wa bar-butlān-i īn ma'nā // [17]
sa'y namāyad wa zūr u buhtān [u] zulm u 'udwān
namūda bāshad bi-sharī 'at-i // [18] nabawī-
'alayhi afzalu l-salāwāt wa-l-salām—maqbūl
nabāshad bar-īn mūjab // [19] iqrār kardam īn
madhkūr bar-sabīl-i hujjat ba-dast-i farzandān-i
bandagān-i īn khānqāh // [20] har-ki aslah
bāshad dādam ta waqt-i hājat 'arz dārad ba yad-
kī hīch afrīda // [21] kā'inan man kāna madkhal
nasāzad wa muzāhim nagardad u taghyīr naku-
nad har-kī madkhal sāzad // [22] wa muzāhim
gardad dar la 'nat-i Khudāy—jalla jalālahü—wa*

(continued on next page)

PLATE 6 *(continued)*

la'nat-i Rasūl-'alayhi l-salām- // *[23] bazūdī khwāhad būd khwānandagān-i maktūb haqīqat dāshad u i'timād namāyand* // *[24] ba-guwāhī jamā 'atī-kī hāzir būdand shahidū bimā [fihi]* // *[25] Jūbān bin-i 'Uthmān Malak bin-i 'Uthmān* // *[26] Hamīd bin-i 'Uthmān Bāzārlū bin-i 'Uthmān* // *[27] Fātima Khātūn bint-i 'Uthmān Māl Khātūn bint-i 'Umar Beg* // *[28] Malak bint-i 'l-Malak . . . bint-i Aqbāshlū* // *[29] wa kataba 'anhum bi-amrihim wa rizā'ihim mutāla'a kunandagān-i madhkūr Makaj-rā az-mulk-i man sammā (or: sum-miya) fī* // *[30] al-waqt dānand īn tawqī-'i'timād namāyad—in shā'a-llāhu Ta'ālā fī awāsit-i shahr-i Rabī'i l-awwali sanata arba'a wa 'ishrīna wa sab'a mi'ata bi-hamdi-llāhi wa-l-khayr.* // *[31] [Marginal verification notes:] Shahida bi-mazmūnihī . . . ghafara-llāhu lahumā* // *[32] Shahida bi-dhālika Turkhān bin-i Sulaymān. [Marginalia: Sultan bin Orhan, Süleyman bin Orhan, İbrahim bin Orhan, Mahmud bin Abu Bekr . . . , Cemaleddin el-Hafız, Mehmed bin Mahmud, Abdulvahid bin Mehmed el-Sivasi].*

TRANSLATION: Urkhan son of Uthman: Shuja al-din Urhkan the son of Fakhr al-din Uthman, in health and satisfaction, bequeathed the entire region of Makaja (Mekece) with the distinct and well known boundaries, in all honesty to meet with God Almighty . . . [to the] Eunuch Sharaf al-din Muqbil,who is my liberated slave, in order to expend what is in the interests of the traveling dervishes, the poor, the strangers and mendicants, and those in search of knowledge, who will be residing in that sufi lodge, whatever is the result of this endowment, should be spent in their interest, and whoever is not the beneficiary of the endowment nor worthy. . . . The readers should know that I have given the trusteeship of Makaja to the offsprings of the servants of this sufi lodge, to whomever is best [qualified]. To this Sharaf al-din Muqbil, I later . . . consigned the aforementioned trusteeship, so that he may serve from the original proceeds and such like—to be used by traveling people—that he may serve as much as is in his power, and for the purpose of service to the trusteeship, to take twenty [?] from the total income. No creature born [including my offspring and inheritors is worthy of. . . . This Trusteeship will be inherited by the children of the servants of the sufi lodge, whoever be of their lineage, generation after generation, and century after century. Whoever begins a dispute about this [matter], and attempts to prove this wrong, and would have shown violence, slander, cruelty, and injustice, [he] will not be accepted in the Prophetic Law [may the best of peace and greetings be upon him]. On this matter, I [have] pledged. This afore-mentioned, in the manner of proof, I gave to the offspring of the servants of this sufi lodge, whoever is worthiest, so that in time of need, it can be offered for sale [?] *[arz darad]*. No creature born, whosoever, should make an intervention, or interrupt [this bequest] or change [it]. Whoever makes an intervention and inter-rupts it, will soon be cursed by God, Exalted be His glory, and the Prophet,

(continued on next page)

PLATE 6 *(continued)*

peace be upon him. The readers of the truth will know and will trust the testimony of the crowd which was present. They witnessed what was there: Çoban the son of Uthman; Malik the son of Uthman; Hamid the son of Uthman; Pazarlu the son of Uthman; Fatima Hatun the daughter of Uthman; Mal Hatun the daughter of Umar Beg; Malik the daughter of al-Malik; the daughter of Akbaşlı. And he wrote about them, on their order and to their satisfaction. The aforementioned readers will consider Makaja [to be] among the property established as a Waqf. They will trust this endowment. God willing. [Written] in mid Rabi' al-awwal of the year 724. Praide be to God. [Marginalia: Sultan the son of Orhan, Süleyman the son of Orhan, İbrahim the son of Orhan, Mahmud bin Abu Bekr . . . , Cemaleddin el-Hafız, Mehmed bin Mahmud, Abdulvahid bin Mehmed el-Sivasi].

SOURCE: Uzunçarşılı, "*Gazi* Orhan Bey Vakfiyesi" (1941), pp. 280–281.

---

suggests a well-directed state in formation with a level of administrative development designed to cope with the polyglot, multiconfessional and multiethnic entity that was growing under their leadership. That this was yet another means by which local Christians found themselves gradually integrated into the Ottoman polity is clear. From Christian slave military commander (à la Balabancık), to manumitted slave administrator (Şerefeddin Mukbil), to member of the Ottoman ruling elite in one generation, must have been a well-established pattern by which the state moulded a political caste. An alternative route to integration was to join the Ottomans as Christians (*Köse* Mihal and Saroz), and then at some future point either they or their descendants converted to Islam. This indicates the immediate integration of various ethnic elements in the formation of the new society.

Whatever differences initially existed between those early Ottomans who were Christians and those who were Muslim, were superseded by the alliance they had formed to reap the shared benefits of their predatory culture. Once they had formed their confederacy, the next stage in the historical pattern of assimilation was cultural mergence, or the adoption of the ruler's religion by the Christian Ottomans.

As noted above, it is hard to square the 1324 *vakfiye* with the later chronicle accounts depicting Orhan and his father Osman alternatively as simple peasants, shepherds or nomads.[70] This document suggesting the existence in 1324 of a developed political structure simply does not accord with any of the explanations. As will be subsequently demonstrated this is but one thread in a string of examples drawn from the

fourteenth and early fifteenth centuries which point in the direction of
the need for an alternate thesis to problematize the emergence of the
Ottoman dynasty. At the very least this suggests the possibility that our
search for the origins of the Ottomans must be focused not on the early
fourteenth century, but rather on the second half of the thirteenth. Is it
possible that Spandugnino is correct in placing the emergence of Osman
in the wake of the Byzantine withdrawal from Bithynia in 1261? If so,
this could help account for the level of advanced structural formation
reflected in the 1324 charter.

Thus, the contradictions raised necessitate a brief digression into the
intriguing question of just who Osman, the founder of the dynasty,
really was? Given the fact that he had slaves and eunuchs in his
entourage is it possible that he could have been a Seljuk, Ilhanid, or Germiyan *gulam* (slave) sent to the frontier? This seems possible, although
certainly unprovable. There is an intriguing passage in a letter from
Timur to Bayezid I which is copied in Şaraf al-Din 'Ali Yazdi's *Zafer-
name* (a life of the Central Asian conqueror), in which the Ottoman
ruler is addressed as: "But you whose true origin ends in a Türkmen
sailor, as all the world knows," suggesting even a possible origin from
one of the maritime principalities (Aydın or Menteşe) for the first
Ottoman ruler.[71] In a similar vein, the same work contains the text of a
letter addressed by Timur to Bayezid whom he addresses as Keesur (Caesar), in which he attempts to bring Bayezid down to earth by reminding
him of his origins, as follows:

> Where thy race and lineage endeth, is known to all men. It is there-
> fore worthy of thy condition, that though advance not toward the foot
> of presumption and that thou throw not thyself into the abyss of afflic-
> tion and calamity.[72]

This, too, raises the possibility of humble (even slave) origins for the
founder of the dynasty. From the fact that he clearly had a close relationship with a number of local Christian rulers in Bithynia, and was
using slave administrators in his own entourage, the traditional view of
this ruler as a simple peasant herdsman is in serious need of revision.

As will shortly be demonstrated, the extant fourteenth-century
Ottoman foundation charters *(vakfiyes)* preserve a variety of elaborate
classical Islamic titles which they bestow on Orhan, Süleyman *Paşa,* and
Murad. Based on these charters, all of which were drawn up between
1324 and 1360 (almost one hundred fifty years prior to the emergence of
the Ottoman dynastic myth identifying them as members of the Kayı
branch of the Oguz federation of Turkish tribes), we may posit that the
use of such Arabic titularies points to a possible indication that the early

Ottomans may have seriously fancied themselves to be the lineal successors of the Abbasids and the Seljuks. In addition, the frequent use of the seemingly spurious title of King of the Kings of the Arabs and the Persians [meaning and all other peoples], raises the intriguing possibility that the Ottomans at this point in time were contemplating an Arab rather than a Turkish lineage for themselves. Colin Imber has reported (and rejected) a tradition found in Ibn Hajar al-'Asqalani's *Inba' al-ghumr bi-abna' al-'umr,* a work written between 1400 and 1450 (prior to the first recordings of the official Ottoman dynastic myth), to the effect that "it is said that their [the Ottomans] origin is from the Arabs of the Hijaz."[73] This finds an echo in Enveri's *Düsturname,* a mid-fifteenth-century work (written ca. 1465), where he names the proto-ancestor of the Ottomans as a "companion of the Prophet called 'Iyad,' living in the Hijaz."[74] These two references raise, at the very least, the possibility that the first Ottoman rulers did in fact flirt with the claim of descent from a companion of the Prophet in the Hijaz. To have done so would simply mean that they were following a typical pattern of seeking legitimation. Bearing in mind that all of these references predate the emergence of the official Ottoman genealogy, this is a possibility warranting further study.

If correct, this interpretation would go a long way toward explaining the seeming incongruities represented by the 1324 charter document which is written in the style of classical Islamic chanceries and which shows Orhan Bey as bestowing property upon the person of his (or his father's) own manumitted eunuch, in the same year that his siege of Bursa is cocommanded by a slave named Balabancık and that the city's surrender is negotiated by a former Christian Ottoman commander named *Köse* Mihal with an advisor to the Byzantine ruler named Saros (who subsequently becomes an Ottoman himself). It would help explain the seeming incongruity of finding the newly surrendered city of Bursa hosting a thriving *Akhi* hospice, complete with learned scholars from the Arabic-speaking world, just five years after its conquest (at the time of Ibn Battuta's visit in 1331). At the very least these seeming incongruities raise the intriguing possibility that prior to creating a Turkish genealogy for themselves the earliest Ottoman rulers flirted with the option of staking their claim for legitimacy on the basis of an equally fictitious descent from the Hijaz and a companion of the Prophet Mohammed.

Returning now to our examination of the accounts written by travelers to Bursa in the Ottoman period, the second visitor to the city was the Greek Orthodox Metropolitan of Thessaloniki, Gregory Palamas, who spent four days as a prisoner in Bursa in 1355. His work, which says nothing specific regarding either the city or its administration, is important in providing the first direct testimony on the presence of a Greek

Orthodox community among its inhabitants. That these Christians who "although surrounded by barbarians" came to meet with Palamas were the offspring of the preconquest populace seems logical.[75] That they were living in a city whose ruler Ahmedi tells us was the great *gazi* Orhan who gave all conquered Christians the choice of conversion or death, throws doubt on the historicity of the account preserved in Ahmedi's *mesnevi*. Rather, in keeping with the well-established Islamic practice of *aman* (guaranteed safety of persons and possessions), Bursa had surrendered and its inhabitants were accordingly left secure in their civic status.

The last of our trio of fourteenth-century visitors to the Ottoman capital of Bursa was another captive, the Bavarian soldier Johann Schilt-berger who, following his capture, had been enrolled as a member of the Janissary Corps. His 1397 description provides one intriguing detail on the city. According to Johann Schiltberger, "The city contains . . . eight hospices/charity homes *(spitaler)* where poor people are received, whether they be Christians, idolaters (Muslims), or Jews."[76] This suggests that there was already a well-developed urban base supporting a social welfare system whose benefits were open to all regardless of religion in the fourteenth century. By the sixteenth century, that is, by the point in time at which the official chronicle accounts of the dynasty began to be composed, this system has been replaced by one in which Muslims, Christians, and Jews established separate pious foundations for their respective communities.

There can be little doubt but that the hospices *(spitaler)* described by Schiltberger are the Bursan equivalent of the *hânegâh* or *imarets* (soup kitchens) which Orhan had constructed in 1324 in the village of Mekece. While that endowment's charter deed specified that it was intended for the use of the traveling poor, strangers, the indigent, dervishes, and men of learning, Schiltberger now adds the very interesting observation that such establishments in the fourteenth century were not designed exclusively for Muslims, but were open to Christians and Jews as well (a possibility also not excluded by the wording of the 1324 Mekece *vakfiye*). In so doing, he indirectly confirms the presence of Christians (noted earlier by Palamas) and Jews among the inhabitants of Bursa at the end of the century.

Interestingly, a fifteenth-century French visitor to Bursa, Bertrandon de la Broquière, who spent ten days in the city in 1432, provides a similar description of this institution in the following passage:

> There are very nice places like hospitals. In three or four of these, bread, meat and wine are distributed to those who want to take them in God's name.[77]

We may easily account for the fact that Schiltberger's eight hospices in 1397 have been reduced to three or four by the time of Broquière's visit forty-five years later in 1432. For in the interim, Bursa had been sacked, pillaged, and burned on two occasions. First, by a son of the central Asian conqueror Timur in 1402–1403, and then a decade later in 1413 by Mehmed Karamanoğlu, the leader of a rival Principality in Anatolia. The havoc thus caused is known to have damaged or destroyed many of the city's princely foundations.[78] The destruction thus wrought was never fully repaired since the Ottoman focus by then had shifted to the Balkans, the site of their new administrative center Edirne.

While neither the 1324 foundation deed nor Broquière in 1432 specifically state that the hospices were serving both the Muslim and non-Muslim poor, neither exclude this possibility. Indeed Broquière's comment to the effect that "bread, meat and wine are distributed to those who want to take them in God's name," implies this must have been the case. As a Christian, he might be expected to note the fact had these charitable institutions excluded his coreligionists. More problematic is the menu of items he lists as being provided in Bursa's soup kitchens. Specifically, his mention of "wine" along with the bread and meat is known to have been the standard fare. This, if true, would represent a real departure from the norm and one not confirmable on the basis of the surviving documents. Even here, our knowledge of the latitudinarian practices associated with the heterodox dervish orders in this period does not allow us to exclude wholly the possibility that the menu provided by Broquière may be correct.

Once again, it is the early sixteenth-century Italian chronicle written by Theodore Spandugnino, a descendant of the imperial Byzantine family of Cantacuzene, which adds another layer of evidence in support of the above interpretation. Spandugnino, who as discussed earlier had lived for some time in the Ottoman Empire and made several extended visits to its capital of İstanbul (in the last quarter of the fifteenth and opening decade of the sixteenth century),[79] provides the following informative description of the imperial foundation endowed by Mehmed II in his new capital.

> Among the churches [mosques] and hospitals *[imarets]* in Europe *(Grecia)* is that of Mehmed in Constantinople, a superb building, with his tomb nearby. The hospital is open to all, Christians, Jews and Turks; and its doctors give free treatment and food three times a day. . . . The official in charge of this great Imaret (Marath) is called the *"Müteveli"* (Mutevoli). . . . These Turks, large and small, are constantly engaged on such pious and charitable works—far more so than we Christians.[80]

What does seem apparent is that in the fourteenth and fifteenth centuries the social welfare network created by the Ottoman rulers was open to all irrespective of religious affiliation. This fourteenth-century phenomena is not all that exceptional when we bear in mind that such institutions were an essential element in addressing the needs of the urban poor, which in turn prevented social unrest, and ultimately contributed to the process of integration. As Ömer Lütfi Barkan's pioneering study on the colonizing role of the *derviş* lodges in this period showed, it was institutions such as this which brought Christians and Muslims together in the formative period of the state.[81] It may have been no coincidence that the earliest recorded act of such charity, the hospice established in Mekece in 1324, was placed by Orhan in the hands of a manumitted slave (himself almost certainly a former Christian), nor that the deed clearly states that following the death of its first *mütevelli* (administrator), the eunuch Şerefeddin Mukbil, he will be succeeded by the most able of the children of the [Christian] slaves attached to the *hânegâh*. This is an indication of the inclusive rather than exclusive nature of the early Ottoman system of social welfare which was developed to serve the needs of both the rural and urban poor. We may hypothesize that such foundations were one means by which the process of gradual assimilation, followed by religious conversion, was facilitated in this period. Indeed, a survey of sixteenth-century *vakıfs* in Bithynia established that many such foundations established in the fourteenth century were placed in the hands of [Christian] slaves *(gılmans)* and their descendants.[82]

For an era of Bursa's history when our primary sources are extremely limited, consisting solely of the aforedescribed traveler's accounts and *vakfiyes* (religious endowment documents), we must thoroughly examine each surviving contemporary document if we hope to tentatively construct a meaningful picture of Ottoman society at this time. Turning from our discussion of the extant travelers, we must focus once again on those fourteenth-century *vakfiyes* that have survived for *imarets/hânegâhs* in the city of Bursa and other Bithynian towns.

After the above described 1324 foundation charter, the next oldest such dated document regarding an endowment established by a member of the Ottoman dynasty is an *vakıfname* dated June 1360, where Orhan establishes the Hacı Karaoğlan *zaviye* (dervish lodge) in İznik in memory of his son Süleyman *Paşa* who had been killed in a hunting accident in Thrace. In this *vakfiye* (written in Arabic), the ruler Orhan names *Hacı* Karaoğlan and his descendants as *mütevellis* (administrators) of the foundation in perpetuity.[83] Of particular interest are the titles accorded Orhan in this document which was drafted just twenty-three years after the 1337 Bursa inscription. He is described as:

The most praised one, and the exalted master, the king of the peoples of nations, the king of the kings of princes of the world, witness of
Islam, protector of mankind, regulator of the principles of justice and
equity, the vanquisher of those who exalt themselves in acts of injustice, the help of the warriors of Islam, refuge of the frontier fighters, the
annihilator of infidels and heretics, the sultan of the *gazis,* the killer of
oppressors, the protector of the religion of God and the helper of the
creatures of God, the hero of the state and the world and religion,
Orhan Beg, son of Osman, son of Ertuğrul.[84]

While still titling himself "Hero of the World and of Religion" and
"Sultan of the *Gazis*" (as in the 1337 inscription), Orhan no longer
refers to himself as "*Gazi* son of the *Gazi*." Far from it, by 1360 Orhan
Beg, has come to think of himself (to the extent this inscription reflects
that process) as "*mâliki riqab al-umam*" (the Possessor of the necks of
nations). In less than a generation, Orhan has progressed from being
solely the "Sultan of the *Gazis*" to the ruler of a state whose subjects
are composed of Muslims, Christians, and Jews. This is a remarkable
transformation and may well reflect the fact that by this date the
Ottoman state has indeed become a blend, representing a heterogeneous commingling of Muslims (many of whom are converts), Christians, and Jews. It hardly supports the idea of a *gazi* state devoted to
killing those Christians who refuse the invitation to convert to Islam.
The use of this title "Possessor of the necks of nations" is fully in keeping with the theory of Ottoman growth postulated on the basis of
Aşıkpaşazade's chronicle.

This explication is strengthened by an examination of the witnesses whose names are attached to the 1360 *vakfiye*. Of the nine individuals so named, one is identifiable as a convert (Şahin bin 'Abdullah), one is a Christian eunuch (Evrenkoş Hadım), and the third
appears to be a Greek Christian named Zağanos.[85] The remaining six
witnesses also appear to have been members of Orhan's immediate
entourage, one of whom is identified as İlyas *al-matbahi* (a kitchen servant or cook named İlyas), while the others are named respectively:
Yusuf bin Musa, Hasan bin Mustafa, *Şeyh Mecnun* bin Hasan (the
Enamored of God Sheikh, son of Hasan), *El Tutan* (Landholder), and
Sekban Karaca (Karaca the Dogkeeper). To say the least there is something slightly incongruous about finding a eunuch, a Christian, a convert to Islam, an Enamored of God Sheikh, a cook and a keeper of the
dogs, among the witnesses to a document which provides its donor an
assemblage of names worthy of any of the Abbasid Caliphs or Seljuk
Sultans. But given that the endower is titled in the same document as
the "Possessor of the necks of nations," this assemblage of individuals

may well reflect (better than any other surviving document), the actual heterogeneous social formation of Ottoman society in the closing years of Orhan's reign.

Also of interest are the list of titles which this *vakfiye* records for Süleyman *Paşa,* the son of Orhan. He is called:

> The Deceased whose sins are forgiven, the auspicious Martyr, Founder of pious deeds, Messenger of good works, Father of abun-

---

PLATE 7
Titles Accorded Orhan *Gazi* in His 1360 İznik *Vakfiye*

TRANSCRIPTION: *Al-mufakhkhar al-a'zam, wa'l-makhdum al-mu'azzam, malik riqab al-umam, malik muluk al-umara' fi'l-'alam, zahir al-islam, nasir al-anam, nazim marasim al-'adl wa'l-insaf, qahir al-mutamarridin bi'l-ihjaf [ijhaf], nusrat al-mujahidin, kahf al-murabitin, qami' al-kafara wa'l-mulhidin, sultan al-ghuzat, qatil al-tughat, nasir din Allah wa'l-mu'in li-khalq Allah, shujā' al-dawla wa'l-dunya wa'l-din, Orhan Beg bin Osman Beg bin Ertuğrul.*

SOURCE: Uzunçarşılı, "Orhan Gazi'nin" (1963), p. 446.

dance, Helper of the weak and poor, Provider for the poor and students, Caretaker of strangers and those seeking help, Possessor of the sword and of the pen, Provider of the banner of knowledge and sovereignty, Commander of the armies of the Believers, Leader of the banners of the warriors for Islam, Regulator of the affairs of religion on the world, Famous of the horizons, the one to whom the care of the dominion of God is bestowed, the second Süleyman, *Gazi Paşa*.[86]

PLATE 8

Titles Accorded Süleyman *Gazi* in Orhan *Gazi*'s 1360 İznik *Vakfiye*

TRANSCRIPTION: *Al-marhum wa'l-maghfur, al-sa'id al-shahid, bani al-khayrat, sa'i al-mabarrat, abu'l-barakat, mu'in al-du'afa wa'l-masakin, murabbi al-fuqara wa'l-talibin, kahf al-ghuraba wa'l-malhufin, sahib al-sayf wa'l-qalam, nasib al-'ilm wa'l-'alam, qayid juyush al-muwahhidin, rayid rayat al-mujahidin, nazim umur al-din fi'l-alamin, mashhur al-afak, al-makhsus bi-'inayat al-malik al-Khallaq, Sulayman (Süleyman) thani ghazi pasha.*

SOURCE: Uzunçarşılı, "Orhan Gazi'nin" (1963), pp. 448–449.

While one may accept most of these appellations as the tribute of a grieving father, what is of interest is once again the fact that were one to remove the name Süleyman and the title *gazi* from this litany, it could be the list of epithets used by any Seljuk ruler. This is not a document which can be easily accepted as originating from a frontier principality in mid-fourteenth century Anatolia. Not only is it written in classical Arabic, the titularies is bestows make it sound as if it was produced in a classical Islamic chancery of the Abbasids by way of the Anatolian Seljuks. Seemingly, within two generations of their emergence the Ottomans had taken on many of the administrative trappings of earlier Islamic dynasties via the medium of the Seljuks.

The next oldest such foundation in the city of Bursa itself is the Hüdavendigar İmaret founded by the ruler Murad I ca. 1365.[87] Also known popularly as the Kaplica İmareti, the oldest surviving copy of the *vakfiye* for this site is one made by the famous *kadı* (religious judge) of Bursa Molla Fenari in the year 1400, which states that it was copied from a version drafted in 1385.[88]

Once again, of particular interest in this document are the titles it records for its founder Murad I and the list of names of witnesses which is appended. Murad I is referred to by the following list of titles:

> The Great Emir, King of the Kings of the Arabs and the Persians [meaning and all other peoples], Protector of the Territories of Allah, Guardian of the Worshippers of God, Champion of the Class of Justice and Benevolence, Sultan son of Sultan, Murad son of Orhan.[89]

Compiled almost one hundred fifty years prior to the point at which the Ottoman rulers could claim the right to be viewed as "King of the Kings of the Arabs and Persians," this title may be nothing more than yet another example of the manner in which such listings bore little relation to reality in the fourteenth century. As such it serves to remind us once again of the rhetorical character of the usage of the title "Sultan of the *Gazis*" on the 1337 inscription.

Also of interest is the list of witnesses appended to this document. Here we see a total of thirty-nine names, among which are a number who are identifiable as first generation converts to Islam. No less than seven of the witnesses bear such names. These include an Umur Beg ibn Koskos *Subaşi* (Umur Beg the son of [the Christian] Koskos the police superintendent), and six individuals bearing the patronym 'Abdullah (slave of God), which in this period marks them as new converts to Islam.[90] Bearing in mind that this document which was initially drawn up in 1385 refers to a witness whose father had been a Christian *subaşi* named Koskos, we may infer that as far back as the reign of Orhan

(1324–1362), there was an already established process where bona fide
Christians were performing administrative functions in the emerging
Ottoman state apparatus. It is even conceivable that following the initial
conquest of Bursa in 1326, Orhan had appointed Umur Beg's Christian
father Koskos as the city's top administrative official. This interpretation
is strengthened by a passage in the work of Gregory Palamas, who upon
visiting the newly conquered Ottoman town of Biga (Pegae) as a captive
in 1354 reports that during the three months of his stay he was hosted
by a prominent citizen, the Hetaeriarch (General) Mavrozoumis. He
describes the treatment he enjoyed in the following terms:

> I . . . and all the others who were with me were offered hospitality by
> Mavrozoumis, who was different from all the rest in kindness. He was
> an Hetaeriarch. He took us under his roof and clothed us when we
> were naked, and fed us when we were hungry, and gave us to drink
> when we were thirsty, and took care of us for three months. Moreover,
> he saved us from the company of barbarians and he invited us to
> preach in the church, as we were wont to do, and to give spiritual com-
> fort both to the native Christians and to those who had been brought
> there in captivity.[91]

PLATE 9
Titles Accorded Murad I in His 1365 Bursa *Vakfiye*

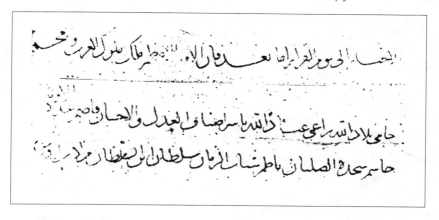

TRANSCRIPTION: *Amir a'zam, malik muluk al-'arab wa'l-'ajam, hami bilad Allah,
ra'i 'ibad Allah, nasir asnaf al-'adl wa'l-ihsan . . . sultan bin sultan Murad bin
Urkhan (Orhan).*

SOURCE: Gökbilgin, "Murad I" (1953), pp. 223–224.

PLATE 10
List of Witnesses Signatory to Murad I's 1365 *Vakfiye*

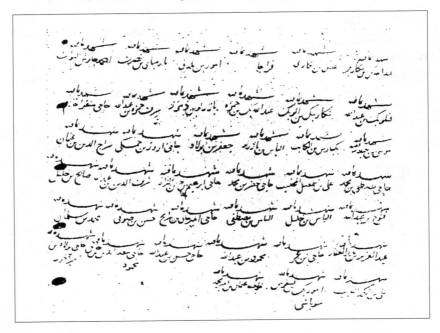

TRANSCRIPTION: *[Line 1] Shahida bi-ma fihi [bears witness to its contents] 'Abdullah bin Beker Beg // [2] SBF 'Abda bin Şikari // [3] SBF Karaca // [4] SBF Umur bin Bulduk[?] // [5] SBF Baybars bin Nüsret // [6] SBF Ahmed Çavuş el-Bevvab // [7] SBF Kutlu Beg bin 'Abdullah // [8] SBF Bengar Beg bin Alo[?] Beg // [9] SBF 'Abdullah Beg bin Hamza // [10] SBF Pazarlu bin Dimitroz[?] // [11] SBF Şirin Hamza bin 'Abdullah // [12] SBF Hacı Sungur [?] al-Hadım // [13] SBF Musa bin Haydar // [14] SBF Begbars bin el-Katib // [15] SBF İlyaz bin Pazarlu // [16] SBF Cafer bin Pulad // [17] SBF Hacı Evroz [Evrenoz?] bin Çemiski // [18] SBF Sarajeddin bin Osman // [19] SBF Hacı Mustafa bin Mehmed // [20] SBF 'Ali bin İsmail el-Muhtesib // [21] SBF Hacı Hızır bin Mehmed // [22] SBF Hacı İbrahim bin Hasan el-Bezzaz // [23] SBF Şerefeddin bin 'Abdullah // [24] SBF Salih bin Halil // [25] SBF Fettah bin 'Abdullah // [26] SBF İlyas bin Halil // [27] SBF İlyas bin Mustafa // [28] SBF Hacı Emirhan bin Rakh[?] // [29] SBF Hasan bin Sabuni[?] // [30] SBF Mehmed bin Süleyman // [31] SBF 'Abdulaziz bin 'Abdulgafar // [32] SBF Hacı bin Ömer // [33] SBF Mahmud bin 'Abdullah // [34] SBF Hacı Hasan bin 'Abdullah // [35] SBF Hacı Sadeddin bin Hacı Mehmed Fakih[?] // [36] SBF Hacı Pulad bin Emirahor // [37] SBF 'Ali bin Nukud al-na-ib // [38] SBF Umur Beg bin Koskos/Kosfos[?] Subaşi // [39] SBF Hevace Osman bin Emire Mehmed.*

SOURCE: Gökbilgin, "Murad I" (1953), p. 233.

From the manner in which Mavrozoumis is described in this passage, it seems quite likely that he was the Ottoman *Subaşı* (Military Governor/Police Chief) in mid-fourteenth-century Biga,[92] that is, the Bigan equivalent of Koskos in Bursa. Clearly, Christians were fulfilling important Ottoman administrative positions in Bithynia in this period, just as they were to do in the Balkans a century later.[93]

This assessment is confirmed by yet another contemporary document, preserved among the acts of the Patriarch of Constantinople, which seems to suggest that as late as 1340 there were also Christians serving as judges in Ottoman Bithynia.[94] The actual text of his 1340 letter, written to the same community in İznik whom two years earlier the Patriarch had allowed to remain covertly Christian (even if they had become overtly Muslims), reads:

> Greetings from the Patriarch to the Clergy, Monks and Christian Population: How much we suffer about your situation, and, of that of all Christians among the Barbarians, is impossible to say. We keep praying to God that he change into serenity the tempest which punishes our errors and that he return the evil against the enemy. We have confidence as long as you strive to serve God. Doubtless the enemy dominates you but you remain the masters of your souls and of the choice of good. As we learned from the *Judge* you remain loyal and we pray to God that you persevere in order to deserve the blessing which he reserves for those he loves. May his grace protect you.[95]

As for the "sons of 'Abdullahs,'" whether they were free Christians who had converted or manumitted slaves is not determinable; however, from the fact that they appear as witnesses to an imperial *vakıf*, we may certainly infer that they were incorporated as members of the Ottoman ruling elite in Bursa when this document was drawn up. Once again we are face-to-face with another of the earliest surviving Ottoman documents which illustrates the manner in which both Christians and first generation converts appear to be playing important roles in the fourteenth-century Ottoman world. Here, too, we have evidence supporting the interpretation that in the first century of Ottoman rule assimilation of non-Muslims was easy and frequent and that one's former Christian status does not appear to have hindered advancement in the emerging Ottoman polity. This is normal in the formative stages of most states and in some ways parallels practices seen in the opening century of the Umayyad dynasty in former Byzantine Syria and Egypt.

One thing is certain: all of the earliest surviving Ottoman documents suggest that both Christians (*Köse* Mihal prior to his conversion, Koskos the *Subaşı* of Bursa, Mavrozoumis the *Subaşı* of Biga, and the unnamed Judge in Iznik are such examples) and recent converts (Köse Mihal following his conversion, Saroz, and Evrenos), together with slaves (Balabancik) and manumitted slaves who were also former Christians (the eunuch Şerefeddin Mukbil), played key administrative roles during the formative years of the Ottoman state. Seemingly, in the first half of the fourteenth century both Christians and ex-Christians found a niche in the emerging Ottoman polity. Indeed, the impression one gets is that the early Ottoman state was one in which religious affiliation was clearly less important than the creation of a working infrastructure and the potential service one could perform. This spirit of latitudinarianism appears to have been a key aspect of early-fourteenth-century Ottoman rule.

The hypothesis as to the heterogeneous nature of the Ottoman ruling class in the opening decades of the fourteenth century would be easy to test if in that period the Ottoman administrative apparatus had developed the practice of compiling *tahrir defters* (cadastral surveys) which recorded the names of all the *erbab-i timars* (Ottoman military administrators) in each region. Aided by such records it would be possible to quantify the input of the local Bithynian population into the formation of the Ottoman polity. Unfortunately, if such records were being kept in that period they have not survived.

However, the process we have been following is confirmable in the following century when administrative practice had come to require the compilation of such periodic cadastral surveys. The earliest extant *tahrir defter* is one which was drawn up in Albania in the year 1431, almost a full century after the events we have been discussing. Published in 1954 by Halil İnalcık, this important register has not received the kind of attention by scholars that its contents warrant. What it establishes is that at the time of its compilation there were numerous Christian *timar*iots serving the Ottoman state in Albania. It also establishes that there were numerous second generation Muslim fief holders who are identified as the sons of Christian fathers.[96] Specifically, a total of 16 percent of the *timars* in the province were held by Christians, 30 percent were in the hands of Muslims from Anatolia (there is no way to determine what number of these were second or third generation converts), and the majority of the remainder were held by Muslim *gulams* (converted Christian slaves).[97] This practice of using Christians as administrators (which my own work has demonstrated disappeared by the opening decades of the sixteenth century),[98] is without doubt a continuation of fourteenth century ones begun in Anatolia. Stated differently, from the fact that in the third decade of the fifteenth century we know that there were Christian administrators in large numbers in Albania, we may posit that they are following in the tracks of several generations of earlier Christian administrators who served the developing Ottoman polity in its formative century. Just as the fourteenth-century Bithynian frontier had accommodated Christian administrators, a century later in the frontier province of Albania the same phenomenon is traceable. To argue differently would mean defending the idea that what in the fourteenth century had been a purely Muslim endeavor, somehow by the fifteenth century had come to include Christians, who were once again excluded by the sixteenth century. That this was not the case is clear from an argument advanced in a critical article written by İnalcık, his "Ottoman Methods of Conquest."[99] In this work he describes the fifteenth-century Ottoman utilization of Balkan Christian administrators in the following terms:

> The Ottoman record books of the fifteenth century show that not only many Ottoman Beys in the government of the provinces but also a considerable number of *timar*iots in the main Ottoman army during the fifteenth century were direct descendants of the pre-Ottoman local military classes or nobility [Note: read Christians]. It is rather surprising to find that in some areas in the fifteenth century approximately half of the *timar*iots were Christians. . . . These proportions were no doubt higher in these areas in the first years after the conquest.[100]

In yet another path-breaking study, his 1954 article on the origin of Christian *timar*iots in the fifteenth-century Balkans, İnalcık convincingly argued that the Ottoman policy of conquest consisted of incorporating large numbers of Greek, Slavic, and Albanian Christians into the *timar* system.[101] He further pointed out that in this early stage in the fifteenth-century Balkans the Ottoman *tahrir defters* establish beyond any doubt that the state in no way followed a policy of attempting to Islamicize either the peasant populations (who were left in their places), or the former members of the ruling elite (who were given positions in the Ottoman administration). While İnalcık discussed the manner in which members of the Byzanto-Balkan military aristocracies were subsumed into Ottoman service in a number of articles, it was only in 1991 that he began to describe the phenomena using the term *İstimâlet*, or the policy of "meeting halfway," by providing concessions to Balkan Christians as a means of ensuring their loyalty.

> . . . In the early period of their expansion, the Ottomans pursued, primarily in order to facilitate conquest, or to make the indigenous population favorably disposed, a policy called *istimâlet*. It was intended to win over the population, peasants and townspeople, as well as military and clerics, by generous promises and concessions, sometimes going beyond the well-known, tolerant stipulations of

Islamic Law concerning non-Muslims who had submitted without resistence [aman]. Within this policy of istimâlet, the Ottomans, especially during the first transition period, maintained intact the laws and customs, the status and privileges, that had existed in the pre-conquest times, and what is more unusual, they incorporated the existing military and clerical groups into their own administrative system without discrimination, so that in many cases former pronoia-holders and seigneurs in the Balkans were left on their fiefs as Ottoman timar-holders.[102]

İnalcık seemed oblivious of the fact that he was describing a practice which is hard to equate with the idea that the early Ottomans were gazis intent on spreading Islam via the sword.

As we have previously seen in the course of our discussion of the Ottoman usage of the term gaza, Balkan Christians were not only serving as sipahis or timar-holders in this period, but in some areas even made up the majority of the auxiliary forces known as the akıncıs/gazis.[103] In short, well into the fifteenth century one could still be a Christian without losing eligibility as a member of the Ottoman ruling elite and/or its military contingents.

What is really rather surprising is that none of the scholars (including İnalcık himself), who have addressed the topic of the origins of the Ottoman state have discussed the full ramifications of this phenomenon. If in the fifteenth-century Balkans a percentage of the members of the Ottoman ruling class were Christians, this certainly reflects the continuation of a status quo established during the course of the previous century in Bithynia. Is it possible that the lack of scholarly attention paid to both the 1431 tahrir from Albania and to the implicit message of the İnalcık articles, stems from the fact that there simply is no way to accept their testimony and still cling to the underlying assumption of Wittek's "Gazi Thesis"? Stated differently, that a thesis which posits the reasons for Ottoman success as emerging from a dedication to spreading Islam at the expense of Christians is impossible to sustain if the ruling elite of the state thus formed is composed of an admixture of Muslim and Christian administrators.

Nor does the fifteenth-century reality in the Balkans easily conform to a theory which posits the Bithynian position of the Ottomans as having attracted a steady flow of manpower (both newly arrived nomads, plus gazis and administrators) from other Anatolian Turkish principalities and Muslim lands, in the preceding century. Had that been the case it seems apparent that there would have been no need to incorporate large numbers of unconverted Christians in the administration of the Balkans a century later.

As hopefully has been demonstrated in the present study, all indications from the surviving fourteenth-century documents seem to substantiate the interpretation that Ottoman society in the state's formative years was one in which Muslims and Christians commingled under a veneer of earlier Seljuk administrative practices. This was a frontier society in flux. As such, it found a place for everyone, free or slave, Muslim or Christian, who had anything to contribute to its growth.

Nor may we overlook the role played by non-Muslim women who married several of the early Ottoman rulers and gave birth to several sultans as well. As may be seen in Appendix 3 we know little about the women of the dynasty in its opening century. However, what information we possess points clearly to the key role of non-Muslim born women in the assimilation of the Bithynian Christian and Muslim populations. In the same fashion that the Ottoman rulers frequently married local (or slave) Christian women, we may posit that the practice was widespread among other members of the Ottoman ruling elite in the state's formative period.[104] That this was definitely the case with the descendants of *Köse* Mihal is clear from an *ihticacname* (a document of complaint in a court case) which is dated 1573. There we see that Mihal and his son 'Ali Bey had both been married to non-Muslim women who subsequently converted to Islam: *a)* Mihal's wife was Hurrem *Hatun* the daughter of 'Abdullah (*bint-i 'Abdullah* meaning daughter of the slave of God, that is, a convert); and, *b)* his son 'Ali Bey's wife was Mahatib *Hatun* the daughter of 'Abdullah.[105]

The role of manumitted slaves in late-fifteenth-century Bursa provides one additional avenue of investigation which must be studied. Specifically, given the large numbers of freed slaves who appear in the earliest extant Ottoman sources from the state's first capital, it seems likely that we may be faced with a long-standing tradition. Namely, captives in war, after a period of economic or household slavery seem to have regularly adopted the religion of the rulers and gained their freedom. This is inferred from the pioneering studies of Halil İnalcık on the earliest surviving *kadı* (religious) court records from Bursa. There (in numerous documents from the late fifteenth century), we see a surprisingly large number of manumitted slaves, who are now Muslims, engaging in all aspects of the city's economic life. Here, too, we must be faced with a continuation of a process which dates from the founding era of the state.[106] If we recall the example of Şerefeddin Mukbil, the freed eunuch Orhan appointed as *Mütevelli* (administrator) of his *vakıf* in Mekece, and that of the *kul* Balabancik who served Osman, it is apparent that this practice existed from at least the opening decades of the fourteenth century.

The various groups discussed above are all clearly discernible in the work of the fourteenth-century Byzantine chronicler Nicephorus Gregoras, who, in describing the nature of Bithynian society at the end of the opening decades of Ottoman rule identifies the following elements:

> Therein all the Bithynians came together, all the barbarians who were of [Orhan's] race, and all the *"mixobarbaroi"* [offspring of mixed Greek and Turkish marriages] and in addition all those of our race whom fate forced to serve the barbarians.[107]

This statement leaves little doubt but that the Ottoman expansion into Bithynia had been accompanied by the widespread union between Muslim men and local Christian women which had resulted in the appearance of the *mixobarbaroi*, (the offspring of such mixed marriages). While not directly referring to those local rulers (e.g., *Köse* Mihal) who had opted for becoming Ottomans themselves, Gregoras' mention of "all those of our race whom fate forced to serve the barbarians," is vague enough to include both those who were enslaved, and those who of their own free will chose to incorporate themselves into the emerging Ottoman polity.

SIX

Christian Peasant Life in the Fifteenth-Century Ottoman Empire

The working hypothesis of this chapter is that the history of peasant life during the formative years of the Ottoman Empire (fourteenth and fifteenth century) is a virtual tabula rasa, a largely unknown canvas, upon which scholars (depending upon their predilections) have tended to project backwards in time either a sixteenth-century-based Ottoman reality or a nineteenth-century Balkan nationalist agenda. Given the obvious dearth of contemporary sources, Ottomanists have generally assumed that a picture drawn on the basis of sixteenth-century material is equally valid for the preceding two hundred years; whereas, Balkan nationalists have tended to assume that the less than pleasant reality of early-nineteenth-century peasant life must indeed reflect an unbroken continuity equally valid for all periods of the *Tourkokratia*. Both approaches share a static vision of society for what this study will suggest was a dynamic and constantly evolving reality, one which, upon close examination of the surviving fragmentary source material, bears little relationship to either.

Implicit in this alternative approach is a rejection of the idea that the Ottoman state in its formative centuries was either solely "Turkish," or, for that matter, purely "Islamic" in nature. Rather, it was a multifaceted society where ability and service were rewarded, with little concern paid to one's religion, and none whatsoever to ethnicity or social status at birth. It may best be described as a predatory confederacy which expanded like a giant amoeba, subsuming all that was useful and reshaping it as necessary in light of changing needs.

Equally implicit is a rejection of the idea that the ethnic Turkish input into the evolving Ottoman polity was numerically predominant, that is, that the unquestionably Turkish dynasty which ruled it was supported in its opening centuries by a majority Turkish element in its population admixture. To the contrary, the evidence to be examined points to the likelihood of a chronic shortage in manpower resulting in the utilization of large numbers of indigenous Christians throughout all levels of society in the fourteenth and fifteenth century.

Rather, the hypothesis underlying this chapter is that what eventually was to emerge as a classical Islamic dynasty, did so less as a result of developments during its formative period than due to the impact of its having annexed the traditional Arab heartland of the Islamic world at the end of the second decade of the sixteenth century. Thereafter, we see the implantation of a centuries' old Islamic bureaucratic tradition to a body which had theretofore been a vibrant, syncretic, multiethnic, multicultural entity. In this sense, the question of who conquered whom is debatable.

Following its incorporation of the older Islamic heartland a new Ottoman amalgam occurred, and with the passage of time the state accordingly adopted a more traditional Islamic character. Viewed from this perspective, it is no coincidence that the tradition of Ottoman historical writing is largely a development of the post-Arab conquests in the opening decades of the sixteenth century. Consequently, much of what we think we know about early Ottoman history is less a reflection of reality than it is of attempts to restyle the Ottoman past into earlier molds of what an ideal Islamic state should be.

In the same manner that we must attempt to escape from this later historiographical tradition, we must likewise focus our examination on the Balkans rather than Anatolia. For, while originating in the latter, the Ottoman state came of age in the Balkans and only really began to turn its attention fully (with the exception of the Yıldırım Bayezid interlude at the end of the fourteenth century) to eastern Anatolia and the heartlands of the Islamic world in the sixteenth century. From the early 1350s forward, the primary Ottoman focus was Balkan oriented and it is in that steady westward movement that we must begin searching for the institutional origins underpinning Ottoman success prior to the point in time at which they began to be obscured by a classical Islamic veneer.

In other words, the Ottoman polity in its formative centuries was nurtured and grew in the late-Roman, Byzantine Christian milieu of the Balkans, a fact which is every bit as important in explaining its pre-sixteenth-century institutional development as the legacy it inherited from earlier Islamic states in Anatolia.

It is within this revisionist, indeed, heretical view of the early Ottoman past (one bearing a far closer relationship to Herbert A. Gibbons and George Arnakis than to Paul Wittek, M. Fuat Köprülü, and Halil İnalcık), that the present chapter seeks to weave a series of vignettes relating to fifteenth-century Ottoman Christian peasant life. It does so on the assumption that the status quo thus reflected is a continuation of practices which developed in the preceding two centuries. As such, its portrait is closer in time to the reality it seeks to depict than those based on the later Ottoman chronicle tradition. To the extent it succeeds, it will illustrate the need for fleshing out a more dynamic portrait of the manner in which fifteenth-century peasant life in the Ottoman state evolved.

The ensuing analysis is based primarily upon a series of surviving *Tahrir Defters*, or Ottoman tax registers, from the Aegean island of Lemnos (Limnos), dating from the years 1490–1520,[1] supplemented by material drawn from similar sources preserved for the hinterland of Salonica (Selanik) in Macedonia,[2] and the Maçka valley of Trebizond (Trabzon) in northeast Anatolia.[3] As will become increasingly apparent, the insights thus provided literally fly in the face of traditional Ottomanist, or, for that matter, Balkan nationalist wisdom.

The most useful source for our purposes is *Tapu-Tahrir Defter #25*, a seventy-two page *mufassal* (detailed) survey of Limnos compiled in the year 1490, just a decade after the final reestablishment of Ottoman rule of this key northern Aegean island which lies directly astride the entrance to the Dardanelles. Unique among the corpus of close to fifteen hundred surviving Ottoman tax registers, *TT #25* not only lists all sources of income derived from the island, but, even more usefully for our purposes, each *akçe* (small silver coin) thus collected is accounted for among the disbursements it lists for the island's *timar*iots (fief holders). The result is a balanced budget which allows us to reconstruct late fifteenth-century life on Limnos in greater detail than for any other part of the Ottoman realms.[4] The present study, while focusing on this *tahrir*, compares its contents with those of a second *mufassal* survey of the island which was drawn up in 1519.[5] The fortuitous survival of these two registers, together with four later detailed surveys of the island, allows us to engage in a comparative approach which is unavailable in such detail for any other Ottoman province. When one factors into this equation that, as an island, Limnos' boundaries did not change over time (unlike those of most Ottoman administrative districts), we have an ideal case study within which to examine changes in peasant life. By the same token, as an island, Limnos was relatively isolated and hence, not subject in this period to Muslim settlement and the consequent phenomenon of religious conversion which often accompanied incorporation into the Ottoman realm.

As such, the 1490 Limnos *tahrir*, which is one of the earliest of a handful of surviving fifteenth-century *mufassal* registers, allows us to reconstruct in some detail the administration, economy, and even lifestyles of a given segment of Ottoman ruled Christian peasant society in an era for which we have almost no extant narrative sources. The picture which emerges is not only surprisingly detailed, but contains numerous elements which either challenge conventional wisdom or allow us to fill in heretofore missing pieces in the canvas of fifteenth-century Ottoman peasant life.

Limnos, due to the dual factors of its key strategic location and its role as the sole source of the highly prized medicinal earth known by the Ottomans as *tin-i makhtum,* or "sealed earth" (the *terra sigillata* of the Italians and the *terra Lemnia* described by ancient writers such as Pliny and Galen), was not a typical Aegean backwater. The possession of the island was a key *casus belli* in the long drawn out Ottoman-Venetian conflict which stretched from 1463–1479. Indeed, so hotly contested was its possession that when it was ultimately ceded by the Doge to the Porte, a special series of clauses relating to its status were actually incorporated into the ensuing peace treaty.[6]

Its role as the site of *tin-i makhtum,* coupled with its housing two of the best natural harbors in the Aegean, highlight its strategic value, and consequently might well lead one to infer that its defense must have been a high priority for the Ottomans. In keeping with known practice, we might well expect to see a significant military presence guarding the island's two major fortresses of Palio Kasri and Kotzinos, together with a naval presence in the Gulf of Mudros.[7] This in keeping with conventional wisdom which divides Ottoman society into a Muslim ruling class, the *askeri,* who performed the dual functions of soldiers and administrators, in return for which they were remunerated by revenues derived from the second major division of society, the *re'aya,* or taxpayers, whose efforts provided the revenues which financed the state apparatus. Applying this model to Limnos, we would expect to see the island's local Christian peasant population working to pay the expenses of its Ottoman military administrators, or fief holders.

To the contrary, the testimony of the 1490 Limnos *tahrir* is sharply at odds with this standard perception of the Ottoman system. It establishes that it was the local indigenous Christian peasant population who bore the primary responsibility for the island's defense. Thus, the heads of the island's six hundred fifty Christian peasant families (with the exception of those exempted from taxation due to physical liabilities such as blindness, old age, or leprosy) were all performing auxiliary military duties for the state in return for which they paid their personal taxes at a reduced rate. The services they performed ran the gamut from fortress guards, cavalrymen, sentinels, pilots, and sailors (groups who collectively accounted for one-third of the adult Christian population), to periodic sentry and lookout duties at the series of *Viglas,* or stone watch towers or huts which dotted the island's coast. In short, the Christian *re'aya* of Limnos were all armed and actively involved in duties generally assumed to have fallen within the preserve of the Muslim *askeri,* or ruling class.[8]

Even more startling is the fact that the official Ottoman presence on Limnos in 1490 consisted solely of a twenty-one man Janissary garrison (most of whom are identifiable as native Greeks by birth who had been recruited into Ottoman service via the *devşirme,* or periodic levies of Christian youths).[9] To say the least, it is apparent that neither the traditional Ottomanist or Balkan nationalist explanations of Ottoman administrative practices can account for the late-fifteenth-century Limniot reality. A situation in which newly conquered Christians are being utilized by their new rulers to ensure the security of the newly conquered territory does not conform to the existing model of Ottoman practice. When we add to this portrait the fact that Limnos lacked even the basic rudiments of an Ottoman bureaucratic presence (there was no *kadı,* or religious judge, on the island in 1490); what we have seen was clearly the widescale participation in the island's defense on the part of the local Christian peasant population, we are faced with a situation which is at odds with standard interpretations of Ottoman practice, and with the Balkan nationalist view of forced subjugation of Christian peasants.

Nor is what we see on Limnos in this period unique to the island. My own studies on selected rural areas of Macedonia and on the Maçka valley of Trabzon in Anatolia, have traced similar practices in those areas as well.[10] Further, as was discussed earlier, the pioneering study of Halil İnalcık on the earliest extant *tahrir,* the 1430 *icmal,* or summary register, from Albania;[11] as well as his extremely important, albeit underutilized, articles on the fifteenth-century Christian *timar*iots (Ottoman fief holders) in the Balkans,[12] and on the early Ottoman methods of conquest,[13] all strongly point to a fifteenth-century Ottoman reality in which one's religious affiliation was of very little import—neither serving to limit one's military contribution to the state, nor prohibiting entry into the *askeri* class. In point of fact, it was this policy of "accommodation," or *"istimâlet,"* which accounts to no small extent for the success enjoyed by the Ottomans in establishing and maintaining their rule in the overwhelmingly Christian Balkans.[14]

Clearly what is called for here is a reappraisal of our understanding of all aspects of fifteenth-century Ottoman rule—one based on surviving contemporary sources rather than on the backward projection of later practices. One thing appears certain, fifteenth-century Ottoman rule of conquered peoples was not primarily based on force of arms. Rather, it worked with and because of the active participation of a wide variety of newly conquered Christians from both the peasantry and former ruling class. That members of the island's late-Byzantine aristocracy were likewise performing military duties on Limnos is inferable from the fact that the peasant auxiliaries were serving under the command of their own officers, some of whom even appear in the 1490 *tahrir* with their former Byzantine military titles, for example, *Kondostavlo*, or, the "Count of the Stables." From the Latin *comes stabuli*, or "count of the stable," this was adopted by the Byzantines as the military title *Konostaulos* in the late thirteenth century. The individual so named in the 1490 register was clearly a member of the island's hereditary aristocracy who had entered Ottoman service complete with his former military rank and title.[15]

Likewise, the actual auxiliary military roles fulfilled by the Limniot populace were nothing new. From the *kanunname* (local law code) which prefaces the second detailed tax register for the island, that of 1519, it is clear that such paramilitary duties were a continuation of pre-Ottoman practice on Limnos and that they were maintained at the express desire of the peasants themselves. The following passage from the *kanunname* establishes this fact:

> After the people of the villages of the said island [Limnos] have fulfilled the Holy Law imposts and the customary levies in the legal manner, it is their customary duty to keep watch and defend the sentry posts on the seacoast around the island. They have Imperial Orders exempting them from the remainder of the customary levies and customary imposts [because of these services]. On behalf of the *Sancak Begs*, the *Subaşıs* (local administrators) who live among the peasants, have been collecting an annual fee called *oturak* (sedentary) in place of their providing the customary coastal defense. This distressed the peasants who complained of this recent innovation imposed upon them and in response the *oturak* was [ordered] lifted from them. Let them defend the coast in places where it is necessary and useful as they have traditionally done.[16]

What we see here is nothing less than an extremely solicitous and responsive government. Peasants appeal to the head of state, complaining against a new practice (which runs counter to tradition) that has been imposed by local administrators, and the appeal is decided in their favor by the Sultan. Stated differently, we see Christian peasants actively seeking to maintain a traditional role as auxiliary military forces, defending what has just recently become the territory of their new Muslim ruler. While we may infer that their interest in so doing was primarily motivated by a desire to maintain the tax breaks thus accorded, they are also expressing their willingness to fight (and presumably die if necessary) for the state they are now part of. In turn, the new ruler of Limnos reacts in a manner that suggests he had no doubts about the Limniot's loyalty as new Ottoman subjects. He upholds their traditional (pre-Ottoman) practice and overturns the decision of his own administrators in so doing. One fact is certain: the armed Christian peasants on Limnos outnumbered their ostensible Ottoman rulers, the Janissary garrison, by a ratio of more than thirty to one.

This decision hardly suggests a state apparatus overwhelmed with a surplus of trained military and administrative manpower. Rather, it raises the possibility that the rapid Ottoman expansion in the late fifteenth century had not only outstripped the center's ability to defend its newly acquired territories, but it also had made it impossible to absorb such areas into any kind of centralized administrative system. The answer, just as it had been throughout the preceding two hundred years, was accommodation *(istimâlet)*. Stated differently, by the late fifteenth century the expanding Ottoman juggernaut was moving with such speed that it dictated the utilization of preexisting Byzantine manpower and defense systems to administer and safeguard even such a key strategic acquisition as the island of Limnos.

This Ottoman willingness to seek accommodation with its new subjects can not but have played a pivotal role in the ease with which newly conquered areas were absorbed into the still growing Ottoman society. This fact, coupled with the security accorded by the *Pax Ottomanica* (after several centuries of Byzantine decline), and what was (as we shall subsequently see) a relatively light tax burden, made it possible for peoples divided by language, culture, custom, and religion, to find a niche under the ever spreading Ottoman umbrella.

What this suggests is the possibility that we need to begin thinking in terms of a new paradigm for early Ottoman history. One in which local society and practice define the center, rather than one which featured a centralized bureaucracy imposing its will on the state. While the latter may well explain the reality of the sixteenth century and thereafter, what we see earlier is a series of ad hoc remedies that accomodated local custom and practice. This approach allows us to account for the great disparity we see in the evolving Ottoman administrative apparatus of the fourteenth and fifteenth century.

In his study on *The Late Medieval Balkans,* the American Byzantinist, John Fine (following İnalcık), has stressed that Ottoman accommodationist practices of this nature were seen throughout the Balkans in the fourteenth and early fifteenth century, as part of the transitional or "vassalage" stage which existed prior to the imposition of direct

Ottoman rule.[17] In so doing, he is emphasizing that Ottoman growth was the result of a predetermined method of conquest, rather than a flexible reaction necessitated by severe manpower shortages caused by the speed of conquest having outstripped the supply of trained manpower. The case study of peasant life on Limnos points to the likelihood that the Ottoman accommodationist stance resulted more from need than premeditation.

The *kanunname* (law code) prefacing the 1490 Limnos *tahrir* provides us an extremely interesting example of the manner in which the flexibility shown by the Ottomans must have made it easy for Christian peasants (unaccustomed to the right to appeal administrative decisions) to accept the new rulers. In this instance, the peasants of the island appeal to higher authority over what they viewed as an unfair tax practice stemming from a peculiarity of the animal husbandry practiced on Limnos.

> And as regards the sheep dues *(adet-i ağnam):* Because the climate of the island is temperate and it is not excessively cold, they [the peasants] are apparently not accustomed to separating their rams from their ewes. For this reason their lambs are not particular to one season. Were they to be counted along with the sheep it would cause the peasants some distress; because they were desirous of and agreed to pay one *akçe* per head of sheep, their lambs were not counted with them. It was recorded that only their sheep be counted and that one *akçe* be paid per head of sheep.[18]

This passage allows us to infer that the normal Ottoman practice of levying the tax on sheep meant that the animals were generally counted at a time of year when there were no lambs. However, the Limniots point out that the climate on the island is temperate and therefore they are not in the practice of ever separating the ewes from the rams which means there is never a time when there is no lamb population. They further argue that this means that they would be paying the "sheep tax" on lambs together with their full grown animals, and they request that only their sheep be subject to the *adet-i ağnam*. The compiler of the local law code *(kanunname)* finds their argument persuasive and records that only full grown sheep on Limnos will be taxed at the rate of one *akçe* (small silver coin) per head.

To say the least, the tax system reflected in this passage was clearly one in which the peasant taxpayers had the right of appeal. Moreover, when they presented a logical argument, the tax collector responded with a degree of understanding not normally associated with that profession. He chose not to cause them "some distress" and recorded in the *tahrir* that the island's lambs were to be exempted from the annual *adet-i ağnam* levy. Here, too, we see the principle of *istimâlet* (accommodation) as a keystone of Ottoman policy as late as the end of the fifteenth century.

When we turn to an examination of the actual list of taxes paid by the agricultural peasants of Limnos, we see that, in addition to the right of appeal, they enjoyed another right normally not associated with medieval taxation, specifically, they paid their personal taxes on a graduated scale in keeping with their net worth. The 1490 *tahrir* lists individual taxpayers in one of three categories: "poor," "of average means," and "well to do"; it shows that they were paying their *(ispence)* capitation tax and *(harac/cizye)* land tax in keeping with their actual economic status rather than on a flat per capita rate.[19] Indeed, when we carefully examine the traceable linkages between the taxes paid by individuals in the three categories and their ownership of livestock such as sheep and swine, it is apparent that there really was a factual basis for determining at which rate one was assessed. Stated differently, those individuals in the "well to do" category own more animals than those "of average means," while those shown as "poor" own little if any livestock. By comparing the taxes paid by individuals in 1490 and 1519, it is actually possible to trace changes in the economic status of individual families. Some families who are shown as "poor" in 1489 are listed as "of average means" a generation later. This suggests that the taxes imposed by the Ottoman authorities were not so harsh as to limit the possibility of upward social mobility.

The portrait which emerges, one which encompasses such features as the utilization of Christian peasant soldiery, who were subjected to a seemingly humane (by medieval standards) graduated tax system (which included the right of appeal), is hardly in keeping with standard interpretations which have tended to emphasize the gap between the rulers and the ruled. Once again, it is the fact that such understanding has all too often been based on the backward projection of a later reality which has tended to cloud our views of fifteenth-century peasant life.

Before continuing with our analysis of peasant society in light of the testimony preserved in the extant Limnos *tahrirs,* it may be useful to cite but one example of the manner in which this particular source sheds light on the ruling, or *askeri* class as well. Earlier studies tell us that members of the Janissary Corps (who comprised the provincial ruling class) were not allowed to marry and raise families prior to the seventeenth century, a change which when implemented is often cited as a cause for decline of this institution. Here, too, a careful comparative reading of the Limnos *tahrirs* (as well as those from Trabzon), illustrates the fallacy of this belief. Not only were fifteenth-century provincial Janissaries marrying and producing offspring, but they were being granted *timars* (fiefs), which were being inherited by their sons as well.[20] This was yet another way in which the indigenous inhabitants became Ottomans, as, given the complete absence of a Muslim population on the island, its Janissaries were intermarrying with the local Christian population. By extension, the offspring of such unions (our second generation of *timar*iots), were the island's Muslims administrators, who were ruling over their Christian cousins. Such second generation Janissaries are identifiable from the fact that they appear in the registers under the rubric of *veled-i kul* (the technical term for Janissary offspring in this period). The second extant Limnos *tahrir*, that of 1519, lists a total of five such *veled-i kuls* who are shown as either holding *timars* which their fathers had possessed in 1490, or, in one instance, actually sharing a *timar* with a father who was also listed in the earlier register. Clearly, in this period provincial Janissaries had already begun to emerge as a hereditary group.[21] Can this be yet another sign of the manpower shortages which were earlier posited as being a key feature of Ottoman life in this era of rapid conquest and expansion?

A self-perpetuating provincial ruling class in place by the end of the fifteenth century would call for some serious reexamination of long-held beliefs relative to the nature of Ottoman administration. At the very least, the clashes some scholars have described as occurring between the *devşirme*-origin Janissaries and native Turkish *timar*iots, might rather have been in that era power struggles between first generation Janissaries and the native born Muslim offspring of their predecessors.

The testimony of the fifteenth-century *tahrirs* in this regard is substantiated by the late fifteenth-century account written by Konstantin Mihailovic, a former Janissary who describes his service in the corps in a work entitled: *Memoirs of a Janissary*. Mihailovic clearly states that fifteenth-century Janissaries were both marrying and leaving their property to whomever they wanted. His observation in this regard is fully borne out by the extant fifteenth century *tahrir* from Limnos.[22]

It is via an examination of the heretofore largely unexplored testimony of the *tahrirs* relative to the phenomenon of religious conversion, that another long-held belief is challenged. Ottomanists have largely ignored the question of religious conversion in their discussions. There are a variety of reasons to account for this: on the one hand, the evidence is scattered and the process of extracting it and shaping it into a meaningful portrait is time consuming. For Turkish scholars, it almost appears as if there is an unspoken taboo against drawing attention to a process which demonstrates the less than ethnic purity of the Turkish populace.

For Balkan nationalist scholars, who all too often view the Ottoman past through the decidedly skewed prism of nineteenth-century ideologies, the most common explanation advanced is that of course there were Christians who converted to Islam—they did so when faced with the choice of conversion or death, or, alternatively to escape the additional tax burdens imposed on non-Muslim subjects.

The testimony of the *tahrirs* in this regard is wildly at odds with all these explanations. On Limnos, as well as in Macedonia and Trabzon, they show a scattering of Muslim peasants sprinkled among the fifteenth-century inhabitants of otherwise Christian villages.[23] These individuals are invariably identified as converts *(mühtedi)* or new Muslims *(nev müslüman)*, whose presence is most notable due to the fact that they were clearly exempt from the personal taxes paid by either Muslim or Christian agriculturalists. The pattern is unmistakable: Christian peasants who converted to Islam were rewarded by what appears to have been a lifetime exemption from taxation. By the second generation the exemptions have been lifted and the offspring of the convert families are shown as paying the normal land usage tax *(çift resmi)* levied on Muslim peasants. Seemingly, in this period there was an economic incentive provided those Christians who chose to accept the religion of the state. The relatively few Christian peasants who opted for this alternative suggests that the personal tax load must not have been so onerous as to make this a particularly attractive option.

The adoption of such a policy by the Ottoman rulers once again suggests that the available pool of potential Muslim settlers was limited and that the offer of a lifetime tax exemption to Christian converts may have been intended to ensure a minimal Muslim presence in newly conquered areas. A detailed examination of the surviving *tahrir defters* for Limnos, the Strymon region of Macedonia and the Maçka valley of Trabzon, establishes that this practice was in place during the last decades of the fifteenth and the opening decades of the sixteenth century. Thereafter, even when a Muslim peasant is listed as a "convert" or "new Muslim," they are shown as paying the normal taxes of any other Muslim agriculturalist.

The *tahrir* entries for several villages, examined in the course of this study, list a single convert family in the late fifteenth century, although on the island of Limnos in 1490 there is only one such "new Muslim," a Mahmud of Imros, listed.[24] By the 1520s many of the same villages are shown as having two or three such "convert" families. When we move to the 1550s, the same sites often are shown as having five or six Muslim families. This trend suggests that the administrative practice of granting a lifetime tax exemption to Christian converts to Islam may have had the desired effect and gradually began to produce a more significant Muslim presence over time.

Though no document establishing this policy is known to have survived, the testimony of a wide sampling of the earliest extant *tahrirs* from exclusively Christian regions of the Balkans and Anatolia, firmly establishes its existence. Once again, we are faced with an early practice which, due to the fact that it has been abandoned by the second half of the sixteenth century, has been overlooked by scholars who have projected their understanding of later Ottoman institutions back in time. May it not have been that as the move to a more centralized system occurred in this period, the practice of *İstimâlet* (accommodation) as a means of ensuring the cooperation of newly conquered peoples became obsolete. In its place, we begin to see that Christians are increasingly treated as they had been in earlier Islamic states.

How significant was this tax break induced religious conversion and to what extent does it account for the Muslim populations of predominantly Christian areas in the Balkans and Anatolia? While there is no way to measure the answer quantitatively, it may well have been that such converts, together with the offspring of provincial Janissary families, may have been the seed out of which many later Muslim communities sprang. Bearing in mind that even in the opening decade of the twentieth century the regions we are discussing (central Macedonia in the Balkans, the Aegean islands, and Trabzon in Anatolia) were areas whose populations were predominantly Christian, such a scenario is possible. Underlying this analysis is a belief that Turkish settlement per se was a relatively limited phenomenon in these regions.

It is by a comparison of known late Byzantine agricultural production on Limnos with the contents of the 1490 and 1519 Ottoman *tahrirs,* that we may gain additional insight into what may only be termed a burgeoning cash economy in the opening decades of the *Turkokratia.*

For the period immediately prior to the Ottoman occupation our major sources of information on the island's economy are the extant monastic records of the various Athonite foundations who possessed dependent houses *(metochia)* on Limnos. Spanning the late eleventh through the fifteenth century, these records consist primarily of lists *(praktika)* of the monastic holdings and the peasants who farmed them in villages scattered throughout the island. Most useful for our purposes are the published records of the monasteries of Dionysiou, Lavra, and Vatopedi, which establish these three Athonite foundations as major landowners on the island. Focusing on their extant *praktika* from the late fourteenth and early fifteenth century, it is possible to project a profile of the island's economy as it existed on the eve of the Ottoman annexation.[25]

The portrait which emerges is one of an economy devoted primarily to agriculture and animal husbandry, where property fell into one of three categories: a) cultivated fields, the size of which was expressed in the Byzantine measurement of the *modioi,* b) vineyards, and c) pasturage or grazing land for livestock. In addition, the *praktika* make frequent references to mills (both wind and water), wine presses, and a large number of *mandras* (sheep folds), which allow us to posit the existence of grain/cereal crops, a grape/wine industry, and livestock in the form of sheep and cattle.[26]

While relatively little detail of a direct nature regarding the specific agricultural crops grown on Limnos is provided, wheat and vegetables are mentioned. Further, the descriptions of individual peasant holdings often note the fact that a particular house had a garden and one or more fig trees. From the frequent and detailed descriptions of the livestock holdings of both the peasants and the monasteries, it is clear that the sheep and its by-products were a particularly important aspect of the island's economy in the late Byzantine period.

The *kanunname* (law code) prefacing the 1490 *tahrir* provides a detailed list of taxes collected on the island which allow us to flush out several additional crops grown on Limnos. These included the fact that the *öşür* (tithe) was to be collected on both olives and almonds, as well as *şira* (grape syrup/wine), wheat, barley, straw/fodder, broad beans, chick peas, flax, fruit, and vegetables. As for livestock, as we have seen, the *kanunname* recorded the manner by which it had been determined that sheep were to be assessed annually at the rate of 1 *akçe* per head, and thereby allows us to determine that this was the single most important aspect of the Limniot economy (there were 24,509 sheep on the island in 1490). The *adet-i ağnam,* collected from this animal, accounted for no less than 20 percent of the total taxes collected. While not specifically mentioned in the *kanunname,* the list of taxes paid by each village also included the *resm-i huk,* or swine tax, which, given the fact that it, too, was levied at 1 *akçe* per animal, allows us to calculate that there were 832 hogs on the island in 1490.[27]

While the sheep, with its by-products of wool, butter, cheese, and so forth is an economically viable animal, the same cannot be said of the hog. Given the fact that this animal is primarily a source of edible meat and leather, it was basically a luxury item in medieval peasant societies. Therefore, the presence of close to 1.5 hogs per household on the island suggests the relative economic well-being of the late-fifteenth-century Limniot peasantry.

Though not specifically taxed, the 1519 *kanunname* lists levies on both cattle and horses among its customs regulations *(gümrük)* governing animals exported from the island. From the fact that the Christian military auxiliaries on Limnos included cavalry units *(müsellem)*, which the *kanunname* states were expected: "in times of need to respond to the summons of the Subaşi with their horses and uniforms/weapons for the Sultan's service *(ki atlariyle ve donlariyle vakt-i hacette subaşı ma'rifetle hizmet-i padişah eda ederler)*, we may deduce the importance of this animal.[28] Richard Pococke, the eighteenth-century English traveler, reports that at the time of his visit (ca. 1745), the island had: "a strong middle sized race of horses, which are remarkable for walking fast."[29] That this native Limniot breed was still extant at the end of the Ottoman period is indicated by a passage in the statistical work compiled by the Frenchman Vital Cuinet ca.1890, where he lists five hundred horses among the livestock figures he provides for the island.[30]

An in-depth comparative examination of the data provided in the 1490 and 1519 *tahrirs,* relative to what were primarily cash crops such as its wine and honey production, as well as its growing cottage textile industry, allows us to begin to discern both the vibrancy and growth of the Limniot peasant economy in the late fifteenth and early sixteenth century. As a case in point, the development of an indigenous textile industry occurred as follows: In the 1490 *tahrir,* flax *(kettan)* is listed as a taxable crop in the single village of Livadskhori. Were it not for the fact that this crop was to emerge in the following generation as a major component of the island's economy, this isolated appearance would be of little interest. However, the 1519 survey records taxes on flax being paid by over half of the island's seventy-five villages. In addition, two other textile related items, cotton *(pembe)* and silkworms *(güğül),* are both among new levies appearing in this register. Here, we see the initial stages of what in later centuries was to become a major cottage textile industry on Limnos. When Pococke visited in 1745 he noted that the:

> Great part of the island is hilly, but the plains and valleys are fruitful, produce great quantities of corn and wine, and some silk and cotton, which they manufacture at home, making a sort of stuff of silk and flax mixed, which is much used for shirts, and is called Meles *(melez),* and a sort of silk-like guaze, very light and transparent, called Brunjuke *(Bürümcük),* which is much used by the ladies for their undergarments.[31]

Clearly, the introduction of flax in 1490, followed by that of cotton and silkworms in 1519, provided the raw materials for the subsequent cottage industry of *Meles* (made of silk and flax) and *Brunjuke* (a kind of tulle silk) were to emerge.

The detail with which the 1519 *kanunname* (unlike that of 1490) provides data on the custom taxes for each item exported off the island for sale, including livestock, wine, "honey, butter, cheese and whatever else of this type of good leaves the island," together with the amounts of customs revenues generated from such sales, all point to an extremely vibrant and growing economy in the opening decades of the sixteenth century. Limnos was a surplus producer and exporter of everything produced on it, including: wine, horses, cows, sheep, honey, butter, cheese, and similar items, wheat, onions, garlic, barley, chick peas, and other grains. This surplus production allows us to infer a relatively high standard of living for the Limniot peasantry by medieval standards.[32]

Our ability to reconstruct the island's economic life in 1490 stems in its entirety from the fact (discussed earlier) that all revenues derived from Limnos are shown as being expended on it in the form of the fiefs provided its military administrators. Whereas normal Ottoman practice dictated that a portion of each area's revenues were expended locally in the form of the stipends assigned its local *timar*iots, some sources of revenue generally went to the either the Imperial Treasury or the Privy Purse. Among these revenue sources normally earmarked for the center, were the *cizye/harac* (land tax) paid by non-Muslims, as well as the revenues from taxes on livestock such as sheep, together with the extraordinary levies *(avariz-i divaniye)* and customs revenues *(gümrük)*.

Within a generation this unique status had changed and the 1519 *tahrir*'s law code establishes that henceforth the island's *cizye*, together with its sheep taxes *(adet-i ağnan)* are assigned to the Imperial Treasury *(hassa-i hümayün)*, while its customs revenues *(gümrük)* are earmarked for the Privy Purse *(mal-i padişah)*.[33] This is a sign of the centralization which is beginning to replace the earlier policy of accommodation.

When one computes the percentages of the 1490 revenues generated on Limnos represented by the combined *cizye*, *adet-i ağnam*, and *gümrük* levies, they account for 55 percent of the total incomes assigned to the island's administrators. Consequently, we might well expect that the alienation of these revenues in 1519 would necessarily result in an increase in rates on the remaining taxes. This assumption is fully supported by the taxes listed in the 1519 *tahrir*, which establish that by the time of its compilation the peasants of Limnos were paying almost double (even allowing for the continuing devaluations of the *akçe*), the taxes paid by their fathers a generation earlier. What we see here may be nothing more than another example of the Ottoman practice of accommodation *(istimâlet)*, whereby in the immediate postconquest era a special treatment was accorded the island. By 1519 such accommodationist practices have been left behind and we now begin to see signs of an increasing centralization.

Though this examination has focused primarily on Limnos, in a number of earlier studies, I have shown that similar changes were transpiring simultaneously in both the Anatolian region of Trabzon and in the agricultural hinterland of Selanik in Macedonia.[34] Based on a comparison of subsequent developments in each of these three regions, it is possible to trace a number of distinct changes relative to the rule of Christian peasants between the late fifteenth and mid-sixteenth century. These include the following:

The removal of most non-Muslim peasants from auxiliary military roles, accompanied by the loss of tax breaks their earlier service had accorded them: By the mid-1520s all the Christian auxiliaries on Limnos have fully reverted from their semimilitary status to that of the traditional peasant, or *re'aya*. Henceforth, they are indistinguishable in the *tahrirs* from the remainder of the Christian peasantry. Viewed differently, the rather blurry distinctions between the ruling and the ruled, which are evident in the late fifteenth century, have disappeared to be replaced by the more classical Islamic distinction between the Muslim rulers and the subject Christians.

The above change is accompanied by a steady increase in the number of Muslim officials identifiable in the *tahrirs:* These include *imams* (prayer leaders), *kadıs* (religious judges), *subaşıs* (police), and so forth, and highlight once again the firm establishment of a more traditional Islamic rule over subject peoples: If our earlier hypothesis relative to the fifteenth-century shortages of trained manpower, due to the rapid expansion under Mehmed II (1451–1481), is correct, this phenomenon suggests that the chronicle accounts describing Bayezid II (1481–1512) as having instituted a more Islamic bureaucracy, may be true.

The practice of taxing Christian peasants in a graduated manner in keeping with their net worth (by assessing their *cizye/harac* and *ispence* levies in different amounts for those classed as "poor," "of average means," and "wealthy") has disappeared: In its place Christian peasants pay their personal levies at one set rate (that formerly paid by those "of average means"). This, too, points to the imposition of a developing centralized traditional Islamic system in place of one whose roots are more likely to be found in pre-Ottoman, that is, late-Byzantine practice.

The absorption of the provincial Janissaries and their descendants into the traditional Ottoman ruling structure: Generally the manner in which fifteenth-century provincial Janissaries are listed in the *tahrirs* allows us to identify them as such, due to the fact that they had yet begun to utilize Muslim surnames and thereby appear with a Muslim proper name and their place of origin, for example, Yusuf Midilli. This manner of notation allows us to infer that the Janissary Yusuf had originally been a Greek Christian from the Aegean island of Mytilene. When in the next generation the same *timar* (fief) is shown to be in the possession of *Ahmet veled-i Yusuf* (Ahmed the son of Yusuf), or *Ahmed veled-i kul* (Ahmed the son of the slave meaning Janissary), we may infer that we are faced with married Janissaries whose *timars* are being passed along to their native born Muslim offspring. However, if thirty years later the income of the same fief is listed as going to an individual with both a Muslim proper name and patronym (e.g., Mehmed the son of Ahmed), there is no way of clearly identifying such an individual as the offspring of a Janissary. From this time forward, we may no longer state with certainty that provincial Janissary posts were passing from father to son. It may be that restrictions prohibiting marriage had by the mid-sixteenth century been imposed on provincial Janissaries in order to ensure the availability of *timars* for each new generations conscripts.

By the 1530s, the practice of granting a lifetime tax exemption to first generation Christian peasant converts to Islam has ceased. This practice which is readily traceable in predominantly Christian areas in the late fifteenth and early sixteenth century, is no longer discernible after the 1530s. Although, from the growing number of Muslims in villages, which had earlier housed such convert families, we may posit the interpretation that the intent of the fifteenth-century Ottoman administrators, who by providing such an economic incentive to conversion, had sought to introduce a Muslim element into otherwise Christian villages, had worked.

The *kanunnames,* prefacing the fifteenth-century *tahrirs* (as our discussion of Limnos has shown), which were initially intended to serve as actual reflections of an evolving tax system, had, by the mid-sixteenth century become static documents which were simply copied from one register to another with no changes: While in the earliest surviving fifteenth-century provincial law codes, one can trace actual changes in the rates of taxation and production over time, this is no longer possible by the late 1530s. From that time forward (with rare exceptions), the *kanunnames* were just copied verbatim into each new register. It was as if they were "frozen" in time, for they no longer bore any relation to whatever the tax system they purported to describe may have been.

Also frozen are the amounts of taxes actually shown as being collected. That is, despite what is known to have been a period of steady inflation, the actual *akçe* amounts shown as being levied remain static: Whereas in the late-fifteenth- and early-sixteenth-century registers we see a steady increase in taxes levied (together with a steady growth in cash crops: such as *zaferan* [saffran] in Macedonia, wine in Trabzon, and the textile industry on Limnos), from the mid-sixteenth century forward the tendency is simply to copy the same list of taxes from each preceding register into its successor.

Finally, by the second half of the sixteenth century, the *tahrir* system virtually collapses and upon close examination it becomes apparent that later registers (particularly *mufassals*) were often simply verbatim copies of those they were intended to replace: This spells the collapse of a system which the evidence at hand suggests was actually functioning in the second half of the fifteenth and opening decades of the sixteenth century. By the 1530s, the system already had begun to stagnate and by the end of the century it had literally fossilized into a meaningless bureaucratic practice, which finally disappeared altogether in the following century. Unfortunately, for the *defter*ologist, the overwhelming majority of the extant *mufassal* registers are those compiled in the mid-sixteenth century at a time when the system was already in decline. One thing is certain: it is via the examination of the handful of extant registers compiled during the reigns of Mehmed II (1451–1481) and Bayezid II (1481–1512), that we may gain the greatest insight into the real intent of these tax registers.

Clearly, fifteenth-century Ottoman peasant reality was a far more syncretic and dynamic one than that seen in the sixteenth century and thereafter. It was typified by an accommodationist stance vis-à-vis the majority of Christian population, one in which religion was only marginally a barrier to either military or administrative advancement. The present study has suggested that this policy of *istimâlet* may well have stemmed from the speed of the Ottoman conquests placing serious strains on the supply of trained military and administrative manpower. It was a need which accounted for the large-scale utilization of both Christian peasants and their former rulers in the expanding Ottoman administration. Typified by a flexible tax system which preserved earlier practices, the ensuing new Ottoman order must have looked particularly attractive to a Christian peasantry long abused during the preceding centuries of Byzantine decline.

It may well have been this accommodationist, indeed syncretic fifteenth-century Ottoman reality, rather than the abundance of an overgrowing influx of Turks, to which we must look for an explanation of Ottoman success in embracing the multitude of peoples divided by culture, language, religion, and history.

If correct, this analysis points to the possibility that among the numerous reasons advanced to account for the long-drawn-out Ottoman decline, we might consider adding the final establishment of a more classical Islamic bureaucracy to what had previously been a more elastic Ottoman polity. If so, two factors are deserving of further study.

First, a detailed examination of the reign of Bayezid II (1481–1512) is called for. Later chroniclers stress that it was this ruler who turned away from the more accommodating postures espoused by his father, Mehmed II (1451–1481), and began the practice of consolidating his father's conquests into a more centralized bureaucracy. To date, there is not a single study devoted to this key ruler, although the fact that the loss of military and semimilitary status for numerous Christians occurred during his rule, suggests that the chronicler's depictions may well be correct in this regard.

Second, the generation following the conquest of the key Arab areas of Syria and Egypt, that is, the post-1517 era, is deserving of further study. Here, too, the chroniclers make mention of the fact that large numbers of Arab bureaucrats and religious scholars began flocking into the Ottoman heartland in the wake of the conquest. One thing is certain, it was only after 1517 that the Ottoman state may have come to encompass a majority Muslim population. It seems logical to assume that many of these new Arab immigrants, schooled as they were in the administration of older Islamic societies (which had ruled minority Christian populations for centuries), found their way into all branches of the Ottoman bureaucracy.

Indeed, within two decades of their arrival, signs of their growing impact on the evolving Ottoman bureaucracy are apparent even in the terminology employed in the *tahrir defters*. By the 1540s we begin to discern a heavy influence of Arabic tax-related terminology on what had theretofore been a system which made heavy use of Greek, Slavic, and Persian names for taxes, weights, and measures. Suddenly, the hybrid admixture of the earlier terminology has been replaced and we find a standardization of Arabic dominated terms transplanted as far west as the Balkans.

A case in point is the manner in which the decidedly un-Islamic practice of recording the tax on swine in Christian regions changes. In the pre-1517 registers it is referred to variously by the Persian *resm-i canavar* (the monster tax), or *resm-i huk* (the swine tax), and in some areas by the Turkish *resm-i domuz* (swine tax). In all post-1550 registers (regardless of region), these terms have given way to the standard Arabic term: *resm-i hınzır* (the swine tax). Similar changes in the crop names recorded in the *tahrirs* occur as well. These changes highlight what must have been the growing impact of earlier Islamic practice.

Can it be that the Ottoman *uç* (border/frontier) society of the fourteenth and fifteenth century had grown with ease partially as a result of its openness to change and willingness to embrace any and all who could contribute to the success of its endeavor, regardless of religion? Whereas, having by the late fifteenth century grown into a highly centralized empire, it then began to act like a more traditional Islamic state, one in which sharing the religion of the ruler became a prerequisite for state service and advancement. Finally, with the absorption of the heartlands of the Arab world it shed even more vestiges of the syncretism and accommodationism which characterized the state in its formative period. While, a great deal of study is called for before this idea can be advanced from the realm of hypothesis, one thing is certain: there is a dynamism traceable in the Ottoman rule of fifteenth-century Christian peasants which is no longer discernible a century later.

One thing is indisputable: the time when we could project sixteenth-century (or later) Ottoman practices back in time and pretend that they were equally valid for the fifteenth century is past. Equally true is the fact that none of the standard explanations for the origins, growth, and expansion of the Ottoman polity are fully satisfactory in accounting for the snapshots of Christian peasant life provided us by the testimony of the late-fifteenth-century tax registers.

SEVEN

The Last Phase of Ottoman Syncretism— The Subsumption of Members of the Byzanto-Balkan Aristocracy into the Ottoman Ruling Elite

> Know that the Grand Vezir is, above all, the Head of the vezirs and commanders. He is greater than all others; he is in all matters the Sultan's absolute deputy. . . . In all meetings and in all ceremonies the Grand Vezir takes his place before all others.
>
> —İnalcık, *The Ottoman Empire*
> (Quoting the *Kanunname*
> (Law Code) of Mehmed II.)

The full degree to which the Ottomans subsumed member of the Byzantine and Balkan nobility into the highest reaches of their own administration can best be illustrated via an examination of the individuals who rose to the position of Grand Vezir in the second half of the fifteenth and opening decades of the sixteenth century.

On May 29, 1453 the Byzantine Emperor Constantine XI Palaiologos fell defending the walls of Constantinople against an Ottoman attack led by the twenty-one-year-old Sultan Mehmed II. Constantine XI died without an heir; his two marriages had been childless. Had the Ottoman attack on that day not spelled the end of the Byzantine Empire, Constantine XI in all likelihood could have been succeeded by one of the three sons of his deceased elder brother. As events turned out, all three were taken into Palace Service by the conqueror, following the fall of the city.[1]

In 1470, within seventeen years of the fall of the city, one of Constantine's nephews emerged from behind the walls of the Seraglio, at the age of twenty-seven, as Mesih *Paşa*, Admiral of the Ottoman fleet and Sancak Beğ (Governor) of the Province of Gallipoli. In 1481 Mesih *Paşa* was appointed by Mehmed's successor, Bayezid II, to the post of Grand Vezir, or Chief Minister of the Ottoman government, a post he held for two years. In 1499 he was elevated to the Grand Vezirate once again, and died in office in 1501.[2]

Mesih *Paşa*'s brother, rechristened as the Ottoman Has Murad *Paşa*, was a personal favorite of Sultan Mehmed II. In 1472, nineteen years after the city's fall, he obtained his first major administrative appointment as *Beylerbey*, or Governor-General, of *Rumeli* (the Balkans). A year later, on August 4, 1473, while leading one wing of Mehmed's army against the Akkoyunlu leader Uzun Hasan, Has Murad *Paşa* died in an ambush; he was crossing the Euphrates River in eastern Anatolia.[3]

As for the third of Constantine's nephews, his subsequent career is harder to trace. There is, however, a possibility that when he emerged from the Palace he did so as Gedik Ahmed *Paşa*, who in 1473 was named Grand Vezir by Mehmed II. While little is known about the early years of Gedik Ahmed *Paşa*, the Turkish scholar Mükrimin Halil Yınanç has cited unnamed Western sources claiming that he was of Palaiologan origin.[4] More recently, the 1985 study on the Serbian region of Vranje by Aleksandar Stojanovski, has established that Gedik Ahmed *Paşa* was a member of the minor Serbian aristocracy. In Stojanovski's study of a fifteenth-century cadastral survey *(tahrir defter)*, a *timar* (fief) holder is listed as the newly converted "father of the illustrious Gedik Ahmed *Paşa*." This identification, while undermining Yınanç's suggestion of Palaiologan ancestry for Gedik Ahmed *Paşa*, would make him a member of the Serbian military aristocracy, since his father is shown to have previously held a *pronoia* (fief).[5]

In short, two individuals who, but for the vagaries of battle on May 29, 1453, might well have been crowned one day as Byzantine Emperors, instead found themselves at the pinnacle of power in the very state which had brought an end to the millennium long Byzantine polity. They did so via the simple expediency of following the path of religious and linguistic acculturation and, in a state which at that juncture was in need of their services, found all doors open as a result.

Nor were the brothers "Palaiologos" unique in this respect. For in the half century between the fall of Constantinople and the Ottoman conquest of the heartland of the Arab world in 1516–1517, several other Ottoman Grand Vezirs were drawn from among the children of the former Byzantine and Balkan nobilities. These include: Mahmud

Paşa twice Grand Vezir for a record seventeen years under Mehmed II [formerly a scion of the Byzanto-Serbian noble family of the Angelović]; Ahmed *Paşa* Hersekzade [formerly Prince Stjepan Hersegović, son of the Duke of St. Sava], who was married to a daughter of Sultan Bayezid II., and held the office on five separate occasions; *Hadım* (Eunuch) 'Ali *Paşa,* the son of Radošin Ostoya, a minor noble from Bosnia, who served as Grand Vezir twice (first in 1501–1502 and then again between 1506–1511); Dukaginzade Ahmed *Paşa,* the son of the Albanian Duke of Menebor, who held office briefly in 1514–1515; and finally *Hadım* (Eunuch) Sinan *Paşa,* a descendant of the Bosnian noble family of the Borovinič, who was appointed to the office twice between the years 1515–1517 .

Scholarship to date has generally failed to differentiate these individuals from the larger group of *devşirme*-origin Vezirs who rose to prominence under Mehmed II (and who were to dominate the office for the next one hundred fifty years). In the period under study, this group included such Grand Vezirs as Rum Mehmed *Paşa,* Davud *Paşa,* İshak *Paşa,* and Koca Mustafa *Paşa.* Such individuals were originally Christian peasant youths, captured in warfare, or collected in periodic levies by Ottoman officials (the process known as *devşirme*), who, following several years of training in Islam and Turkish in one or another of the various Palace Schools, generally emerged as Ottoman officials. They came to dominate the highest levels of government to such an extent, that the late Turkish scholar, İsmail Hakkı Uzunçarşılı, stated that (with the exception of four Turkish-born Vezirs), the remainder of the thirty-four Grand Vezirs who served between 1453 and 1600 were all *devşirme* conscripts.[6] What Uzunçarşılı and later scholars writing on this period have overlooked was the fact that between 1453–1516 several of those individuals which they termed *devşirme* conscripts were in fact members of the preexisting aristocracies who were incorporated into Ottoman service.

By uniting all non-Turkish Grand Vezirs together under the *devşirme* rubric, Uzunçarşılı (as the present study seeks to demonstrate), was blurring an important distinction. If the standard interpretation of the rationale behind the *devşirme* practice is correct, namely, that the Ottomans sought to insure the absolute loyalty of the higher echelons of their administrators through the formation of a kind of slave *(kul)* hierarchy, which, cut off from all ties with their former backgrounds, would form a sort of Sultanic Praetorian Guard, then the least likely candidates would be members of the former Byzantine and Balkan aristocracies. Such individuals not only knew their own pasts, but also their original Christian identities were also known to their contemporaries. This fact is reflected in some of them using their new Muslim proper names in conjunction with Turkified forms of their original Christian surnames (e.g., Hersekzade, Dukaginzade, etc.). The practice of subsuming members of the local Christian nobilities predates the *devşirme* system, which only came into being at the end of the fourteenth century, a fact noted by Halil İnalcık when he wrote that the roots of the *devşirme* system may be traced to the much earlier "practice of taking into Palace service or into the army the young sons of members of the local military class in conquered areas."[7] This phenomenon is seen as early as the opening decade of the fourteenth century when Osman *Gazi,* the founder of the Ottoman dynasty, was assisted in his Bithynian conquests by local Christian lords such as *Köse* Mihal.

What changed under Mehmed II (1451–1481) was that for the first time the highest offices in government, including that of the Grand Vezirate, now became open to such former members of the Greek, Bulgarian, Serbian, and Albanian aristocracies.[8] This is not to say that they monopolized such offices, only that they shared them with other members of the Ottoman ruling class. To view such individuals as *devşirme* conscripts is an error in attribution. For, while the *devşirme* converts, who rose to power from the late fourteen century forward were generally of peasant origins, and who were cut off from their roots when they were retrained as Ottomans, this was not the case with the individuals who are the subject of this chapter's discussion. In contrast, what I would term the "Byzantine and Balkan aristocrats turned Vezirs," were drawn from the highest strata of the preconquest nobility. As such we might expect that they would have been among those individuals first eliminated by the conquerors, who could have viewed them as potential focal points for any kind of restorationist movement on the part of the defeated enemy.

On the contrary, following the ultimate defeat of Byzantium, the confidence of the Ottoman rulers Mehmed II (1451–1481), Bayezid II (1481–1512), and Selim I (1512–1520), was such that they felt able to subsume even members of the defeated ruling dynasty into the highest levels of their own state's elite. Their willingness to do so (despite the potential risks), must also have been prompted by need. That is, as the rulers of an ever-growing polity centered in the Balkans, the overwhelming majority of whose inhabitants shared neither the religion nor the language of the rulers, the Ottoman Sultans needed administrators who could at least speak the languages of the people they ruled. What better source of trained manpower than the newly converted and educated Ottomans drawn from the very families who had ruled the area for centuries? If the descendants of the former rulers found a niche in the Ottoman hierarchy, might this not encourage their former subjects to do so as well? Whatever their rationale, the Ottomans opted for "continuity" to an extent which seemingly lacks a direct parallel in either the contemporary fifteenth-century world, or in modern society. This sense of confidence and desire for continuity is also reflected in the fact that Mehmed II and later Ottoman rulers at times styled themselves as *Kaysar* (Caesar), *Basileus* (King—the primary title used by the Byzantine Emperors), *Padişah-i Kostantiniye* (Emperors of Constantinople), and as *Padişah-i Rum* (Emperors of the Romans), all titles which clearly underline a belief in their role as inheritors of universal power.

As illustrated in table 7.1, the second half of the fifteenth century was a particularly syncretic era for the Ottomans. This is reflected in the backgrounds of the individuals who held the post of Grand Vezir between 1453–1516. Among them were a Christian renegade (Zaganos *Paşa*), *devşirme* conscripts (İshak *Paşa,* Rum Mehmed *Paşa,* Davud *Paşa,* and Koca Mustafa *Paşa*), freeborn Muslim Turks (Koca Sinan *Paşa,* Karamani Mehmed *Paşa,* and Çandarlı İbrahim *Paşa*), and the group we are primarily concerned with, the former members of the Byzantine and Balkan aristocracies who either of their own free will opted to become Ottomans (Hersekzade Ahmed *Paşa* and Dukaginzade Ahmed *Paşa*), or who were taken as hostages or captives (Mahmud *Paşa,* Gedik Ahmed *Paşa* [?], Mesih *Paşa,* Hadım 'Ali *Paşa* and Hadım Sinan *Paşa*). The extant Ottoman sources are generally silent in regard to the early lives of all these individuals, and this is particularly so for those of non-Turkish origin.

For a knowledge of the ethnic and religious backgrounds of the Byzantine and Balkan aristocrats turned Vezirs, we must turn to what other contemporary but non-Ottoman observers recorded about them. In this respect, a most important source is the sixteenth-century work of the Byzanto-Italian chronicler Theodore Spandounes (Spandugnino), a longtime resident in the Ottoman capital, who had spent part of his boyhood as a ward of his greataunt Mara/Maria, the daughter of the Serbian Despot George Branković and widow of the Ottoman Sultan Murad II, in the town of Ješevo in Macedonia,[9] and who was also a close relative of both the Palaiologan Mesih *Paşa* and the son of the Duke of St. Sava in Bosnia, Hersekzade Ahmed *Paşa*. Spandounes, himself a descendant of the Imperial Byzantine family of the Cantacuzenes, was a grand-son of the sister of the three Palaiologan Princes, about whose careers he writes the following:

> Mehmed also sent a force to lay siege to Rhodes. It was led by one Mesih Pasha *(Messit bassa)*, who was of the house of Palaiologos. He was a brother of my father's mother. At the capture of Constantinople

TABLE 7.1
Ottoman *Vezir-I A'zams* (Grand Vezirs), 1453–1516

Name	Dates of Service	Origin	Geographical Origin and Family Name
İshak *Paşa* [?]	1453: June–July [?]	Christian slave: *Devşirme* conscript	Unknown: Greek or Croat
Zaganos *Paşa* [?]	1453: August [?]	Greek Renegade	Unknown
Mahmud *Paşa*	1453–1468	Byzanto-Serbian: Nobility	Serbia; Angelović, the Thessalian branch of the Serbian Despotate
Rum Mehmed *Paşa*	1468–1470	Greek Christian: *Devşirme* Conscript	Greek or Albanian: Captured in 1453 at the conquest of Constantinople
İshak *Paşa* [second term]	1470–1472	Christian Slave: *Devşirme* Conscript	Unknown: Greek or Croat
Mahmud *Paşa* [second term]	1472–1474	Byzanto-Serbian: Nobility	Serbia; Angelović, the Thessalian branch of the Serbian Despotate
Gedik Ahmed *Paşa*	1474–1476	Byzantine or Serbian: Nobility	Imperial family of the Palaiologos or Serbian nobility?
Hoca Sinan *Paşa*	1476–1477	Muslim Turkish	İstanbul: Son of Hızır Beğ, the first Ottoman Kadı of İstanbul
Karamani Mehmed *Paşa*	1477–May 1481	Muslim Turkish	Konya in Anatolia

(continued on next page)

TABLE 7.1 *(continued)*

Name	Dates of Service	Origin	Geographical Origin and Family Name
Mesih *Paşa*	1481–1482	Byzantine: Nobility	Member, Imperial family of the Palaiologos
İshak *Paşa* [third term]	1482	Christian Slave: *Devşirme* Conscript	Unknown: Greek or Croat
Davud *Paşa*	1483–Feb. 1497	Albanian Christian: *Devşirme* Conscript	Albanian: family name unknown
Hersekzade Ahmed *Paşa*	March 1497–August 1498	Bosnian Nobility	Son of the Duke of St. Sava in Bosnia
Çandarlı İbrahim *Paşa*	September 1498–August 1499	Muslim Turkish Veziral family	Last in the line of Çandarlı Vezirs from İznik in Anatolia
Mesih *Paşa* [second term]	1500–1501	Byzantine Nobility	Member, Imperial family of the Palaiologos
Hadım 'Ali *Paşa*	1501–1502	Christian Eunuch: Minor Nobility	Bosnia: Family of Ostoya from the village of Drozgometva
Hersekzade Ahmed *Paşa* [second term]	November 1502–September 1506	Bosnian Nobility	Son of the Duke of St. Sava in Bosnia
Hadım 'Ali *Paşa* [second term]	1506–1511	Christian Eunuch: Minor Nobility	Bosnia: Family of Ostoya from the village of Drozgometva
Hersekzade Ahmed *Paşa* [third term]	July 1511–September 1511	Bosnian Nobility	Son of the Duke of St. Sava in Bosnia

(continued on next page)

TABLE 7.1 *(continued)*

Name	Dates of Service	Origin	Geographical Origin and Family Name
Koca Mustafa *Paşa*	October 1511– October 1512	Christian Slave: *Devşirme* Conscript	unknown
Hersekzade Ahmed *Paşa* [fourth term]	November 1512– October 1514	Bosnian Nobility	Son of the Duke of St. Sava in Bosnia
Dukaginzade Ahmed *Paşa*	December 1514– March 1515	Albanian Nobility	Son of the Albanian Duke of Menebor
Hadım Sinan *Paşa*	June 1515– September 1515	Bosnian Christian Slave: Eunuch Nobility	Bosnian: Noble family of the Borovinić
Hersekzade Ahmed *Paşa* [fifth term]	October 1515– April 1516	Bosnian Nobility	Son of the Duke of St. Sava in Bosnia
Hadım Sinan *Paşa* [second term]	April 1516– January 1517	Bosnian Christian Slave: Eunuch Nobility	Bosnian: Noble family of the Borovinić

SOURCE: Information in this table is drawn primarily from: Danişmend, *İzahli Osmanli* (1971); Süreyya, *Mehmed Süreyya's* (1996); Osmanzade, *Hadiqat ül-vüzera* (1969); and articles on individual Grand Vezirs found in *The Encyclopaedia of Islam*, the *İslam Ansiklopedisi*, *Türkiye Diyanet Vakfı İslam Ansiklopedisi*, Uzunçarşılı, *Osmanli Tarihi* (1943); Reindl, *Manner um Bayezid 1983*).

he had been taken by the Turks along with his two brothers. He was only ten at the time, and they were all made Turks. Mesih rose to the rank of Pasha."[10]

In a later passage, in which he describes Sultan Bayezid II's campaign against the Aegean island of Mytilene in 1501, Spandounes adds the following regarding Mesih *Paşa*'s subsequent career:

> This Mesih, for all that he was the brother of the mother of my father, was a fierce enemy of the Christians; and in the course of his operations at Mytilene he broke his neck.[11]

Spandounes' observation regarding the former Palaiologan Prince "being a fierce enemy of the Christians" may also be inferred from the fact that Mesih *Paşa*, alone of the fifteen Grand Vezirs under study, made the pilgrimage to Mecca, a practice incumbent upon good Muslims, but one which the duties of office seldom allowed high-ranking Ottomans in this period to observe. That he did so at the height of his career (in the interim between his two terms in office) suggests that this individual, who might have become the Emperor of Eastern Christendom, had indeed become a devout practicing Muslim.[12]

Spandounes was likewise related by marriage to Hersekzade Ahmed *Paşa*, the son of the Duke of St. Sava in Bosnia. Here, Ahmet *Paşa*'s eldest brother Ladislas was married to a woman named Anna, who was a sister of Spandounes grandfather.[13]

Recalling our earlier discussion of the sources utilized by Spandounes:

> . . . I was able to consult two of the nobility who were on most intimate terms with the Emperor of the Turks; they were among my closest friends and my relations, men of rare talent and great knowledge of these matters.[14]

It is clear that our author was naming his relatives the two-time Ottoman Grand Vezir Mesih *Paşa*, and the son-in-law of Sultan Bayezid II, the five-time Grand Vezir Hersekzade Ahmed *Paşa*. By stating that they were "among my closest friends and my relations," Spandounes makes it clear that regardless of their having assumed a new religion, culture, and names, members of the former Byzantine nobility were still fully aware of their past and maintained ongoing relations with members of their former Christian families.

Another such example was Mahmud *Paşa* [Angelovič], a scion of the Byzanto-Serbian nobility, who was captured while a youth and raised in the Ottoman Palace in Edirne. His subsequent extraordinary career was marked by extremely close contacts with a number of different members of his original family. Five case studies (among many which might be cited) will serve to illustrate this fact:

On his maternal side, Mahmud *Paşa*, was the Serbian-born grandson of the Byzantine nobleman Marko Yagari. As such he was a cousin of the late-Byzantine philosopher George Amirutzes, who in 1461 was serving as the *Protovestiarius* (Counselor) of David Komnenus, the Emperor of Trebizond. When Mahmud *Paşa* led Sultan Mehmed's land army against Trebizond, he negotiated the surrender of the city with none other than his own cousin. It is likely that Amirutzes' subsequent long career in the Ottoman Palace was also due to these familial links.[15]

On his paternal side, Mahmud *Paşa* was the son of Michael Angelovič of Novo Brodo, a scion of the Serbian branch of the Thessalian

Byzantine despot dynasty.[16] Thus, in March 1458, when Mahmud's brother Michael was removed by the Bosnian Queen (who was the daughter of the despot of Serbia), and replaced by a Catholic Bosnian, the Serbian aristocracy contacted Mehmed II and offered him suzerainty over Serbia. Who better to settle the Serbian question than the former Byzanto-Serbian Mahmud *Paşa*, who was sent by the Sultan for that very purpose?[17] The architect of direct Ottoman rule in Serbia was himself the Serbian-born Angelović.[18]

Mahmud *Paşa*'s brother Michael Angelovič, who remained a Christian, was at his brother's side throughout most of his career. When, late in life (1471) Mahmud *Paşa* (disillusioned by his fall from power) seems to have plotted against Ottoman interests with the Venetians, his brother Michael was also deeply involved.[19]

As had his brother Michael, Mahmud *Paşa*'s mother (who also remained an Orthodox Christian), joined her son the Vezir in the Ottoman capital. We may infer that she too found favor in the Sultan's eyes as a *ferman* (imperial edict) issued by Mehmed II in 1462 bestows upon her the Monastery of Prodromos Petros in Konstantiniye (İstanbul).[20]

In 1460 when the Ottomans moved against the Despots of Mistra, one of Mehmed's commanders was his Grand Vezir, Mahmud *Paşa*. The Byzantine chronicler Sphrantzes relates how following the conquest of the town and fortress of Gardiki, the inhabitants, who had resisted Ottoman calls for surrender, were put to the sword. The only exception were their leaders, the family of the Bokhales, who were spared a similar fate only due to the entreaties of Mahmud *Paşa*, because "Manuel Bokhales' wife was his second cousin."[21]

Not only did Mehmed II seemingly approve of these ties, on occasion he encouraged them (by the bestowal of property on Mahmud's Christian mother), and when appropriate (such as in the Serbian case) he used them to his political advantage. It was the level of trust which he had in Mahmud that prompted the contemporary Ottoman chronicler Tursun Beg describing events in 1461 to write: "Mahmud *Paşa* was now at the height of his glory. It was as though the Sultan had renounced the sultanate and bestowed it on Mahmud."[22]

While there is some dispute as to when Mehmed elevated Mahmud *Paşa* to the post of *Vezir-i Azam* (Grand Vezir),[23] a close reading of the account provided by Kritovoulos (a former Byzantine official who entered Mehmed's court circle and wrote a history in Greek of the early years of his reign, 1453–1467), leaves no doubt but that by late 1453 the Ottoman administration was headed by the former Byzanto-Serbian nobleman Angelović.[24] Kritovoulos (in a heading left out in the Riggs translation), clearly states that Mahmud *Paşa* was "brought into the rank and office of Zaganos" as the individual "who took charge of the affairs of the Great Sultan" in the summer of 1453.[25] As a close advisor and confidant of Mehmed at that time, Kritovoulos' account is based on firsthand knowledge and therefore must be deemed credible given the absence of any other contemporary account which contradicts him. The only real question is whether or not, following the fall of the city and the removal of Çandarlı Halil *Paşa* from the post of Grand Vezir he was replaced briefly (for two or three months) first by İshak *Paşa* and later by Zaganos *Paşa*. On this question, the sixteenth-century chronicler, Küçük Nişancı [Ramazanzade] (d. 1571) relates the early career of Mahmud *Paşa* in the following terms: "He became *kadiasker* and, in *Rebiülevvel* 857 (1453), immediately after the conquest of Constantinople, became Grand vizier in place of Halil *Paşa* [Candarlı]."[26] In so doing, he strengthens the account provided by Kritovoulos.

Once Mahmud *Paşa* assumed office, he is described by Kritovoulos in terms which leave no doubt whatsoever that he was acknowledged by his contemporaries as a member of the former Byzantine aristocracy. Mahmud *Paşa*, the new Vezir was:

> A man named Mahmud, who had formerly belonged to the Roman nation on both his father's and his mother's side. His paternal grandfather, Philanthropinos, had been ruler of Hellas [Central Greece], with the rank of Caesar. This man had so fine a nature that he outshone not only all his contemporaries but also his predecessors in wisdom, bravery, virtue, and other good qualities. He was very quick to recognize spontaneously what needed to be done, even when another told him of it, and still quicker in carrying it out. He was also eloquent in addressing a crowd, able in commanding men, and still more clever in making use of things and in finding a way out of difficulties. He was enterprising, a good counselor, bold, courageous, excelling in all lines, as the times and circumstances proved him to be. For from the time he took charge of the affairs of the great Sultan, he gave everything in this great dominion a better prospect by his wonderful zeal and his fine planning as well as by his implicit and unqualified faith in and goodwill towards his sovereign. He was thus a man of better character than them all, as shown by his accomplishments.[27]

That Mehmed concurred with the glowing testimonials provided by Kritovoulos and Tursun Beg may be inferred from the fact that Mahmud *Paşa* was to remain in office for the next fifteen years (1453–1468). Following his first dismissal in 1468, he was recalled to the post for two more years in 1472. His seventeen years at the pinnacle of the state's administrative apparatus was unequalled by any other Grand Vezir in the more than six hundred years of Ottoman history. There can be little doubt that when Mehmed II (in the passage given at the beginning of this chapter) described the office and its power in his *Kanunname* (Law Code), he had Mahmud *Paşa* in mind.

Although many of the former Byzantine nobility, who subsequently rose to positions of power in the Ottoman state were originally captives (e.g., Mahmud *Paşa,* Mesih *Paşa* and Has-Murad *Paşa*), or, in an earlier period, hostages demanded by the court to ensure the loyalty of their families who, having accepted Ottoman suzerainty were left in their own lands as vassals, this was not always the case.

In this regard, the career of Hersekzade Ahmed *Paşa* is particularly illuminating. The favorite son of Duke Stjepan Vukčič-Kosača (1405–1466), a great Bosnian *Vojvoda,* who ruled southeast Bosnia/Herzegovina (from his title "Herceg," or "Duke" of St. Sava his domains were called "Hercegovina" and his descendants "Hercegovič"),[28] he was born in Castel Nuovo in the mid-1450s. On his mother's side he was descended from the family of the Dukes of Bavaria (Duke of Payro meaning Bayern). While earlier scholarship often maintained that he had been sent to Mehmed's court as a hostage, the Bosnian historian Hazim Sabanovič has established that the future Ahmed *Paşa* spent his childhood in Castel Nuovo, aside from a period when he was being educated in Dubrovnik, where he was known as Prince Stjepan. He was still in Castel Nuovo in 1472, at which time he had a falling out with his older brother the Herceg (Duke) Vlatko, who had seized his share of their father's inheritance. In response, Prince Stjepan went on his own to İstanbul, converted to Islam and took the Muslim name Ahmed, but kept a hybrid Slavonic-Ottoman Turkish form of the family name Hercegovič-Hersekzade (literally, 'Son *[zade]* [of the] Duke *[hersek]*). His subsequent rise was meteoric: first mentioned in a *ferman* (imperial edict) of Mehmed II's dated 1477 as the "servant of my kingdom Ahmed Beg," in the following year he served in the Sultan's retinue as a *Mir-i 'Alem* (Commander) in the Albanian campaign. By 1481, when still in his mid-twenties, he was married to Princess Hundi *Hatun,* the daughter of the new ruler, Sultan Bayezid II, and had been promoted to the post of *Beylerbey* (Governor-General) of Anatolia.[29] He was later to assume the post of Grand Vezir on no less than five occasions between the years 1497 and 1516. In short, Prince Stjepan/Hersekzade Ahmed *Paşa* was one of the leading Ottoman statesmen of the era. He attained these achievements not after a long period of training in the Ottoman Palace as a child, but rather by opting to become an Ottoman as an adult. Even then he did not give up his usage of the Venetian title *Gentilhuommo Nostra* (Our Nobleman), which had been granted to his father.

The case of the two members of the Bosnian nobility who rose to power as eunuchs in the Ottoman court is of particular interest. They were the Bosnian-born *Hadım* (eunuch) 'Ali *Paşa* (son of Radošin Ostoya, who was a minor aristocrat from the village of Drozgometva), who was elevated to the office by Bayezid II on two occasions: first from 1501–1502 and then again between 1506 and 1511,[30] and *Hadım* Sinan *Paşa*, a member of the Bosnian aristocratic family of the Borovoničs, who also held the office on two separate occasions: first for only two months in 1515 and then again for nine months in 1516–1517.[31] While both the Byzantine and Ottoman courts contained eunuchs, it was the former which drew upon the sons of the Balkan nobility in that capacity.[32] In contrast, the more common Ottoman practice in later centuries was to use white eunuchs who were generally slaves from the Caucasus and black eunuchs who were slaves from the Sudan. The appearance of two Bosnian slave eunuch Grand Vezirs in the early sixteenth century may well reflect the continuation of earlier Byzantine practice.

The final member of the group of Christian aristocrats turned Ottoman Grand Vezirs was the Albanian Ottoman known as Dukagin-zade Ahmed *Paşa*, who held the office under Sultan Selim I between December 1514 and March 1515. According to the nineteenth-century biographer Mehmed Süreyya: as young men he and his brother responded to reports of Mehmed II's having praised them by saying "if only they were Muslims," left Albania, traveled to İstanbul, converted to Islam, took the names Ahmed and Mahmud respectively, and entered Palace service. Mahmud died shortly thereafter, but Ahmed rose through the Ottoman bureaucracy together with a hybrid Turkified version of his Christian family name: Dukaginzade, or the Son of Duke Jean [*Duka* (Duke)—*gin* (Jean)—*zade* (son of)]. The original Duke Jean, the grand-father of Ahmed, had been a Neapolitan Anjou vassal who held territory in Northern Albania.[33] Dukaginzade Ahmed *Paşa* was married first to Ayşe *Hanım* Sultan (a granddaughter of Sultan Beyezid II) and later to Fatma Sultan (a daughter of Sultan Selim I).

Interestingly, it appears that while the surnames of Mahmud *Paşa* (Angelovič) and Mesih *Paşa* (Palaiologos), both of whom were taken as young captives into Ottoman service, were known by their contempo-raries, they were not used during their careers as Ottoman officials. In contrast, the family names of those two Balkan nobles who opted of their own free will to join the Ottoman court as adults (Hersekzade and Dukaginzade) continued to be used throughout their lifetimes. It is likely more than coincidence that both Hersekzade Ahmed *Paşa* and Dukag-inzade Ahmed *Paşa* were married to daughters of the Ottoman rulers

Bayezid II and Selim I respectively, the only two Grand Vezirs in the period under study to be so honored.

An examination of the fifteen individuals who held the position of Grand Vezir for one or more terms of appointment between 1453 and 1516 reveals a number of interesting features. First, no less than six and possibly seven of them were members of what we have termed the "Byzantine and Balkan aristocrats turned Vezirs." (Listed chronologically in the order they served: Mahmud *Paşa*, Gedik Ahmed *Paşa* [?], Mesih *Paşa*, Hersekzade Ahmed *Paşa*, Hadım 'Ali *Paşa*, Dukaginzade Ahmed *Paşa* and Hadım Sinan *Paşa*). Collectively, they held the office for no less than thirty-five of the sixty-three year period under study.

Their terms were interspersed with those of five other former Christians, who had entered Ottoman service either via the *devşirme*, as war captives, or on their own initiative. These included: Zaganos *Paşa*, Rum Mehmed *Paşa*, İshak *Paşa*, Davud *Paşa* and Koca Mustafa *Paşa*, who held the office for a total of nineteen years.

In addition, there were also three Vezirs of Anatolian Turkish origin: Hoca Sinan *Paşa* who served in 1476–1477, Karamani Mehmed *Paşa* from Konya who held the office between 1477 and 1481; and, Çandarlı İbrahim *Paşa* from İznik who was Grand Vezir between 1498–1499.

For 60 percent of the period, or thirty-eight of the sixty-three years under study, the office was dominated by three individuals: the former Byzanto-Serbian aristocrat Mahmud *Paşa* [Angelovič], who between the years 1453 and 1474 was Grand Vezir for a total of seventeen years (one term of fifteen and a second of two years); the Albanian Christian *devşirme* conscript Davud *Paşa*, who held the office for fourteen years between 1483 and 1497; and, the Bosnian son of the Duke of St. Sava, Hersekzade Ahmed *Paşa*, whose five appointments between the years 1497 and 1516 totaled seven years.

In the post-1516 era two factors combine to bring an end to what I have termed the period of the "Byzantine and Balkan aristocrats turned Vezirs." First, there was the obvious factor of time: while, as we have seen, following the ultimate defeat of Byzantium in 1453, and subsequent fall and incorporation of the remaining semiindependent Balkan states, numerous members of the former Byzantine aristocracy were subsumed into the higher reaches of the Ottoman administrative bureaucracy, by the second decade of the sixteenth century the last such (Hersekzade Ahmed *Paşa*) had died. This brought an end to the phenomenon we have been examining.

Second, by 1516 the *devşirme* system had developed to the point that henceforth its members were to increasingly fill the office of *Vezir-i 'Azam*. While the second half of the fifteenth century had witnessed the assimilation of members of the former aristocracy into the Ottoman elite, in the sixteenth and seventeenth century the positions they had once filled went to former Christian peasant children, who, raised as Ottomans, now came to monopolize the Grand Vezirate and other high-ranking state offices.

Stated differently, the Balkan aristocrats had by now been fully subsumed into the Ottoman polity. Their descendants were native born Muslims whose subsequent careers are indistinguishable from those of other high-ranking Ottoman families.

CONCLUSIONS

For generations of students who were forced to memorize the date of May 29, 1453, as one of history's great "fault-lines," the point in time at which the eastern Roman/Byzantine Empire came to a sudden and traumatic end, the implications of the present study are several.

First and foremost is the extent to which the fifteenth-century Ottoman polity subsumed rather than destroyed its predecessor states. The phenomenon we have discussed via a case study of Ottoman Grand Vezirs who served between 1453 and 1516, was repeated at literally all levels of the state apparatus in the period between 1299 and 1516. In the same manner that high-ranking former aristocrats found niches as Ottoman administrators, so, too, did members of the lesser nobility, many of whom were turned from Byzantine and Balkan fief *(pronoia)* holders into Ottoman-*timar*iots (fief holders).[34] From the beginning of the sixteenth century forward the cumulative effect of the ongoing religious and cultural assimilation, coupled with the dominance of the *devşirme* conscripts and the conquest of the Arab world, meant that the state's administrative manpower needs could be drawn from a far larger pool of both Christian peasant conscripts and native born Muslims.

This chapter has highlighted the need to discard any approach to this period which reads a modern understanding of religion into the past. The apparent ease with which Byzantine and Balkan aristocrats adopted the religion of their new rulers suggests that the latter-day stigma of "turning Turk" must have been viewed differently in the fifteenth-century Ottoman world. The manner in which such former Christians maintained ties with those family members who had not converted raises the possibility that the *Realpolitik* of the era fully embraced the concept of: *cuius regio eius religio* as the operative maxim.

Finally, this examination has suggested that the time has come to begin reevaluating the idea that a change of religion on the part of the ruling elite should necessarily be equated with a major "fault-line." In the same manner that we recognize the continuity of the Roman Empire in the east under Byzantium, despite the religious upheaval of replacing pagan beliefs with Christianity, we might be well advised to begin focusing on the continuity between the Byzantine Empire and its successor state, the Ottoman Empire.

When we do so it becomes clear that the process of subsuming members of the former ruling elites into Ottomans, one which began with figures such as the local nobles of Bithynia (e.g., *Köse* Mihal, Saros, et.al.) at the beginning of the fourteenth century, culminated in the early sixteenth century by which time the descendants of the Byzanto-Balkan aristocracy had been completely transformed into the Ottoman elite. From now on their offspring (with the rare exception of families such as the Hersekzades and Dukaginzades) are no longer identifiable as anything but what they had become: native born Muslim Ottomans.

EIGHT

The Nature of the Early Ottoman State

To the reader who has come this far two trends should be apparent. First, there is a small (but by no means inconsiderable) body of evidence pointing to the upmarket (high Islamic) character of the early Ottoman state at a very early period. The testimony of the 1324 *vakfiye* (endowment charter) from Mekece (which establishes the presence of an Islamic chancery complete with slave administrators and eunuchs in the opening decades of the state's history), coupled with the description provided by Ibn Battuta as to the Islamic character of the city of Bursa in the wake of its conquest (1331), as well as the clear parallels between the titles found on fourteenth-century Ottoman inscriptions *(kitabes)*, with those of the other Anatolian Beyliks, suggest that the early Ottoman state has already incorporated aspects of Islamic formal administrative culture to a higher degree than has previously been recognized. Second, as I have pointed out, these high Islamic tendencies (somewhat paradoxically), were coexisting with the extensive recruitment and utilization of both free Christians and recent converts into the elite of the newly forming Ottoman polity.

I find this situation, particularly the role of free Christians in the opening decades of fourteenth-century Bithynia (e.g., *Köse* Mihal, Koskos the *Subaşı,* Mavrozoumis, the Christian Judge in İznik, etc.), coupled with the presence of large numbers of free Christian *timar*iots, and the subsumption of the former Balkan and Byzantine nobility in the fifteenth century, difficult to square with Wittek's insistence that it was a "*gazi* ethos" which served as the underlying raison d'être for Ottoman growth and expansion. Religion (Islam), far from being the driving mechanism of the emerging Ottoman polity, repeatedly appears to have given way to practical considerations. As a case in point, we may recall the treatment accorded by Orhan to the Byzantine ruler of Bursa when, following the surrender of that city in 1326, he accepted a ransom of thirty thousand florins for the captives, rather than insist (as Ahmedi tells us a good *gazi* must) upon conversion to Islam or death.

Our reexamination of the *Gazi* Thesis has shown Wittek to have taken undue liberty with his use of both Ahmedi's *mesnevi* and his interpretation of the 1337 inscription *(kitabe)* from Bursa. It would appear that he did so in an attempt to advance his single-minded insistence that religious zeal was indeed the primary factor in accounting for fourteenth century Ottoman territorial expansion. A closer examination of these same sources has suggested that the terms *gaza* and *gazis* were used synonymously with *akın* and *akıncı* in that period, and that all were primarily used to describe the manner in which booty and slaves accrued to the Ottoman leaders and their followers. That later writers endowed these terms with a specific religious connotation signals a shift in identification. The testimony of the earliest sources point to inclusion rather than exclusion. In other words, Osman and Orhan were far more interested in accommodation with their Bithynian Christian neighbors than in converting them to Islam. This was the key first step in a process which ultimately resulted in cultural assimilation. In this earlier practice, the evidence supports the idea that sharing the religion of the rulers was neither a prerequisite for admission to, or service in, the Ottoman ruling elite in the fourteenth and early fifteenth century.

Throughout this period a primary source of Ottoman manpower was conversion. Whether facilitated by a state policy of kindness and good treatment (for the peasants), or a desire to share in the spoils of conquest and *Realpolitik* concerns (for the local Byzantine nobility), ever-increasing numbers of Bithynian (and later Balkan) Christians, inspired primarily by the promise of shared booty, opted to join the Ottoman banner. The manumission of slaves, gradual assimilation and intermarriage were all to become means whereby the Ottoman manpower base was provided with a steady flow of religious and cultural converts. In the ensuing process of assimilation, religious conversion seems to have consistently preceded linguistic and Ottoman cultural assimilation, followed by Turkification.[1]

The melting pot that was Ottoman Bithynia in the opening decades of the fourteenth century stemmed from a conscious or unconscious awareness on the part of the early Ottoman rulers that some form of common identity was needed in what otherwise was a multireligious, polyglot, multiethnic society. With the passage of time and successive generations of converts the indigenous population was religiously Islamicized, linguistically Turkified, and culturally Ottomanized.

Ottoman society became a synthesis of classical Islamic administrative practices (discernible from the outset), that were inherited from Seljuk, Ilhanid and neighboring Turkish principalities, which together with the Muslim population forged out of the Bithynian melting pot produced a new society. The resulting amalgam in the fourteenth and fifteenth centuries was one in which Christians and Muslims (many of whom themselves were converts), worked together to spread the Ottoman banner initially westward into the Balkans and then later east to the heartlands of Islam. The centralized empire which emerged by the mid-sixteenth century (drastically reshaped in the wake of the conquest of the older Islamic states), was one which bore an ever decreasing relationship to the frontier society of the fourteenth and early fifteenth centuries.

In point of fact, this description of the Ottoman state as one formed from a heterogeneous symbiosis or takeover of classical Islamic institutions inherited from earlier Muslim states in Anatolia, with both the Muslim population of the region and an ever-increasing number of Christians and Christian converts to Islam, is not a designation which is likely to attract many adherents among either contemporary Balkan or Turkish historians. Both groups (due to their retrospective reading of history) would prefer to think of the Ottomans as "modern" Turks. That is, Balkan nationalists are fixated on their view of the conquering Turk with sword in hand presenting their hapless Christian victims with the choice of "conversion or death," rather than one in which a significant portion of the traditional ruling class was co-opted into the Ottoman elite; whereas, today's Turks (a la Köprülü) want to cling to the idea that somehow the Ottoman polity was a purely Turkish creation, that is, a state whose essence was Turkishness wrapped in an Islamic veneer.

On the key question of who the Ottoman elite were in the fourteenth century, the surviving contemporary sources suggest that they were a hybrid admixture formed from Anatolian Muslims and local Bithynian and later Balkan Christians. As such, Herbert A. Gibbons, W. L. Langer and R. P. Blake, and George Arnakis (only the last of whom had direct access to the primary Ottoman sources), seem to come closer to what must have been the historical reality than any of their successors in the scholarly debate.

There is an ironic twist to this interpretation; it would suggest that the real secret of Ottoman success may have stemmed from the failure of its early rulers to adhere to the traditional Islamic concept of the *gaza*. Osman and Orhan, rather than attempting to pressure the local Christians of Bithynia into accepting Islam or subjugating them to the yoke of a tolerated *cizye* (poll tax) paying community, simply left the issue of religion open. One joined their banner as either a Christian or a Muslim and made their mark on the basis of ability. When in 1973, Halil İnalcık described the fourteenth-century Ottomans as "a true 'Frontier Empire,' a cosmopolitan state, treating all creeds and races as one,"[2] he highlighted what appears to be the real secret of Ottoman success in its formative period.

Viewed through the lens of surviving fourteenth- and early-fifteenth-century sources, the emerging Ottoman polity was one in which culture and ideology were (from the outset) the vehicle through which the administrative apparatus of earlier Islamic dynasties was passed on to the new entity. Islam was the religion of the rulers from the time of Osman forward. What was different about Osman and his immediate successors was the fact that they in no way sought to impose their own faith upon those who, attracted by the prospect of booty and slaves, flocked to their banner. On the contrary, in the first one-hundred-plus years of the state, one's religion in no way determined whether or not one could join their endeavor and/or serve as a member of its ruling elite. Muslims (many of whom were converts) and Christians rose to positions of prominence on the basis of performance not belief.

From the fact that many such Christian Ottomans (or their offspring) subsequently converted, it is not historically implausible to suggest that by the second half of the fourteenth century continued advancement in the administrative system may have been facilitated by sharing the religion of the ruler. By the second half of the fifteenth century this latitudinarian attitude had gradually given way to one in which sharing the religion of the rulers became an essential prerequisite for membership in the ruling class. This change was made easy by virtue of the fact that with the passage of time the offspring of the early Christian Ottoman nobility had opted for the religion of the rulers. It was in this period that the Ottoman dynastic myth was created. By now the state had evolved to the point that it projected itself (and therefore its founders) as a leading Islamic dynasty in line with the Abbasids and Seljuks. At that point in their development, it became convenient to shed their actual history for ideological purposes. One way to assuage its new found orthodoxy was by projecting an Islamic past back in time. Increasingly, the early Ottoman rulers were depicted as *gazis* who had striven from their inception to expand the realm of Islam at the expense of their Christian neighbors.

This view of the early Ottoman state can partially be explained in terms of a severe manpower shortage, or, more specifically a dearth of individuals with the skills and experience necessary to ensure military expansion, with a commensurate administrative apparatus. This view is seemingly in disagreement with those scholars who have viewed Ottoman growth as stemming primarily from a steady flow of Muslim Turcomans who were attracted by the new state's proximity to Byzantium and the opportunity to participate in the *gaza*. For, while there may have indeed been many nomads joining the Ottoman banner, it was their lack of the necessary skills to administer the growing state which must account in part for the discovery of many Christians in both military and administrative positions first in fourteenth-century Bithynia and later in even larger numbers in the Balkans.

While all would agree that it is only by distancing ourselves from an ex post facto approach, and attempting to view the early Ottomans within the time and space they occupied, that it is possible to gain a clearer insight into their origins, I would argue that we must go one step further and disabuse ourselves of the idea that the *gaza* and the tribal origins of the Ottomans provide a useful framework for understanding the Ottoman emergence and growth in fourteenth-century Bithynia.

Assuming for the moment that the scenario as to the nature of the early Ottoman state which has been set out above is viable, namely, that in its opening decades the Ottoman polity was one in which a group of Muslim (Osman) and Christian (*Köse* Mihal and Evrenos) warriors came together and elected the ablest of their number, Osman, as leader of their joint endeavor designed to enrich themselves with booty and slaves taken primarily (but by no means exclusively) from their Christian neighbors. That in this formative period, one's religion played no visible role in whether or not one was considered an Ottoman, rather what made one an Ottoman was the effectiveness of his contribution to the shared endeavor of conquest and booty. Further, that, somewhat paradoxically, the new entity's administrative apparatus was, from the outset, largely adopted from the Seljuk—Ilhanid tradition, that is, from its earliest days the Ottoman polity possessed a healthy dose of members of the *ulema* (Muslim educated religious class), inherited from these states, in keeping with the religion and culture of its ruler, Osman. Finally, that the evolving administrative apparatus was also shaped (in keeping with the "accommodationist" policies of the rulers), by numerous practices inherited from the states who earlier had ruled the various peoples now gathered under the Ottoman umbrella.

Consequently, the urban structure of the early Ottoman polity was one in which all the trappings and experience of the preceding three centuries of Anatolian history, that is, the high Islamic culture and administration as passed from the Abbasids to the Seljuks and Mongol Ilhanids, is apparent. In contrast to the typical experience in earlier

Islamic states, the demands on the ground (shaped by the twin facts of rapid conquest and a lack of adequately trained manpower) meant that the new entity's ruling elite was paradoxically open to both Muslims and Christians. By contrast, the overwhelmingly Christian peasantry were absorbed into a tax and administrative system which was familiar due to its wholesale adoption of earlier Byzantine and Balkan practices. The resulting hybrid was the early Ottoman state.

What is difficult to account for is the anomaly of a state which from its inception shows clear evidence of possessing many elements of the high Islamic bureaucratic tradition, but which lacked the parallel distinctions between a Muslim ruling elite and Christian subjects, which had been developed in earlier Islamic states. Here, I can only repeat the suggestion that this seeming anomaly stemmed from the lack of adequate manpower resources necessary to feed the amoeba-like growing Ottoman entity, that is, its rapid growth required the linguistic and administrative skills of the preexisting Christian ruling elite; and by the very manner in which the state had been initially construed, that is, the collective nature of the new endeavor that was formed by a small group of Muslim and Christian rulers in Bithynia.

Three short case studies will suffice to illustrate the fact that the explanation here advanced, in addition to being viable, further sheds important light on a variety of questions and issues which have heretofore plagued scholars working on the period.

First, how can we account for the less than total adherence to Islamic practice which is most noticeable in the life of the fourth Ottoman ruler, Bayezid I (1389–1402)? Recalling our discussion of Ahmedi's passages on this ruler's life, it is clear that both the Byzantine and Ottoman chronicle traditions are united in stressing the dissipated life-style followed by Bayezid I, one which included a heavy reliance on alcohol, a spurning of even the basic Islamic practice of public ritual prayer, and the utilization of an ever-increasing number of Christian troops to assist in his conquests of neighboring Muslim states. While earlier studies have linked this to the influence of his Serbian wife, Olivera and her brothers Stefan and Vuk, and even commented upon the fact that Bayezid's sons were named İsa (Jesus), Musa (Moses), Süleyman (Solomon), and Mehmed (Mohammed), thereby raising the question as to whether the choice of such names may not in fact have represented a "general current which dominated the spirit of the time and even the court of the Sultan,"[3] they have been unable to fit this important ruler comfortably into the *gazi* explanation of the origins of the state. Can it be that Bayezid, rather than being viewed as some kind of aberration (as Ahmedi and later Ottoman writers alleged), was in fact simply the logical outcome of the manner in which the Ottoman state had developed in the course of the fourteenth century? His dissipated life-style may have been the norm rather than the exception. There are other under-studied aspects of his reign which suggest that this hypothesis is worthy of serious scholarly attention.

As a case in point, we may cite the example of a preacher in Bayezid's reign who, from a mosque in the capital city of Bursa, even went so far as to declare from the pulpit that Jesus was in no way a lesser prophet than Mohammed. Then, when an Arab member of the *ulema* pointed out to the congregation the fallacy of this view from the perspective of the Islamic science of exegesis, the congregants rejected his intervention in favor of their own preacher's position. It seems clear, from the manner in which this seeming heretical declaration was wholeheartedly accepted by the populace of Bursa, that they were at a stage where a doctrine preaching that Islam and Christianity were basi-cally one religion was acceptable.[4] In short, as late as the end of the fourteenth century, even in the city of Bursa (which already had the infrastrucure of mosques, medreses, and *imarets* associated with formal Islamic practices), support for a kind of "Islamochristian" syncretism was conceivable.

Another element not previously worked into this equation is that even a member of Bayezid's own family also seems to have felt that there was little difference between the two faiths. From the testimony of two contemporary Byzantine chroniclers, George Sphrantzes and Doukas, it is clear that Bayezid had five sons (leaving aside the pretender, Mustafa). In addition to Mehmed, Isa, Musa, and Süleyman, he had a fifth son named Yusuf (Joseph). Following the defeat at Ankara, Yusuf (com-pletely ignored in the later Ottoman chronicles), who was an adolescent, ended up at the court of the Byzantine Emperor Manuel, where he con-verted to Christianity and took the name Demetrios, before falling vic-tim to an outbreak of the plague.[5] While differing on the detail they pro-vide, both Sphrantzes and Doukas leave no doubt as to the outline presented above, namely, the fifth son of Bayezid died a Christian.

Viewed in the light of the aforegoing discussion, the claim of the Bursan preacher that Jesus and Mohammed were equal in their prophet-hoods appears as nothing more than a logical synthesis for a developing society in which Muslims and Christians were both free to practice (and propagate?) their beliefs. If, as has been argued, the Ottoman ruling class of the first generations was made up of both Christians and Mus-lims, and, if the social network system and its culture and values created by the early Ottoman rulers was readily available to members of all faiths, the attempt to create a new "Islamochristian" synthesis may be viewed as nothing more than a normal progression to a course whose roots must be found nearly a century earlier in Bithynia.

The same is true for perhaps one of the most misunderstood aspects of early Ottoman history, the so-called Sheikh Bedreddin Revolt which broke out in Rumeli and Anatolia in 1416. This event, which more accurately should be called the "Börklüce Mustafa Revolt," after its leading figure in Anatolia, is known primarily via the account preserved in the work of the Byzantine chronicler Doukas, where it is portrayed as a social and religious movement, which attracted huge numbers of followers, preached a kind of communal sharing of material goods and stressed fraternization between Muslims and Christians.[6] Stated differently, it was depicted in the contemporary Byzantine sources (and later Ottoman ones) as a revolution whose central doctrine was a kind of bond of charitable Communism, supported by a mystic love of God, in which all differences of religion were overlooked. Before it was brutally suppressed by the state (whose needs had by this time moved it in the direction of assimilation), this movement had begun to spread rapidly among the Muslim and Christian peasantry of western Anatolia and the Balkans. The large-scale social uprising which resulted threatened for a time to become the common faith of all.

While scholars who have studied this phenomenon have generally been perplexed to account for it in light of the "Gazi Thesis," from the perspective of the alternative explanation advanced here, it too seems entirely logical. The end of the fourteenth century was a point in time when the paradox of a state whose urban administrative structure had a high Islamic character, yet whose ruling elite and its peasant population in the countryside were typified by what I have termed an Islamo-Christian syncretism, clashed. Two conflicting tendencies came into conflict and "high" Islam emerged victorious.

In a state formed by Muslims and Christians, in which the role of popular religion had, from its inception, brought Muslims and Christians together (e.g., the hânegâh established by Orhan in the town of Mekece in 1324), this movement was nothing more than an attempt actually to unite the two faiths as one. Recalling that this is a period in which up to half the state officials in some areas of the Balkans (timariots) were Christian, what could be more natural than an attempt to develop a new religious synthesis as a reflection of the actual nature of the evolving political entity? That it was spearheaded by Bedreddin, himself the former kadıasker (religious judge of the army) of Prince Musa, is not surprising. Who, other than a representative of the ruler's religion could advance such a radical doctrine?

Finally, our interpretation can also shed much needed light on the origins and development of the Janissary Corps, a key Ottoman institution whose roots also trace to the late fourteenth century. Given the fact that Christians were de facto exempted from military service as a result of the poll tax they paid, how could one maintain the parity between the two faiths which we have argued marked the formative years of the Ottoman state? While Christian members of the local nobility were given *timars* and easily absorbed into the Ottoman ruling class, the same was not necessarily true of the Christian peasantry.

Implicit throughout this study is my acceptance of the fact that the Ottomans were constantly in need of trained and disciplined manpower in the fourteenth and early fifteenth century. Had there been hordes of Muslim fighters moving into the Ottoman Bithynia in the first half of the fourteenth century, it seems likely that a far different state would have emerged. The indigenous Christian population would have been overwhelmed by the sheer force of numbers and it is extremely unlikely that we would have seen the significant numbers of Christian members of the Ottoman ruling elite that we do. From this perspective the Janissaries were expanded by Murad II in an attempt to meet the ever-increasing need for trained manpower, and, at the same time, to provide an avenue whereby a portion of the male Christian peasantry were both trained militarily and assimilated religiously to the faith of the ruler. Bearing in mind that this development follows the Sheikh Bedreddin revolt, that is, comes in the wake of a movement which threatened the very fabric of what had been for a century in Bithynia a formal Islamic administrative apparatus, it seems likely that one intent of Murad's was to tip the religious balance of the fifteenth-century state once and for all in favor of Islam. Stated differently, the experience of the Sheikh Bedreddin revolt must have convinced the Ottoman rulers that the time when tolerance of unconverted Christians had been a necessary means of ensuring a steady supply of trained manpower for the Ottoman juggernaut (regardless of the faith of its soldiers), had outlived its usefulness. From the 1430s onward, Islam increasingly became a prerequisite for membership in the Ottoman ruling elite. One facet of this change was the regular enrollment of Christian youths (converted to Islam), who in turn were trained as soldiers and military administrators, that is, acculturated as Ottomans.

In the aftermath of the shock waves which emanated from Bedreddin's attempt to create a new Islamochristian confederation as the socioreligious underpinning of the Ottoman polity, Sultan Murad II took steps to ensure that in future no one could fail to see that Islam was the state's religion and that the Ottoman rulers were its sole legitimate dynasty. An anonymous Greek chronicle of the early seventeenth century (which is based on the mid-sixteenth century Italian work of Francesco Sansovino),[7] expresses this new reality by relating how Murad II (after retiring in favor of his young son Mehmed II) had the following dream:

> They say that Murad had a dream one night, which he then related and the Turks believed it to be prophetic: he saw a man dressed in white garments, like a prophet, who took the ring that his son was wearing on his middle finger and transferred it to the second finger; then he took it off and put it on the third; after he had passed the ring to all five fingers, he threw it away and he vanished. Murad summoned his *hodzas [hocas]* and diviners and asked them to interpret this dream for him. They said: "Undoubtedly, the meaning is that only five kings from your line will reign; then another dynasty will take over the kingdom." *Because of this dream it was decided that no members of the old, noble families, i.e., the Turahanoğlu, the Mihaloğlu, or the Evrenos, would be appointed Beglerbegs or Viziers and that they should be restricted to the office of the standard-bearer of the akıncı, i.e., the horsemen who owe military service and receive no salary when they form the vanguard during campaigns. There is another family of this kind called Malkoçoğlu. These standard-bearers are under the command of the beglerbeg. All these families had hoped to reign, but, because of Murad's dream, they were deprived of their former considerable authority.*[8]

Without in anyway arguing for a literal acceptance of this dream story, its symbolic significance is clear. In the same manner that Spandugnino had written earlier of how the initial state had been formed by four Christian and Muslim lords (Mihal, Evrenos, Turahan, and Osman), who came together and chose Osman as the first among equals,[9] now a latter-day anonymous Greek translator of Sansovino relates how (in the aftermath of the final emergence of Islam as the state's formal religion), so, too, the Ottoman rulers shunted off the descendants of their fellow cofounders of the state to the Balkan frontiers in an effort to ensure that there would be no future question as to the primacy of the House of Osman.

Several lines of argument may be advanced in support of the underlying historical synthesis which culminated in the dream story preserved in this anonymous Greek version. First, is the fact that throughout the second half of the fourteenth and fifteenth centuries the Balkans were indeed the primary (if not exclusive) preserve of the great founding families of the Evrenosoğlu, the Mihaloğlu, and (later) the Turahanoğlu. For in an era when the Ottoman rulers customarily sent their sons to serve as governors in the provinces, they did so almost exclusively in Anatolia.[10] The Balkans were left in the hands of their real conquerors, the descendants of the other founding families of the state. It is almost as if there were an agreement between the great ruling families that Anatolia was to be ruled by the descendants of Osman and the Balkans by the heirs of Evrenos, Mihal, and Turahan.[11]

Indeed, we have one source from the opening years of the fifteenth century, the text of a treaty negotiated between Prince Süleyman and the representatives of several Christian states in 1403 (following the defeat of Bayezid I at Ankara), which illustrates the extent of the powers held by Evrenos *Gazi* in the Balkans.[12] The Venetian Pietro Zeno, who negotiated the agreement, reports to the Serenissima that Süleyman's agreement to cede territories in the Balkans was strongly opposed by Vranes (Evrenos *Bey*), who was one of his captains. His objections to giving up territories was joined in by other Ottoman captains who were present.[13] That Evrenos' objections took a concrete form is clear from a later passage in Zeno's account, where he reports that a Venetian citizen, the Marquess of Bodonitza, had obtained some land in the region of Zeitounion (an area ruled by Evrenos), which led his Turkish neighbors to attack him. Zeno further reports that Evrenos "has determined to attack and despoil him of everything."[14] Clearly, the old ruling families viewed the Balkans as their preserve and resented attempts on the part of the ruling Ottoman family to negotiate away what they had conquered by force of arms. The extent to which the dissatisfaction of the Evrenosoğlu and Mihaloğlu families may have contributed to the ultimate defeat and death of Prince Süleyman is unclear.

The anonymous chronicle also relates that none of the members of the Evrenosoğlu, Mihaloğlu or Turahanoğlu families ever appear to have served as *Beylerleys* (Governor-Generals) or *Vezirs* (Ministers) in the Ottoman state, that is, held the highest administrative positions. Yet, the Byzantine and Ottoman chronicle traditions are unanimous in stressing the importance of these noble families. It is almost as if there was a conscious decision not to give the members of these families a stronger claim to legitimacy than they already possessed due to the large military forces at their disposal.[15] Ottoman documents from the reign of Mehmed II attest to the degree of autonomy enjoyed by these families which even allowed them on their own initiative to dispense *timars* (fiefs) to their followers which passed from father to son.[16]

Finally, no single member of the lines of Evrenos, Mihal, or Turahan, appears to have ever been given in marriage to a princess of the Ottoman dynasty.[17] This becomes significant since in the fourteenth and fifteenth centuries the practice whereby the daughters of the Ottoman rulers were used to forge numerous political alliances with local Turkish rulers in

Anatolia was widespread. Could it be that this too reflected a conscious desire not to give any member of those families with a potential claim to rule, anything which could further strengthen their positions?

In addition to Spandugnino and the anonymous chronicle, we have two other sixteenth-century sources which echo their sentiments as regards both the collective nature of the early Ottoman venture and the special status accorded to the descendants of Osman's cofounders. Writing in 1534, the Italian Benedetto Ramberti relates how Osman, having decided to solidify and expand his early territorial gains in Bithynia, shared his vision of the future with two Greeks and a Turk. When they agreed to join his endeavor he promised them that we would always maintain:

> Both themselves and their descendants, in great state and dignity, and suitably to the great benefit which he had received from them: besides this that he would never harm their blood nor that of their posterity through laws that would lay hands upon them even if they should transgress grievously.

Ramberti then adds the interesting detail that in case the Ottoman line would end: "these would pretend to the sovereignty, and therefore they are highly respected."[18]

Three years later, in 1537, an Italian pamphlet coauthored by one Junis (Yunus) Bey and Alvise Gritti (the natural son of a Venetian Doge who was in the service of Sultan Süleyman), reiterates Osman's pledge to "never put a hand in their blood or fail to give them offices."[19]

If these accounts are credible as reflections of what was commonly believed in Ottoman elite circles as late as the mid-sixteenth century, our earlier assessment of the importance of the cofounders and their descendants (based on titles used and accorded them in the late fourteenth century), is further strengthened. One thing seems certain, even two-hundred-fifty years after the founding of the Ottoman polity, the importance of the descendants of Mihal, Evrenos, Turahan, and Malkoç, was still recognized. They were as close to a hereditary nobility as the Ottomans produced. While authors such as Spandugnino, Ramberti, and Yunus Bey/Gritti still noted the Christian antecedents of those whose forefathers were Greek Christians, the actual manner in which the state had been founded had receded into the past and the preeminence of the Ottoman line was firmly established

Indeed by the reign of Mehmed II (1451–1480), the phenomenon we have discussed, the religio-social hybrid Islamochristian entity, which created the early Ottoman state, has disappeared. In its place we have the Ottoman Empire, which, following the conquest of Constantinople in 1453, quickly sheds the last vestiges of syncretism. At the same time, this ruler once and for all removes the possibility that the descendants of the state's cofounders (Mihaloğulları, Evrenosoğulları, Turahanoğulları, etc.), might still recall the days when the Ottoman ruler was nothing more than a first among equals. He does so by drastically curtailing the wealth and power of these families by confiscation of their *vakıf* properties, and by limiting their sphere of action to the western marches in the Balkans.[20]

Nor is it coincidental that it is this ruler, Mehmed II, who for the first time actively encourages the writing of chronicle histories of the dynasty. The resulting accounts (with the exception of Aşıkpaşazade) are highly sanitized and reflect little of what we have seen was the actual nature of the Ottoman state in the first half of the fourteenth century. In its place we are left with a depiction of the early Ottoman rulers as fighters for the faith of Islam *(gazis)*, complete with imperial genealogies linking them to the most important branch of the Turks.

CONCLUSION

To the extent the present study has succeeded in its aim, it hopefully is apparent that a careful utilization of the earliest surviving Ottoman sources allows us to draw an alternate picture to that depicted in the royal chronicles of the late fifteenth century and thereafter. The need for utilizing the earliest surviving records of the Ottoman state should be clear. Given the scarcity of such documentation such attempts will always remain highly speculative. The present study clearly suffers from this limitation. It is however, a preliminary attempt to question the underlying assumptions advanced by Paul Wittek fifty years ago. As such, its limited objective is to free future scholars from the restrictions implicit in the "*Gazi* Thesis" and to pave the way for a discussion of Ottoman Bithynia in the first half of the fourteenth century, which is based on the sources it has utilized. If we had a similar dearth of sources for the period of the American War of Independence, we would not countenance present-day scholarship projecting this nation at the time of World War I backwards in time as a reflection of 1780s reality.

APPENDIX 1

Wittek's Reading of the Titles Conferred on Orhan in the 1337 Bursa Inscription Compared with the Actual Titles Recorded

Title and Translation as Read by Wittek	Actual Title and Translation as Read by Lowry
Sultān	*al-amīr al-kabīr al-mu'azzam al-mujāhid [fi sabīl Allāh]*
[Sultan]	[The Foremost Great Emir, Warrior on Behalf of God]
ibn Sultān al-ghuzāt	*Sultān al-ghuzāt*
[son of the Sultan of the *ghazis*]	[Sultan of the *ghazis*]
ghāzī ibn al-ghāzī	*ghāzī ibn al-ghāzī*
Ghazi, son of Ghazi	Ghazi, son of ghazi
Shujā' ad-daula wa'd-dīn	*shujā' al-dawla wa'l-dīn*
[————————————]	[Champion of the State and Religion]
marzbān al'āfāq	*wa-l afak [munfiq or muttafiq/muttafaq]*
[marquis of the horizons]	[and the Horizons]

Title and Translation as Read by Wittek	Actual Title and Translation as Read by Lowry
baḥlavān-i jihān	*paḥlavān-al-zamān*
[hero of the world]	[Hero of the Age]
Orkḥān bin ʿOthmān	*Urkḥān bin ʿUthmān*
[———————]	[Orhan, son of Osman]

Titles Used by the Ottoman Dynasty in the Fourteenth and Early-Fifteenth Century

Date	Source	Actual Title/Titles Used	Citation
1320	Silver *akçe* (coin)	*Osman bin Ertuğrul*	Artuk, 1980: pp. 27–32
1324	Mekece *Vakıfname* (Endowment Deed)	*Şücaddin Orhan bin Fahrüddin O[sman]*	Uzunçarşılı, 1941: p. 280–
1327	Silver *akçe* (coin minted in Bursa)	*Orhan bin Osman*	Uzunçarşılı, 1947: p. 125
1337	Bursa: *Şehadet Cami*	*Al-amir al-kabir al-mu'azzam al mujahid . . . sultan al-ghuzat, ghazi ibn al-ghazi, shuja' al-dawla wa-l al-afak pahlavan al-zaman Urkhan bin 'Uthman*	Ayverdi, 1966: p. 59
ND	Silver *akçe* (coin minted in Bursa, ca. 1326–1354	*Es-sultan al-'adl Orhan bin Osman*	Artuk, 1974: p. 453–
1348	Orhan Beg's *mülkname* (deed)	*Orhan bin Osman*	Öz, 1938: Vesika I.
1360	İznik *vakıfname* (Endowment Deed)	*Al-mufakhkhar al-a'zam, wa'l-makhdum al-mu'azzam, malik riqab al-umam, malik muluk al-umara' fi'l-'alam, zahir al-islam, nasir al-umam, nazim*	Uzunçarşılı, 1963: p. 438

Date	Source	Actual Title/Titles Used	Citation
ND	Silver *akçe* (coin)	*marasim al-'adl wa'l-insaf, qabir al-mutamarridin bi'l-ihjaf, nusrat al-mujahidin, kahf al-muratibin, qami' al-kafara wa'l-mulhidin, sultan al-ghuzat, qatil al-tughat, nasir din Allah wa'l-mu'in li-khalq Allah, shuja' al-dawla w'l-dunya wa'l-din, Orhan Beg bin Osman Beg bin Ertuğrul*	Artuk, 1974: p. 457
1385	Bursa: Copy of *vakıfname*—1385	*Es-sultan la'a Murad bin Orhan* *Emir-i azam, melik-i mülük al-arab wa'l-a'cem, hami-i bilad-ullah, ra'i-i 'ibad-ullah, naşir-i esnaf-ül 'adl wa'l-ihsan sıfatları ile wa sultan ibn sultan Murad bin Orhan*	Gökbilgin, 1953: p. 220
1388	İznik: *Nilüfer Hatun İmaret—kitabe* (inscription)	*Al-malik al-mu'azzam, al-hakan al-muskerim, sultan ibn sultan Murad bin Orhan*	Taeschner, 1932: p. 131
1389	Silver *akçe* (coin)	*Bayezid bin Murad*	Artuk, 1974: p. 458
1399	Bursa: Ulu Cami *kitabe* (inscription)	*Es-sultan al-mu'azzam Bayezid Han bin Murad*	Mantran, 1954: p. 91

Date	Source	Actual Title/Titles Used	Citation
1403	Bursa: Silver akçe (coin)	Es-sultan bin es-sultan Bayezid Han bin Murad Han	Artuk, 1974: p. 459–60
1410	Copper coin	Timur Han korkan Mehmed bin Bayezid Han	Artuk, 1974: p. 460
1413	Edirne: Silver akçe (coin)	Es-sultan al-malik al-azam Mehmed bin Bayezid	Artuk, 1974: p. 464
1417	Bursa: Orhan Cami kitabe (Restoration inscription)	Sultan bin sultan Mehmed bin Bayezid Han	Mantran, 1954: p. 90
		Sultan al-ghuzat wa'l-mujahidin Orhan Beg bin Osman Beg	
		Es-sultan ibn es-sultan, sultan Mehmed bin Bayezid Han	
1420	Bursa: Yeşil Cami kitabe (inscription)	Es-sultan al-azam wa'l-hakan al-kerim sultan al-şark wa'l-garb wa'l-hakan al'acam wa'l-'arab al-muisid bita'yyid rab al-alemin giyas al-dünya wa'l-din es-sultan bin es-sultan, es-sultan Mehmed bin Bayezid, bin Murad, bin Orhan	Mantran, 1954: pp. 92–93
1423	Bursa: copper coin	Sultan Murad Han bin Mehmed Han	Artuk, 1974: p. 466

Date	Source	Actual Title/Titles Used	Citation
1426	Bursa: *Muradiye Cami—kitabe* (Inscription)	*Sultan wa'l-arab wa'l-acem ta'l Allah fi al-'alam es-sultan bin es-sultan, es-sultan Murad bin Mehmed bin Bayezid Han*	Mantran, 1954: p. 94
1443	Bursa: *Bedrettin Hafsa Cami—kitabe* (Inscription)	*hatun binti sultan Mehmed bin Bayezid han, al-gazi*	Koyunluoğlu, 1935: p. 166
1450	Bursa: *Selçuk Hatun Cami—kitabe* (Inscription)	*Selçuk hatun bint es-sultan ibn es-sultan Mehmed han bin Bayezid gazi han*	Koyunluoğlu, 1935: p. 167

APPENDIX 3

Wives and Mothers of the Ottoman Dynasty in the Fourteenth and Fifteenth Century

Dates	Ruler	Ethnic Origin Of Wife Or Consort Who Produced Successor
1280–1324	Osman	Osman's Mother: Unknown; Mother of Orhan who succeeded him was Mal Hatun (Turkish origin);
1324–1360	Orhan	Mother of Murad I was Nilüfer Hatun who was a Bithynian Greek (daughter of the lord of Yarhisar)
1360–1389	Murad I	Mother of Bayezid I was Gülçiçek Hatun, a Bithynian Greek
1389–1402	Bayezid I	Mother of Mehmed I was Devlet Hatun bin 'Abdullah (a convert, as such either a slave or local Christian);
1413–1421	Mehmed I	Mother of Murad II was Emine Hatun (Princess of the Turkish Principality of Dulkadirli)
1421–1451	Murad II	Mother of Mehmed II was Hüma Hatun (most likely a Greek or Slavic slave)
1451–1481	Mehmed II	Mother of Bayezid II was Gülbahar Hatun (a Pontic Greek from the village of Douvera in Trabzon)

Dates	Ruler	Ethnic Origin Of Wife Or Consort Who Produced Successor
1481–1512	Bayezid II	Mother of Selim I was Ayşe Hatun (Princess of the Turkish Principality of Dulkadırlı)

SOURCES: Alderson, *The Structure of the Ottoman Dynasty* (1956); Lowry, *Studies in Defterology* (1992); Umur, *Osmanli Padişah Tuğralari* (1980).

APPENDIX 4

Provincial Governorships Held by Princes of the Ottoman Dynasty in the Fourteenth and Fifteenth Century

Dates	Şeyzade (Prince)	Province(s) They Served In	Sultan
Unknown	Orhan bin Osman	Sultanönü	Orhan
1329	Murad b Orhan	İzmit	Murad I
1330	Murad b Orhan	Sultanönü	
Unknown	Murad b Orhan	Bursa	
1359	Murad b Orhan	Gelibolu	
Unknown	Halil b Orhan	İzmit (?)	
Unknown	İbrahim b Orhan	Eskişehir	
Unknown	Emir Süleyman b Orhan	Bolu	
1330	Emir Süleyman b Orhan	İzmit	
1336	Emir Süleyman b Orhan	Balıkesir	
Unknown	Emir Süleyman b Orhan	Bursa	
1356	Emir Süleyman b Orhan	Gelibolu	
1381–1389	Bayezid b Murad	Kütahya	Bayezid I
1382–1385	Savcı b Murad	Bursa	
Unknown	Yakub b Murad	Balıkesir	
1393–1403	Mehmed b Bayezid	Amasya	Mehmed I
1403–1413	Mehmed b Bayezid	Bursa	
1390	'İsa b Bayezid	Antalya	

Dates	Şeyzade (Prince)	Province(s) They Served In	Sultan
1402	'İsa b Bayezid	Balıkesir	
1403	'İsa b Bayezid	Bursa	
Unknown	Musa b Bayezid	Kütahya	
1403–1404	Musa b Bayezid	Bursa	
1411–1413	Musa b Bayezid	Edirne	
Unknown	Mustafa b Bayezid	Antalya	
1398	Emir Süleyman b Bayezid	Sivas	
1400	Emir Süleyman b Bayezid	Manisa	
1402–1411	Emir Süleyman b Bayezid	Edirne	
1417–1421	Murad b Mehmed Han	Amasya	Murad II
1444–1446	Murad b Mehmed Han	Manisa	
1406	Kasım b Murad	Amasya	
1415	Mahmud b Murad	Amasya	
1420	Mustafa b Murad	İsparta	
1437–1439	Mehmed b Murad Han	Amasya	Mehmed II
1439–1444	Mehmed b Murad Han	Manisa	
1446–1451	Mehmed b Murad Han	Manisa	
1457–1481	Bayezid b Mehmed Han	Amasya	Bayezid II
1468–1474	Cem b Mehmed Han	Kastamonu	
1474–1481	Cem b Mehmed Han	Karaman	
1481	Şehinşah b Bayezid Han	Konya	
1481–1483	Şehinşah b Bayezid Han	Manisa	
1483–1511	Şehinşah b Bayezid Han	Konya	
1482–1513	Ahmed b Bayezid Han	Amasya	
ca. 1481	Alemşah b Bayezid Han	Menteşe	
1507–1510	Alemşah b Bayezid Han	Manisa	
1484–1502	Korkut b Bayezid Han	Manisa	
1502–1509	Korkut b Bayezid Han	Antalya	
1510–1511	Korkut b Bayezid Han	Antalya	
1511–1512	Korkut b Bayezid Han	Manisa	
1494–1511	Selim b Bayezid Han	Trabzon	Selim I
1511	Selim b Bayezid Han	Semendire	

SOURCES: Umur, *Osmanlı Padişah Tuğraları* (1980); Uzunçarşılı, *Osmanlı Tarihi* (1947); Alderson, *The Structure of the Ottoman Dynasty* (1956), pp. 17–24.

Only one major limitation was enforced; members of the Ottoman dynasty could not be governors of any of the provinces in Rumelia (Europe). This rule only came into force after the Great Interregnum; prior to that Orhan's son Süleyman Paşa had been appointed "Rum Beylerbeyı" ca. 1354, and on his death Murad I followed him in this position. There does not seem to have been any specific reason for this prohibition, but perhaps it may be attributed to a distinction between Anatolia as "Dar'ül İslam" (House of Islam), and Rumelia as "Dar-ul Harb" (House of War). If so, the implication is that, while sons could be used as rulers of settled provinces inhabited by Muslims, it might be dangerous to leave them in permanent command of large bodies of troops on active service. Granted this was the reason, justification for it can be found in the one exception: Selim I entirely misused his European command. Having forced Bayezid II to grant him the "Beylik" of Semendire (Smederevo), he immediately turned the soldiers under his orders against his father [Alderson, *The Structure of the Ottoman Dynasty* (1956), p. 19].

An alternative explanation (the one advanced in the present study) is that the Balkans were indeed the preserve of the great ruling families of the Mihaloğulları, Evrenosoğulları, and Turahanoğulları, while Anatolia remained that of the House of Osman.

Notes

INTRODUCTION

1. Cemal Kafadar, *Between Two Worlds: The Construction of the Ottoman State* (Berkeley, 1995).

2. Paul Wittek, *The Rise of the Ottoman Empire* (London, 1938).

3. Wittek, *Rise of Ottoman Empire* (1938), pp. 14–15, and 43.

4. Wittek, "De la défaite d'Ankara à la prise de Constantinople," *Revue des études islamiques* 12 (1938): 1–34. See in particular pp. 3, and 28.

5. George Arnakis, *Hoi protoi othomanoi* (Athens, 1947).

6. R. C. Jennings, "Some Thoughts on the Gazi Thesis," *Wiener Zeitschrift für die Kunde Des Morgenlandes* 76 (Vienna, 1986): 151–161.

CHAPTER 1. THE DEBATE TO DATE

1. Herbert A. Gibbons, *The Foundation of the Ottoman Empire* (Oxford, 1916). See in particular pp. 27 and 49.

2. Gibbons, *Foundation of Ottoman Empire* (1916).

3. M. Fuat Köprülü, "Anadolu'da İslamiyet: Türk İstilasından Sonra Anadolu Tarih-i Dinisine Bir Nazar ve Bu Tarihin Menba'ları," *Darülfünun Edebiyat Fakültesi Mecmuası* 2 (1922): 281–311, 385–420, and 457–486.

4. Franz Babinger, "Der Islam in Kleinasien—Neue Wege der Islamforschung," *Zeitschrift der Deutschen Morgenlandischen Gesellschaft* [Neue Folge] Band I (Band 76) (Leipzig, 1922), pp. 126–152.

5. Köprülü, "Anadolu'da İslamiyet," 1922, and M. Fuat Köprülü, *Islam in Anatolia after the Turkish Invasion,* trans. and ed. G. Leiser (Salt Lake City, 1993).

6. Friedrich Giese, "Das Problem der Entstehung des osmanischen Reiches," *Zeitschrift für Semitistik und verwandte Gebiete* 2 (1924): 246–271.

7. W. L. Langer and R. P. Blake, "The Rise of the Ottoman Turks and Its Historical Background," *American Historical Review* 37 (1932): 468–505.

8. M. Fuat Köprülü, *Les origines de l'empire ottoman* (Paris, 1935); M. Fuad Köprülü, *Osmanlı İmparatorluğunun Kuruluşu* (Ankara, 1959); and M. Fuad Köprülü, *The Origins of the Ottoman Empire,* trans. and ed. G. Leiser (Albany: State University of New York Press, 1992).

9. Wittek, *Rise of the Ottoman Empire* (1938), pp. 14, 20, and 51.

10. Halil İnalcık, *The Ottoman Empire: The Classical Age, 1300–1600* (London, 1973), p. 5.

11. İnalcık, *The Ottoman Empire* (1973), p. 6.

12. Halil İnalcık, "The Question of the Emergence of the Ottoman State," *International Journal of Turkish Studies* 2, no. 2 (1981–1982): 71–79.

13. İnalcık, *The Ottoman Empire* (1973), p. 7.

14. Ibid., p. 7.

15. Ibid., p. 7.

16. Aşıkpaşazade, *Tevarih-i Al-i Osman,* ed. 'Ali Bey (İstanbul, h.1332/1913), pp. 23–24; F. Babinger, "Mikhaloghlu," *Encyclopaedia of Islam,* new edition, vol. VII (Leiden, 1990), pp. 34–35.

17. İnalcık, *The Ottoman Empire* (1973), p. 8.

18. İnalcık, "Question of Emergence" (1982), pp. 71–79.

19. Ibid., p. 75.

20. Halil İnalcık and Donald Quataert, eds., *An Economic and Social History of the Ottoman Empire, 1300–1914* (Cambridge, 1994), p. 11.

21. Arnakis, *Hoi protoi othomanoi* (1947), pp. 32–33.

22. Ernst Werner, *Die Geburt Einer Grossmacht—Die Osmanen (1300–1481)* (Vienna, 1985). Expanded edition of the work originally published in 1966 and Ernst Werner, *Büyük Bir Devletin Doguğu—Osmanlılar (1300–1482)—Osmanlı Feodalizminin Oluşum Süreci* (İstanbul, 1986), vol. 1. Volume 2 of this work appeared in 1988 as *Halk Ayaklanmaları ve Askeri Feodalizm* (İstanbul, 1988).

23. Speros Vryonis, Jr., *The Decline of Medieval Hellenism in Asia Minor and the Process of Islamization from the Eleventh through the Fifteenth Century* (Berkeley, 1971).

24. Gyula Kaldy-Nagy, "The Holy War *(jihad)* in the First Centuries of the Ottoman Empire," *Harvard Ukrainian Studies* 3–4 (1979–1980): 467–473.

25. Rudi P. Lindner, *Nomads and Ottomans in Medieval Anatolia* (Bloomington, 1983), pp. 2–50.

26. Pal Fodor, "Ahmedi's Dasitan as a Source of Early Ottoman History," *Orientalia Hungaricae* 38 (1984): 41–54. See p. 50.

27. Fodor, "Ahmedi's Dasitan" (1984), pp. 41–54.

28. Jennings, "Some Thoughts on the *Gazi* Thesis," pp. 151–161.

29. Colin Heywood, "Wittek and the Austrian Tradition," *Journal of the Royal Asiatic Society*, no. 1 (1988): 7–25; Colin Heywood, "Boundless Dreams of the Levant: Paul Wittek, the *George-Kreis,* and the Writing of Ottoman History," *Journal of the Royal Asiatic Society*, no. 1 (1989): 30–50. Also see J. Wansbrough, "Paul Wittek and Richard Haklyut: A Tale of Two Empires," *Osmanlı Araştırmaları* 7 and 8 (1988): 55–70.

30. Colin Imber, "Paul Wittek's 'De la defaite d'Ankara a la prise de Constantinople," *Osmanlı Araştırmaları* 5 (1986): 65–81; Colin Imber, "The Ottoman Dynastic Myth," *Turcica* 19 (1987): 7–27; Colin Imber, "The Legend of Osman Gazi," *The Ottoman Emirate, 1300–1389,* ed., E. Zachariadou (Rethymnon, Crete, 1993), pp. 67–76.

31. Şinasi Tekin, "Türk Dünyasında 'Gaza' ve 'Cihad' Kavramları Üzerine Düşünceler [Başlangıçtan Osmanlıların Fetret Devrine Kadar]," *Tarih ve Toplum,* no. 109 (January, 1993): 9–18; Şinasi Tekin, "Türk Dünyasında 'Gaza' ve 'Cihad' Kavramları Üzerine Düşünceler—II ['Gazi' teriminin Anadolu ile Akdeniz Bölgesinde İtibarını Yeniden Kazanması]," *Tarih ve Toplum,* no. 110 (February, 1993): 73–80.

32. Feridun Emecen, "Gazaya Dair: XIV. Yüzyıl Kaynakları Arasında Bir Gezinti," *Hakkı Dursun Yıldız'a Armağan* (İstanbul, 1995): 191–197.

33. Kafadar, *Between Two Worlds*, p. 28.

34. Ibid., pp. 80–82.

35. Colin Imber, "Cemal Kafadar: Between Two Worlds: the Construction of the Ottoman State," *Bulletin of the School of Oriental and African Studies* 60, no. 1 (1997): 211–212.

36. Imber, "The Legend of Osman Gazi" (1993), p. 75.

37. İnalcık, "Question of the Emergence" (1982).

38. Dimitri Kitsikis, *Türk-Yunan İmparatorluğu: Arabölge Gerçeği Işığında Osmanlı Tarihine Bakış* (İstanbul, 1996).

39. Sencer Divitçioğlu, *Osmanlı Beyliğinin Kuruluşu* (İstanbul, 1996).

CHAPTER 2. WITTEK REVISITED:
HIS UTILIZATION OF AHMEDÎ'S *İSKENDERNÂME*

1. Nihad Sami Banarlı, "Ahmedi ve Dasitan-ī Tevârîh-i Mülûk-i al-i 'Osmân," *Türkiyat Mecmuası* 6 (İstanbul, 1939): 49–176; Kemal Sılay, "Ahmedi's History of the Ottoman Dynasty," *Journal of Turkish Studies* 16 (1992): 129–200.

2. Wittek, *Rise of Ottoman Empire* (1938), p. 14; and Silay (1992), pp. 135–136.

3. Colin Imber, *The Ottoman Empire, 1300–1481* (İstanbul, 1990), p. 69.

4. Wittek, *Rise of the Ottoman Empire* (1938), p. 14.

5. Sılay, "Ahmedi's History" (1992).

6. Banarlı, "Ahmedi ve Dasıtàn-ı Tevârîh-i Mülûk-i al-i Osman (1939).

7. Wittek, *Rise of the Ottoman Empire* (1938), p. 14.

8. Tunca Kortantamer, *Leben und Weltbild des altosmanischen Dichters Ahmedi* (Freiburg, 1973), p. 20.

9. Fodor, "Ahmedi's Dasitan (1984), p.41.

10. Fodor, Ibid., p. 43, and V. L. Ménage: "The Beginnings of Ottoman Historiography," in *Historians of the Middle East,* eds., B. Lewis and P. Holt (London, 1962), pp. 168–179.

11. Sılay, "Ahmedi's History" (1992), pp. 135, and 145.

12. Wittek, *Rise of the Ottoman Empire* (1938), p. 14, and Sılay, "Ahmedi's History" (1992), pp. 135, and 145.

13. Sılay, "Ahmedi's History" (1992), pp. 135–136, and 145–146.

14. Ibid., pp. 136, and 146–147.

15. Ibid., pp. 136–137, and 147.

16. Lindner, *Nomads and Ottomans* (1983), pp. 4–5.

17. Sılay, "Ahmedi's History" (1992), pp. 137–138, and 147–148.

18. Kortantamer, *Leben und weltbild* (1973), p. 236.

19. Imber, "Ottoman Dynastic Myth" (1987), p. 11.

20. Sılay, "Ahmedi's History" (1992), pp. 138, and 148–149.

21. Ibid., pp. 138, and 149.

22. Nihal Atsız, *Osmanlı Tarihleri, Vol. I.: Şükrullah 'Behcetüttevarih'* (İstanbul, 1949), pp. 39–76. See p. 53.

23. Sılay, "Ahmedi's History" (1992), pp. 139–140, and 150–151.

24. F. Sümer, "Karaman-Oghullari," *The Encyclopaedia of Islam,* new ed., vol. 4 (1978): 619–625; See p. 623; J. H. Kramers, "Murad I," *The Encyclopaedia of Islam,* new ed., vol. 7 (1992): 592–594.

25. Sılay, "Ahmedi's History" (1992), pp. 139–140, and 150–151.

26. Ibid., p. 140.

27. Ibid., pp. 140, and 151–152.

28. Kur'an, *Süratu'l-baqara* (2): 246–251.

29. Sılay, "Ahmedi's History" (1992), pp. 140–142, and 152–154.

30. Ibid., pp. 142, and 154–155.

31. Ibid., pp. 143, and 155.

32. Banarlı, "Ahmedi ve Dasitan" (1939), pp. 72–74; Kortantamer, *Leben und Weltbild* (1973), pp. 112–116, 124–125, and 420–421.

33. Paul Wittek, "Deux chapitres de l'histoire des Turcs de Roum," *Byzantion* 2 (1936): 285–319; See p. 312; Fodor, "Ahmedi's Dasitan (1984), pp. 41–42, and 52.

34. Wittek, "Deux chapitres de l'histoire" (1936), p.312.

35. Fodor, "Ahmedi's Dasitan (1984), p. 52.

36. Ménage, "Beginnings of Otrtoman Historiography" (1962), p. 169.

37. İnalcık, *The Ottoman Empire* (1973), p. 16.

38. Sılay, "Ahmedi's History" (1992), p. 142, and 155.

39. Ibid., pp. 142–143.

40. Ibid., p. 143.

41. E. J. W. Gibb, *A History of Ottoman Poetry,* vol. I (London, 1900), p. 255.

42. İsmail Hakkı Uzunçarşılı, *Osmanlı Tarihi,* vol. I (Ankara, 1947), p. 322.

43. Mükrimin Halil Yınanç, "Bayezid I," *İslam Ansiklopedisi,* vol. 2 (İstanbul, 1962), pp. 369–392. See pp. 389–390.

44. Hasan Turyan, *Bursa Evliyaları ve Tarihi Eserleri* (Bursa, 1982), see pp. 44–46.

45. Kafadar, *Between Two Worlds* (1995), p. 111.

46. Doukas, *Decline and Fall of Byzantium to the Ottoman Turks,* tran., H. Magoulias (Detroit, 1975), see pp. 87–88.

47. George T. Dennis, ed., and trans., *The Letters of Manuel II Palaeologus* (Washington, D.C., 1977), see pp. 50–51.

48. Dennis, *Letters of Manuel II Palaeologus* (1977), pp. 42–51.

49. Imber, *The Ottoman Empire* (1990), pp. 42–43.

50. S. Reinert, "Manuel II Palaeologos and His Müderris," *The Twilight of Byzantium,* eds., S. Curcic and D. Mouriki (Princeton: Princeton University Press, 1991), pp. 39–51.

51. Imber, "Paul Wittek's 'De la defaite" (1986), pp. 72–73.

52. Sılay, "Ahmedi's History" (1992), pp. 143–144, and 156.

53. Fodor, "Ahmedi's Dasitan" (1984), p. 47.

CHAPTER 3. WITTEK REVISITED:
HIS UTILIZATION OF THE 1337 BURSA INSCRIPTION

1. Wittek, *Rise of Ottoman Empire* (1938), p.14.

2. Ibid., pp. 14–15.

3. A. Memduh Turgut Koyunluoğlu, *İznik ve Bursa Tarihi* (Bursa, 1935), see pp. 163–164.

4. Ibid., p. 163; Robert Mantran, "Les Inscriptions Arabes de Brousse," in *Bulletin D'Etudes Orientales* 14 (1952–1954): 87–114, see p. 90.

5. Tekin, "Türk Dünyasında 'Gaza'" (1993), pp. 73–76.

6. İsmail Hakkı Uzunçarşılıoğlu, *Tokad, Niksar, Zile, Turhal, Pazar, Amasya vilayet, kaza ve nahiye merkezlerindeki kitabeler* (İstanbul, 1927); İsmail Hakkı Uzunçarşılıoğlu, *Afyon Karahisar, Sandıklı, Bolvadin, Çay, İsaklı, Manisa, Birgi, Muğla, Milas, Peçin, Denizli, İsparta, Eğirdir'deki Kitabeler ve Sahip, Saruhan, Aydın, Menteşe, İnanç, Hamit Oğulları hakkında malumat* (İstanbul, 1929).

7. Tekin, "Türk Dünyasında 'Gaza'" (1993), pp. 73–76.

8. Wittek, *Rise of Ottoman Empire* (1938), p. 53, fn. 27.

9. F. Taeschner, "Beitrage zur frühosmanischen Epigraphik und Archaologie," *Der Islam* 20 (1932): 109–186. See pp. 127–137.

10. Wittek, *Rise of Ottoman Empire* (1938), p. 39; Emecen, "Gazaya Dair" (1995), p. 194.

11. Halim Baki Kunter, "Kitabelerimiz," *Vakıflar Dergisi* 2 (1942): 431–455 plus Plates. See pp. 437–438; Kâzım Baykal, *Bursa ve Anıtları* (Bursa, 1950), see p. 174; Ekrem Hakkı Ayverdi, *Osmanlı Mimarisinin İlk Devri* (İstanbul, 1966), see p. 59; Mantran, "Les Inscriptions Arabes de Brousse" (1954), pp. 89–90; Koyunluoğlu, *İznik ve Bursa Tarihi* (1935), p.163.

12. Heywood, "Wittek and the Austrian Tradition" (1988), p. 10.

13. Ahmed Tevhid, "Bursa'da En Eski Kitabe," *Tarihi Osmanı Encümeni Mecmuası*, vol. 29 (İstanbul, 1912), pp. 318–320.

14. Wittek, *Rise of Ottoman Empire* (1938), p. 53, fn. 26.

15. Paul Wittek, *Menteşe Beyliği: 13–15 inci Asırda Garbi Küçük Asya Tarihine ait Tetkik* (Ankara, 1944), see p. 133, fn. 441.

16. Ibid., p. 133, fn. 441.

17. Wittek, *Rise of Ottoman Empire* (1938), p. 15.

18. Mantran, "Les Inscriptions Arabes de Brousse" (1954), p. 90.

19. Ibid., p. 91.

20. Ibid., p. 104.

21. Ibid., p. 27.

22. Robert Mantran, "Les Inscriptions Turques de Brousse," *Oriens* 12 (1959): 115–170. See p. 129.

23. F. Th. Dijkema, *The Ottoman Historical Monumental Inscriptions in Edirne* (Leiden, 1977), see pp. 180, 185, and 186 for three such examples from Edirne.

24. İ. H. Konyalī, *Söğüt'de Ertuğrul Gazi Türbesi İhtifali* (İstanbul, 1959), see pp. 23 and 31.

25. Jennings, "Some Thoughts on the *Gazi* Thesis" (1986), pp. 154–155.

26. Imber, "Ottoman Dynastic Myth" (1987), pp. 7–8; Tevhid, "Bursa'da" (1912), p. 318–320; Kunter, "Kitabelerimiz" (1942), pp. 437–438; and Ayverdi, *Osmanlı Mimarisinin* (1966), p. 59.

27. Kafadar, *Between Two Worlds*, pp. 157–191.

28. Ibid., pp. 193–207.

29. Uzunçarşılı, *Afyon Karahisar* (1929), pp. 7–8.

30. Ibid., pp. 8–9.

31. Ibid., pp. 11–12.

32. Ibid., p. 42.

33. Ibid., pp. 75–76.

34. Uzunçarşılı, *Afyon Karahisar* (1929), pp. 109–112.

35. Ibid., pp. 157–158 and Wittek, *Menteşe Beyliği* (1944).

36. Ibid., pp. 161–165.

37. Ibid., pp. 112–113.

38. İsmail Hakkı Uzunçarşılı, "*Gazi* Orhan Bey Vakfiyesi," *Belleten*, vol. 5 (Ankara, 1941): 277–288; Kafadar, *Between Two Worlds* (1995), p. 61.

39. See *Appendix 2;* Uzunçarşılı, "*Gazi* Orhan Bey Vakfiyesi" (1941), pp. 277–278; İbrahim Artuk and Cevriye Artuk, *İstanbul Arkeoloji Müzeleri Teşhirdeki İslami Sikkeler Kataloğu,* vol. 2 (İstanbul 1974), pp. 453–456; İbrahim Artuk, "Osmanlı Beyliğinin Kurucusu Osman Gazi'ye Ait Sikke," in *Social and Economic History of Turkey,* eds., O. Okyar and H. İnalcık (Ankara, 1980), pp. 27–33; Uzunçarşılı, *Osmanli Tarihi* (1947), p. 125.

40. See Appendix 1.

41. Kunter, "Kitabelerimiz" (1942); Banarlı, "Ahmedi ve Dasitan" (1939).

CHAPTER 4. WHAT COULD THE TERMS *GAZA* AND *GAZI*
HAVE MEANT TO THE EARLY OTTOMANS?

1. Şinasi Tekin, "XIV. Yüzyılda Yazılmış Gazilik Tarikası 'Gaziliğin Yol-ları' adlı Bir Eski Anadolu Türkçesi metni ve Gaza Cihad Kavramları Hakkında," *Journal of Turkish Studies* 13 (1989): 139–204; Emecen, "Gazaya Dair (1995), pp. 191–197.

2. Sılay, "Ahmedi's History" (1992), p. 147.

3. Ibid., p. 137.

4. Imber, "The Legend of Osman *Gazi*" (1993), pp. 73–74.

5. Vasilis Demetriades, "The Tomb of Ghazi Evrenos Bey at Venitza and its Inscription," *Bulletin of the School of Oriental and African Studies* 39 (1976): 328–332; Mehmed Nüzhet, A*hval-i Mihal Gazi* (İstanbul, 1897), see p. 45. In the late 1990s the Evrenos Bey inscription was moved from Yenitza to Thessaloniki for safekeeping. On a recent visit to Thessaloniki (February 2001), Demetriades and I spent a fruitless day searching for its present location, only to conclude that the present-day whereabouts of this most important Ottoman inscription is unknown.

6. Doukas, *Decline and Fall of Byzantium* (1975), pp. 133–134.

7. Benjamin Stolz and Suat Soucek, trans. and eds., *Konstantin Mihailovic, Memoirs of a Janissary* (Ann Arbor, 1975), see p. 177.

8. Donald M. Nicol, trans. and ed., *Theodore Spandounes On the Origin of the Ottoman Emperors* (Cambridge, 1997), see p. 125.

9. Doukos, *Decline and Fall of Byzantium* (1975); J. van Dieten, ed. and trans., *Nikephoros Gregoras—Rhomaische Geschichte,* Books I–XVII (Stuttgart, 1973–1988); Albert Failler, ed. and trans., *Georges Pachymeres Relations Historiques,* Books X–XIII (Paris, ND); Marios Philippidis, trans., *The Fall of the Byzantine Empire* (Amherst, 1980).

10. Sılay, "Ahmedi's History" (1992), p. 136.

11. Ibid., pp. 136–138.

12. See Plate 2 and Halil İnalcık, "Osmanlı İdare, Sosyal ve Ekonomik Tarihiyle İlgili Belgeler: Bursa Kadı Sicillerinden Seçmeler," *Belgeler* 10, no. 14 (1980–1981): 1–91, see pp. 16–17).

13. İsmail Hami Danişmend, *İzahlı Osmanlı Tarihi Kronolojisi,* Cilt I–IV (İstanbul, 1947), pp. 382–383.

14. İsmail Hakkı Uzunçarşılı, "Akıncı," *İslam Ansiklopedisi* I (1950): 239–249, see pp. 239–240; A. Decei, "Akindji," *The Encyclopaedia of Islam,* 2d ed., vol. I (1960): 340. For a different perspective, see: Irène Beldiceanu-Steinherr, "En Marge D'un Acte Concernant le Pengyek et les Aqingi," *Revue des Études Islamiques* 37 (1969): 21–47, see p. 27.

15. Boris Nedkov, *Osmano-turska diplomatika i paleografiia,* vol. 2 (Sofia, 1972), see pp. 175–177, and 320.

16. Ö. L. Barkan, "Essai sur les données statistiques des registres de recensement dans l'Empire Ottoman aux XVe et XVIe siècles," *Journal of the Economic and Social History of the Orient* I (1957): 9–32, see p. 32.

17. See Plate 3. See Nedkov, *Osmano-tarska diplomatika* (1972), p. 320.

CHAPTER 5. TOWARD A NEW EXPLANATION

1. Ménage, "Beginnings of Ottoman Historiography" (1962), pp. 174–175; V. L. Ménage, "The Menaqib of Yakhshi Faqih," *Bulletin of the School of Oriental & African Studies* 26 (1963): 50–54; Halil İnalcık: "How to Read Ashik Pasha Zade's History," in *Studies in Ottoman History in Honour of Professor V. L. Ménage*, eds., C. Heywood and C. Imber (İstanbul, 1994), pp. 139–156.

2. İnalcık, "How to Read Ashik Pasha Zadi's History," *Studies in Ottoman History in Honour of Professor V. L. Ménage*, eds. C. Heywood and C. Imber (İstanbul, 1994), pp. 143–145.

3. Aşıkpaşazade, *Tevarih* (1913), p. 30.

4. Gibbons, "Foundation of Ottoman Empire (1916), p. 48.

5. Joseph de Hammer, trans., *Histoire de l'Empire Ottoman*, trans., J. Hellert, vol. I (Paris, 1835), see p. 152, and fn. 3).

6. Danişmend, *İzahlı Osmanlı* (1947), 1:12.

7. Uzunçarşılı, *Osmanlı Tarihi* (1947), 1:118.

8. İsmail Hakkı Uzunçarşılı, "Evrenos," *İslam Ansiklopedisi* 4 (1964): 413–418, see pp. 414–415.

9. Irene Melikoff, "Ewrenos," *The Encyclopaedia of Islam*, new ed., vol. 2 (1965): 720; Uzunçarşılı, "Evrenos," in *İslam Ansiklopedisi*, vol. 3: 414–418.

10. Aşıkpaşazade, *Tevarih* (1913), p.51.

11. Johannes Leunclavius, "Pandectes Historiae Turcicae," *Patrologiae Graecae* 149 (1866): 718–922, see p. 756. Published in J. P. Migne.

12. Claude Cahen, "Karasi," *Encyclopaedia of Islam*, new ed., vol. 4 (1978): 627–629, see p. 628.

13. Ö. L. Barkan, "Osmanlı İmparatorluğunda Bir İskan ve kolonizasyon metodu olarak Vakıflar ve temlikler: I. İstila devirlerinin Kolonizatör Türk Dervişleri ve zaviyeler," *Vakıflar Dergisi* 2 (1942): 279–386. See p. 342.

14. Lady Goodenough, *The Chronicle of Muntaner*, Hakluyt Society, sec. ser., no. 50 (London, 1921), see pp. 543–544.

15. Wittek, *Rise of Ottoman Empire* (1938), p. 42 and fn. 55.

16. Goodenough, *Chronicle of Muntaner* (1921), pp. 502–506 and 526.

17. Ibid., p. 533.

18. Melikoff, "Ewrenos" (1965), p. 720.

19. F. Babinger, "Turakhan Beg," *Encyclopaedia of Islam*, first ed., vol. 4 (1934): 876–878, see p. 877); H. İnalcık and M. Oğuz, *Gazavat-ı Sultan Murad b. Mehemmed Han* (Ankara, 1978), see pp. 88–91.

20. Vasilis Demetriades, "The Tomb of Ghazi Evrenos Bey at Venitza and its Inscription," *Bulletin of the School of Oriental and African Studies* 39 (1976): 328–332.

21. Demetriades, "The Tomb of *Gazi* Evrenos" (1976), pp. 331–332.

22. Dijkema, *Ottoman Historical Monumental Inscriptions* (1977), p. 25.

23. See Plate 4. See Demetriades, "The Tomb of *Gazi* Evrenos" (1976), pp. 330–332.

24. See Appendix 2.

25. M. Tayyib Gökbilgin, "Mihal-oğulları," *İslam Ansiklopedisi,* vol. 8 (1970): 285–292, see p. 285); citing Uzunçarşılı, *Tokad, Niksar, Zib, Turhal . . .* (1927), p. 25; Nüzhet, *Ahval-i Mihal Gazi* (1897), p.45.

26. See Plate 5.

27. H. A. R. Gibb, *The Travels of Ibn Battuta, A.D. 1325–1354,* vol. II (Cambridge, 1962), see p. 451.

28. İsmail Hakkı Uzunçarşılı, "Orhan Gazi'nin, Vefat Eden Oğlu Süleyman Paşa İçin Tertip Ettirdiği Vakfiyenin Aslı," *Belleten* 27 (Ankara, 1963), pp. 437–451, see p. 438.

29. M. Tayyib Gökbilgin, "Murad I. Tesisleri ve Bursa İmareti Vakfiyesi," *Türkiyat Mecmuası* 10 (1953): 217–234. See p. 220.

30. Taeschner, "Beitrage zur frühosmanischen" (1932), p. 131.

31. Nüzhet, *Ahval-il Mihal Gazi* (1897), p. 45.

32. Artuk, *İstanbul Arkeoloji* (1974), p. 460.

33. Demetriades, "The Tomb of *Gazi* Evrenos" (1976), pp. 330–332.

34. Nicol, *Theodore Spandounes* (1997), p. 142.

35. Beatrice Forbes Manz, *The Rise and Rule of Tamerlane* (Cambridge, 1989), see pp. 73 and 174.

36. Nicol, *Theodore Spandounes* (1997), p.16.

37. Ibid., pp. ix–xi.

38. Ibid., pp. 3–4. [Emphasis is mine]

39. Ibid., p. xvi.

40. Babinger, "Mikhaloghlu" (1990), p. 34.

41. Vryonis, *Decline of Medieval Hellenism* (1971), pp. 341–342; J. Darrouzes, *Les Regestes Des Actes Du Patriarcat De Constantinople* (Paris, 1977), see pp. 142–143.

42. Anna Philippidis-Braat, "La Captivité de Palamas chez les Turcs," *Travaux et Memoires,* vol. 7 (Paris, 1979), pp. 109–222, see p. 171; M. Balivet, "Des 'Kühhan' (Kahin) aux *Xiovai (Xioviç),*" *Byzantion* 52 (1982): 24–59; Elizabeth Zachariadou, "Religious Dialogue Between Byzantines and Turks During

the Ottoman Expansion," *Religionsgespräche im Mittelalter,* eds., B. Lewis and F. Niewöhner (Wiesbaden, 1992), see pp. 291–293.

43. Ménage, "Beginnings of Ottoman Historiography" (1962), pp. 174–175.

44. Halil İnalcık, "The Status of the Greek Orthodox Patriarch Under the Ottomans," *Turcica* 21–23 (1991): 407–436, see p. 409.

45. J. Schacht, "Aman," *Encyclopaedia of Islam,* new ed., vol. 1 (1960): 429–430.

46. Aşıkpaşazade, *Tevarih* (1913), pp. 4–5.

47. Ibid., p. 5.

48. Ibid., p. 11.

49. Ibid., pp. 12–13.

50. Ibid., p.13.

51. Aşıkpaşazade, *Tevarih* (1913), p. 17.

52. Ibid., p. 30.

53. Ibid., pp. 30–31.

54. Gibb, *Travels of Ibn Battuta* (1962), pp. 449–450.

55. Ibid., pp. 451–452.

56. Emecen, "Gazaya Dair" (1995), p. 194.

57. Gibb, *Travels of Ibn Battuta* (1962), p. 450.

58. Ibid., pp. 452–453.

59. Ibid., p. 450.

60. Irène Beldiceanu-Steinherr, *Recherches sur les actes des regnes des sultans Osman, Orkhan et Murad I* (Münich, 1967), pp. 85–89; H.-G. Majer, "Some Remarks on the Document of Murad I from the Monastery of St. Paul on Mount Athos (1386)," in *Mount Athos in the 14th–16th Centuries* (Athens: Institute for Byzantine Research, 1997), pp. 33–39, see p. 33.

61. Uzunçarşılı, "*Gazi* Orhan Bey Vakfiyesi" (1941), pp. 277–288; Beldiceanu-Steinherr, *Recherches sur les actes* (1967), pp. 85–89; and Kafadar (1994), p. 61.

62. Uzunçarşılı, "*Gazi* Orhan Bey Vakfiyesi" (1941), pp. 280–281; Suha Umur, *Osmanlı Padişah Tuğraları* (İstanbul, 1980), p. 79.

63. Ibid., pp. 280–281.

64. Ibid., pp. 280–281.

65. Ibid., pp. 281.

66. See Plate 6. See Uzunçarşılı, "*Gazi* Orhan Bey Vakfiyesi" (1941), p. 282.

67. Aşıkpaşazade, *Tevarih* (1913), p.22.

68. Speros Vryonis, Jr., "Seljuk Gulams and the Ottoman Devshirmes," *Der Islam,* vol. 41 (Berlin, 1965): 224–252, see pp. 240–241.

69. Daniel Sahas, "Gregory Palamas (1296–1360) on Islam," *The Muslim World* 73 (1983): 1–21, see 9–10; Philippidis-Braat, "La Captivité de Palamas" (1979), p. 171; Halil İnalcık, *Hicri 835 Tarihli Suret-i Defter-i Sancak-i Arvanid* (Ankara, 1954), p. 143.

70. Imber, *Ottoman Emirate* (1993); Imber, *Ottoman Dynastic Myth* (1987); Colin Imber, "Canon and Apocrypha in Early Ottoman History," in *Studies in Ottoman History in Honour of Professor V. L. Ménage,* eds., C. Heywood and C. Imber (İstanbul, 1994), pp. 117–137.

71. Gibbons, *Foundation of Ottoman Empire* (1916), pp. 267 and 361.

72. Major Davy, trans., *Sharfuddin Ali Yezdi's Politics and Military Institutions of Tamerlane* (New Delhi, 1972), pp. 53–54.

73. Şevkiye İnalcık, "Ibn Hacer'de Osmanlı'lara Dair Haberler," in *A. Ü. Dil ve Tarih-Coğrafya Fakültesi Dergisi,* vol. 6 (1948), pp. 189–195; pp. 349–358, and pp. 517–529, see p. 190; Imber, "Canon and Apocrypha" (1994), pp. 122–124, and 127–128.

74. Imber, "Canon and Apocrypha" (1994), p. 128, and Mükrimin Halil Yınanç, ed., *Düsturname-i Enveri* (İstanbul, 1928), pp. 73–74.

75. Philippidis-Braat, "La Captivité de Palamas" (1979), pp. 144–146.

76. J. Buchan Telfer, trans., *The Bondage and Travels of Johann Schiltberger, A Native of Bavaria, in Europe, Asia, and Africa, 1396–1427* (New York, 1879), p. 40; Ulrich Schlemmer, ed., *Johannes Schiltberger: Als Sklave im Osmanischen Reich und bei den Tataren, 1394–1427* (Stuttgart, 1983), p. 118.

77. Galen R. Kline, ed., *The Voyage d'Outremer by Bertrandon de la Broquiere* (New York and Bern, 1988), p. 83.

78. Ekrem Hakki Ayverdi, *Osmanlı Mimarisinin İlk Devri* (İstanbul, 1966).

79. Nicol, *Theodore Spandounes* (1997), p. ix–x and 3.

80. Ibid., p. 134.

81. Barkan, "Osmanlı İmparatorluğunda" (1942).

82. Ö. L. Barkan and E. Meriçli, *Hüdavendigar Livası Tahrir Defterleri* (Ankara, 1988); Ayverdi, *Osmanlı Mimarisinin* (1966).

83. Uzunçarşılı, "Orhan Gazi'nin" (1963), pp. 437–438.

84. See Plate 7. See Uzunçarşılı, "Orhan Gazi'nin" (1963), p. 446.

85. Uzunçarşılı, "Orhan Gazi'nin" (1963), p. 442.

86. See Plate 8. See Uzunçarşılı, Ibid., p. 449.

87. Semavi Eyice, "İlk Osmanlı Devrinin Dini-İçtimai Bir Müessesesi Zaviyeler ve Zaviyeli—Camiler," in *İ. Ü. İktisat Fakültesi Mecmuası,* vol. 23, nos. 1–2 (İstanbul, 1962), pp. 3–80, see p. 32.

88. Gökbilgin, "Murad I" (1953), p. 219.

89. See Plate 9. See Gökbilgin, "Murad I" (1953), p.223–224.

90. See Plate 10. See Gökbilgin, Ibid., p. 233; Heath W. Lowry, *Trabzon Şehrinin İslamlaşması ve Türkleşmesi, 1461–1583,* 2d ed. 1998 (İstanbul: Bosphorus University Press, 1981), pp. 119–140.

91. G. Arnakis, "Gregory Palamas Among the Turks and Documents of his Captivity as Historical Sources," *Speculum* 26 (1951): 104–118, see p. 106); Sahas, "Gregory Palamas" (1983), p. 6; Philippidis-Braat, "La Captivité de Palamas (1979), p. 144.

92. Halil İnalcık, *Hicri 835* (1954), p. 143.

93. Ibid.

94. Darrouzes, *Les Regestes Des Acles* (1977), no. 2198; and Lindner, *Nomads and Ottomans* (1983), p. 5.

95. Ibid., p. 153.

96. Halil İnalcık, *Fatih Devri Üzerinde Tetkikler ve Vesikalar* (Ankara: Türk Tarih Kurumu, 1954).

97. İnalcık, *Hicri 835* (1954), p. 159.

98. Heath W. Lowry, *Studies in Defterology: Ottoman Society in the Fifteenth and Sixteenth Centuries* (İstanbul, 1992).

99. İnalcık, "Ottoman Methods of Conquest" (1954).

100. Ibid., pp. 113–114.

101. İnalcık, "Fatih Devri Üzerinde" (1954), p. 141.

102. İnalcık, "The Status of the Greek Orthodox Patriarch" (1991), p. 409.

103. Nedkov, *Osmano-tursica* (1972), pp.175–177 and 320.

104. A. D. Alderson, *The Structure of the Ottoman Dynasty* (Oxford, 1956), pp. 85–100; Umur, *Osmanlı Padişah* (1980).

105. Mahmut R. Gazimihal, "İstanbul Muhasaralarında Mihaloğulları ve Fatih Devrine ait bir Vakıf Defterine Göre Harmankaya Malikanesi," *Vakıflar Dergisi* 4 (1958): 125–137, see p. 130.

106. Halil Sahillioğlu, "Slaves in the Social and Economic Life of Bursa in the Late 15th and Early 16th Centuries," *Turcica* 17 (1985): 43–112; İnalcık, *Osmanli İdare* (1981), pp. 1–91; Halil İnalcık, "Osmanlı İdare, Sosyal ve Ekonomik Tarihiyle İlgili Belgeler: Bursa Kadı Sicillerinden Seçmeler," *Belgeler* 13, no. 17 (1988): 1–41.

107. Gregoras quoted in Speros Vryonis Jr., "Byzantine and Turkish Societies and their Sources of Manpower," in *War, Technology and Society in the Middle East,* eds., V. J. Parry and M. E. Yapp (London, 1975), p. 133.

CHAPTER 6. CHRISTIAN PEASANT LIFE IN THE
FIFTEENTH-CENTURY OTTOMAN EMPIRE

1. Heath W. Lowry, "The Island of Limnos: a Case Study on the Continuity of Byzantine Forms Under Ottoman Rule," in *Continuity and Change in Late Byzantine and Early Ottoman Society,* eds., A. Bryer and H. Lowry (Birmingham and Washington, DC, 1986), pp. 235–259; Heath W. Lowry, "A Corpus of Extant Kanunnames for the Island of Limnos as Contained in the TapuTahrir Defter Collection of the Başbakanlık Archives," *Journal of Ottoman Studies* 1 (1980): 41–60; Heath W. Lowry, "The Fate of Byzantine Monastic Properties Under the Ottomans: Examples from Mount Athos, Limnos & Trabzon," *Byzantinische Forschungen* 16 (1990): 275–311.

2. Heath W. Lowry, "Fifteenth-Century Ottoman Peasant Taxation: The Case Study of Radilofo (Radolibos)," in *Continuity and Change in Late Byzantine and Early Ottoman Society,* eds. A. Bryer and H. Lowry (Birmingham and Washington, DC, 1986), pp. 23–37; Lowry, *Keşişlik* (1993): pp. 15–26.

3. Heath W. Lowry, "Privilege and Property in Ottoman Maçuka during the Opening Decades of the Tourkokratia, 1461–1553," in *Continuity and Change in Late Byzantine and Early Ottoman Society,* eds., A. Bryer and H. Lowry (Birmingham and Washington, DC, 1986), pp. 97–128.

4. Lowry, "The Island of Limnos" (1986), p. 237.

5. Ibid., p. 237.

6. Ibid., pp. 238–241; Julian Raby, "Terra Lemnia and the Potteries of the Golden Horn: An Antique Revival Under Ottoman Auspices," *Byzantinische Forschungen* 21 (1995): 305–342.

7. John Haldon, "Limnos, Monastic Holdings and the Byzantine State: ca. 1261–1453," in *Continuity and Change in Late Byzantine and Early Ottoman Society,* eds., A. Bryer and H. Lowry (Birmingham and Washington, DC, 1986), pp. 161–234. (See map following p. 188).

8. Lowry, "The Island of Limnos" (1986), pp. 244–249.

9. Ibid., pp. 241–242.

10. Lowry, "Fifteenth-Century Ottoman Peasant Taxation" (1986), and Lowry, "Privilege and Property" (1986).

11. İnalcık, *Hicri 835* (1954).

12. Halil İnalcık, "Stefan Duşan'dan Osmanlı İmparatorluğuna: XV. asırda Rumeli'de hiristiyan sipahiler ve menşeleri," in *Fatih Devri Üzerinde Tetkikler ve Vesikalar* (Ankara, 1954), pp. 137–184.

13. Halil İnalcık, "Ottoman Methods of Conquest," in *Studia Islamica* 2 (Paris, 1954): 104–129.

14. İnalcık, "The Status of the Greek Orthodox Patriarch" (1991), p. 409.

15. Lowry, "The Island of Limnos (1986), p. 245.

16. Ibid., p. 246, and Lowry, *A Corpus of Extant Kanunnames* (1980), pp. 48–51.

17. John Fine, Jr., *The Late Medieval Balkans: A Critical Survey from the Late Twelfth Century to the Ottoman Conquest* (Ann Arbor, 1987), see pp. 607–611; İnalcık, "Ottoman Methods of Conquest" (1954), pp. 104–129.

18. Lowry, "The Island of Limnos" (1986), p. 258, and Lowry, *A Corpus of Extant Kanunnames* (1980), pp. 46–47.

19. Lowry, *A Corpus of Extant Kanunnames* (1980), pp. 43–45.

20. Lowry, "The Island of Limnos" (1986), pp. 241–244.

21. Ibid., pp. 243–244.

22. Stolz and Soucek, *Konstantin Mihailovic* (1975), pp. 157–159.

23. Lowry, "The Island of Limnos" (1986), p. 257; Lowry, "Fifteenth-Century Ottoman Peasant Taxation" (1986), pp. 30–31; Lowry, "Privilege and Property" (1986), 101–103.

24. Lowry, "The Island of Limnos" (1986), p. 257.

25. Haldon, "Limnos, Monastic Holdings" (1986), pp. 161–215; Lowry, "The Island of Limnos" (1986), pp. 250–253; and Lowry, "Fifteenth-Century Ottoman Peasant Tradition" (1990), pp. 275–311.

26. Haldon, "Limnos, Monastic Holdings" (1986).

27. Lowry, "The Island of Limnos" (1986), p. 258.

28. Lowry, *A Corpus of Extant Kanunnames* (1980), pp. 51–53; and Lowry, "The Island of Limnos" (1986), p. 245.

29. Richard Pococke, *A Description of the East and Some Other Countries,* vol. 2, part 2 (London, 1745), see pp. 22–23).

30. Vital Cuinet, *La Turquie D'Asie,* vol. 1 (Paris), 1890, see p. 477.

31. Pococke, *A Description of the East* (1745), p. 22.

32. Lowry, *A Corpus of Extant Kanunnames* (1980), pp. 48–50.

33. Ibid., pp. 48–50.

34. Lowry, "Privilege and Property," and Lowry, "Fifteenth-Century Ottoman Peasant Taxation" (1986).

CHAPTER 7. THE LAST PHASE OF OTTOMAN SYNCRETISM—
THE SUBSUMPTION OF MEMBERS OF THE BYZANTO-BALKAN
ARISTOCRACY INTO THE OTTOMAN RULING ELITE

1. Halil İnalcık, "Mesih Pasha," *The Encyclopaedia of Islam,* vol. 6 (1990): 1025–1026; Nicol, *Theodore Spandounes* (1997), p. 46.

2. Ibid., pp. 1025–1026

3. Nicol, *Theodore Spandounes* (1997), p. xvi; Tursun Beg, *The History of Mehmed the Conqueror,* eds. H. İnalcik and R. Murphy (Minneapolis and Chicago: Bibliotheca Islamica, 1978), p. 60.

4. Mükrimin Halil Yınanç, "Gedik Ahmed Paşa," *İslam Ansiklopedisi* 1: 193–199.

5. Aleksandar Stojanovski, *Vranjski kadiluk u XVI veku* (Vranje, 1985).

6. İsmail Hakki Uzunçarşılı, *Osmanlı Tarihi: İstanbul'un Fethinden Kanuni Sultan Süleyman'ın Ölümüne Kadar,* vol. 2 (Ankara, 1943), p. 11.

7. Halil İnalcık, "Ghulam," *The Encyclopaedia of Islam,* vol. 2 (1965): 1085–1091, see p. 1086.

8. Ibid., p. 1086.

9. Nicol, *Theodore Spandounes* (1997), p. xv.

10. Ibid., p. 46.

11. Ibid., p. 61.

12. N. Akbayar and S. A. Kahraman, eds., *Mehmed Süreyya: Sicill-i Osmani* (İstanbul, 1996), p. 1087.

13. Nicol, *Theodore Spandounes* (1997), p. 44.

14. Ibid., pp. 3–4.

15. Franz Babinger, *Mehmed the Conqueror and His Time* (Princeton: Princeton University Press, 1978), p. 115; Colin Imber, "Mahmud Pasha," in *The Encyclopaedia of Islam,* vol. 6 (1986): 69–72; Lowry, *Trabzon Şehrinin* (1981), pp. 5–18.

16. Babinger, *Mehmed the Conqueror* (1978), p. 115.

17. Imber, "Mahmud Pasha" (1986a), p. 70.

18. Tursun Beg, *History of Mehmed the Conqueror* (1978), pp. 41–43.

19. Babinger, *Mehmed the Conqueror* (1978), pp. 115, 147; Theoharis Stavrides, *The Ottoman Grand Vezir Mahmud Pasha Angelovic (1453–1474)* (Unpublished Ph.D. diss., Harvard University, 1996), p. 421.

20. Şehabeddin Tekindağ, "Mahmud Paşa," in *İslam Ansiklopedisi,* vol. 7: 183–188, see pp. 187–188) and vol. 6; Mirmiroğlu, *Fatih Sultan Mehmet II Devrine Ait Tarihi Vesikalar* (İstanbul, 1945), pp. 92–93.

21. Marios Philippides, trans., *The Fall of the Byzantine Empire: A Chronicle by George Sphrantzes, 1401–1477* (Amherst, 1980), p. 81.

22. Imber, "Mahmud Pasha" (1986), p. 70

23. See Babinger, *Mehmed the Conqueror* (1978), pp. 114–115; Halil İnalcık, "Mehmed the Conqueror (1432–1481) and His Time," *Speculum* 35 (1960): 408–427, see pp. 413–414.

24. Kritovoulos, *History of Mehmed the Conqueror,* trans., Charles Riggs (Princeton: Princeton University Press, 1954), pp. 88–89.

25. Diether Roderich Reinsch, ed., *Critobuli Imbriotae Historiae* (Berlin, 1983), p. 88.

26. Howard Crane, ed., and trans., *The Garden of the Mosques: Hafız Hüseyin al-Ayvansarayi's Guide to the Muslim Monuments of Ottoman Istanbul* (Leiden, 2000), p. 212.

27. Kritovoulos, *History of Mehmed* (1954), p. 88–89; Reinsch, *Critobuli* (1983), p. 88.

28. H. Sabanović, "Hersek-zade," *The Encyclopaedia of Islam*, vol. 3 (1971): 340–342.

29. Sabanović, "Hersek-zade" (1971), pp. 340–342.

30. M. Tayyib Okiç, "Hadım ('Atik) Ali Paşa Kimdir?" in *Necati Lugal Armağanı* (Ankara: Türk Tarih Kurumu, 1968), pp. 501–515, see pp. 513–514).

31. Christine Whitehead, "Khadim Sinan Pasha," and "Khodja Sinan Pasha," in *The Encyclopaedia of Islam*, vol. 9: pp. 630–631.

32. Alexander Kazhdan, et al., *The Oxford Dictionary of Byzantium,* 3 vols. (Oxford: Oxford University Press, 1991), pp. 746–747.

33. Akbayar and Kahraman, *Menmed Süreyya* (1996), p. 208; Abdülkadir Özcan, "Dukakinzade Ahmed Paşa," *Türkiye Diyanet Vakfı İslam Ansiklopedisi,* vol. 9 (1994): 550–551.

34. İnalcık, *Hicri 835* (1954).

CHAPTER 8. THE NATURE OF THE EARLY OTTOMAN STATE

1. Heath W. Lowry, *Trabzon Şehrinin İslamlaşması ve Türkleşmesi,* 1461–1583 (İstanbul: Bosphorus University Press, 1981), pp. 119–140.

2. İnalcık, *The Ottoman Empire*, p. 7.

3. Wittek, "De la défaite d'ankara" (1938), pp. 31–32 and fn. 1.

4. Ibid., pp. 31–32 and fn. 1; Gibb, *History of Ottoman Poetry* 1: p. 232–235.

5. Marios Philippides Sphrantzes, *The Fall of the Byzantine Empire* (Amherst, 1980), p. 22; Doukas, *Decline and Fall of Byzantium* (1975), p. 112.

6. Doukas, *Decline and Fall of Byzantium* (1975), pp. 119–122.

7. Elizabeth Zachariadou, *The Chronicle about the Turkish Sultans (of Codex Barberinus Graecus 111) and its Italian Prototype [in Greek]* (Thessalonica, 1960); Elizabeth Zachariadou, "A Note about the Chronicle of the Turkish Sultans," [in Greek] *Hellenika* 20 (1967): 166–169.

8. Marios Philippides, trans., *An Anonymous Greek Chronicle of the Seventeenth Century: Codex Berberinus Graecus 111* (New Rochelle, New York, 1990), pp. 59–60. [Emphasis is mine.]

9. Nicol, *Theodore Spandounes,* p. 15–16.

10. See appendix 4.

11. A. D. Alderson, *The Structure of the Ottoman Dynasty* (Oxford, 1956), p. 19.

12. G. T. Dennis, "The Byzantine-Turkish Treaty of 1403," *Orientalia Christiana Periodica* 33 (1967): 72–88.

13. Ibid., pp. 82 and 85.

14. Ibid., p. 86.

15. Danişmend, *İzahli Osmanlı* (1947), vol. 1.

16. Irène Beldiceanu-Steinherr, "En Marge D'un Acte Concernant le Pengyek et Les Aqingi," in *Revue des Études Islamiques* 37 (1969): 30.

17. Alderson, *Structure of Ottoman Dynasty* (1956), p. 91.

18. Albert Lybyer, *The Government of the Ottoman Empire in the Time of Suleiman the Magnificent* (Cambridge, 1913), p. 242.

19. Ibid., pp. 272–273.

20. İnalcık, "How to Read Ashik Pasha" (1994), pp. 144–146.

Bibliography

Akbayar, N., and S. A. Kahraman, eds. *Mehmed Süreyya: Sicill-i Osmani.* İstanbul, 1996.

Akdağ, Mustafa. "Ankara Sultan Alaeddin Cami Kapısında Bulunan Hicri 763 Tarihli Bir Kitabenin Tarihi Önemi." *Tarih Vesikaları* [Yeni Seri]. Vol. 1, No. 3 (1961): 366–373.

Aktepe, Münir. "Çandarlı İbrahim Paşa." In *Türkiye Diyanet Vakfı İslam Ansiklopedisi* 8 (1993): 214.

Alderson, A. D. *The Structure of the Ottoman Dynasty.* Oxford, 1956.

Alexander, J. C. (Alexandropoulos). "The Lord Giveth and the Lord Taketh Away: Athos and the Confiscation affair of 1568–1569." In *Mount Athos in the 14th-16th Centuries*, 149–200. Athens: Institute for Byzantine Research, 1997.

Arnakis, George. "Gregory Palamas Among the Turks and Documents of his Captivity as Historical Sources." In *Speculum* 26 (1951): 104–118.

———. *Hoi protoi othomanoi.* Athens, 1947.

Artuk, İbrahim. "Osmanlı Beyliğinin Kurucusu Osman Gazi'ye Ait Sikke." In *Social and Economic History of Turkey.* Edited by O. Okyar and H. İnalcık, 27–33. Ankara, 1980.

Artuk, İbrahim, and Cevriye Artuk. *İstanbul Arkeoloji Müzeleri Teşhirdeki İslami Sikkeler Kataloğu.* Vol. 2. İstanbul, 1974.

Aşikpaşazade. *Tevarih-i Al-i Osman.* Edited by 'Ali Bey. İstanbul, h.1332/1913.

Atsız, Nihal, ed. *Aşıkpaşaoğlu Tarihi.* İstanbul, 1992.

———. *Osmanlı Tarihleri, Şükrullah 'Behcetüttevarih'.* Vol. 1: 39–76. İstanbul, 1949.

Ayvansarayi. *The Garden of the Mosques: Hafız Hüseyin al-Ayvansarayi's Guide to the Muslim Monuments of Ottoman Istanbul.* Edited and translated by Howard Crane. Leiden, 2000.

Ayverdi, Ekrem Hakkı. *Osmanlı Mimarisinin İlk Devri.* İstanbul, 1966.

Babinger, F. "Mikhal-oghlu." In *Encyclopaedia of Islam.* New Ed. Vol. 7: 34–35. Leiden, 1990.

———. *Mehmed the Conqueror and His Time.* Princeton: Princeton University Press, 1978.

———. "Turakhan Beg." In *Encyclopaedia of Islam.* First Ed. Vol. 4 (1934): 876–878.

———. "Der Islam in Kleinasien—Neue Wege der Islamforschung." In *Zeitschrift der Deutschen Morgenlandischen Gesellschaft.* Neue Folge. Band I. Band 76, 126–152. Leipzig, 1922.

Balivet, M. "Chrétiens secrets et martyrs christiques en Islam turc: Quelques cas à travers les textes (XIIIe–XVIIe siècles)." *Islamochristiana* 16 (1990): 91–114.

———. "Des 'Kühhan' (Kahin) aux *Xiovai (Xioviç).*" In *Byzantion* 52 (1982): 24–59.

Banarlı, Nihad Sami. "Ahmedi ve Dasitan-ıTevarih-i Müluk-i Al-i-Osman." *Türkiyat Mecmuası* 6 (İstanbul, 1939): 49–176.

Barkan, Ö. L. "Essai sur les donnees statistiques des registres de recensement dans l'Empire Ottoman aux XVe et XVIe siècles." In *Journal of the Economic and Social History of the Orient* 1 (1957): 9–31.

———. "Osmanlı İmparatorluğunda Bir İskan ve kolonizasyon metodu olarak Vakıflar ve temlikler: I. İstila devirlerinin Kolonizatör Türk Dervişleri ve zaviyeler." *Vakıflar Dergisi* 2 (1942): 279–386.

Barkan, Ö. L., and E. Meriçli. *Hüdavendigar Livası Tahrir Defterleri.* Ankara, 1988.

Başbakanlık, T. C., Devlet Arşivleri Genel Müdürlüğü. *Bulgaristan'daki Osmanlı Evrakı ve Orhan Gazi Vakıfları.* Osmanlı Arşivi Daire Baş, no. 17. Ankara, 1994.

Baykal, Kâzım. *Bursa ve Anıtları.* Bursa, 1950.

Beldiceanu-Steinherr, Irène. "En Marge D'un Acte Concernant le Pengyek et les Aqingi." In *Revue des Études Islamiques* 37 (1969): 21–47.

———. *Recherches sur les actes des règnes des sultans Osman, Orkhan et Murad I.* Münich, 1967.

Bryer, Anthony. "Greek Historians on the Turks: the case of the first Byzantine-Ottoman marriage." In *The Writing of History in the Middle Ages. Essays presented to Richard William Southern.* Edited by R. H. C. Davis and J. M. Wallace-Hadrill, 471–493. Oxford, 1981.

Cahen, Claude. "Karasi." In *Encyclopaedia of Islam.* New Ed. Vol. 4 (1978): 627–629.

Cuinet, Vital. *La Turquie D'Asie*. Vol. 1. Paris, 1890.

Danişmend, İsmail Hami. *İzahlı Osmanlı Tarihi Kronolojisi*. Cilt 1–4. İstanbul, 1947.

Darrouzes, J. *Les Regestes Des Actes Du Patriarcat De Constantinople*. Paris, 1977.

Decei, A. "Akindji." In *The Encyclopaedia of Islam*. 2d ed. Vol. 1 (1960): 340.

Demetriades, V. "Athonite Documents and the Ottoman Occupation." In *Mount Athos in the 14th-16th Centuries*, 41–67. Athens: Institute for Byzantine Research, 1997.

———. "The Tomb of Ghazi Evrenos Bey at Yenitza and its Inscription." *Bulletin of the School of Oriental and African Studies* 39 (1976): 328–332.

Dennis, George T., ed. and trans. *The Letters of Manuel II Palaeologus*. Washington, DC, 1977.

———. "The Byzantine-Turkish Treaty of 1403." In *Orientalia Christiana Periodica* 33 (1967): 72–88.

Divitçioğlu, Sencer. *Osmanlı Beyliğinin Kuruluşu*. İstanbul, 1996.

Dijkema, F. Th. *The Ottoman Historical Monumental Inscriptions in Edirne*. Leiden, 1977.

Doukas. *Decline and Fall of Byzantium to the Ottoman Turks*. Translated by H. Magoulias. Detroit, 1975.

Emecen, Feridun. "Gazaya Dair: XIV. Yüzyıl Kaynakları Arasında Bir Gezinti." In *Hakkı Dursun Yıldız'a Armağan*, 191–197. İstanbul, 1995.

Erzi, Adnan. "Bursa'da İshaki dervişlerine mahsus zaviyenin vakfiyesi." *Vakıflar Dergisi* 2 (İstanbul, 1942): 423–429.

Erzi, H. Adnan. "Osmanlı Devletinin Kurucusunun İsmi Meselesi." *Türkiyat Mecmuası* 7–8 (1942): 323–326.

Eyice, Semavi. "İlk Osmanlı Devrinin Dini-İçtimai Bir Müessesesi Zaviyeler ve Zaviyeli—Camiler." *İ. Ü. İktisat Fakültesi Mecmuası* 23, nos. 1–2 (İstanbul, 1962): 3–80.

Failler, Albert, ed. and trans. *Georges Pachymeres Relations Historiques*. Books 10–13. Paris: Institut Français D'Etudes Byzantines, nd.

Fine, John, Jr. *The Late Medieval Balkans: A Critical Survey from the Late Twelfth Century to the Ottoman Conquest*. Ann Arbor, 1987.

Fleet, Kate. *European and Islamic Trade in the Early Ottoman State: The Merchants of Genoa and Turkey*. Cambridge, 1999.

Fodor, Pal. "Ahmedi's Dasitan as a Source of Early Ottoman History." *Orientalia Hungaricae* 38 (1984): 41–54.

Gazimihal, Mahmut R. "İstanbul Muhasaralarında Mihaloğulları ve Fatih Devrine ait bir Vakıf Defterine Göre Harmankaya Malikanesi." *Vakıflar Dergisi* 4 (1958): 125–137.

Gibb, E. J. W. *A History of Ottoman Poetry*. Vol. 1. London, 1900.

Gibb, H. A. R. *The Travels of Ibn Battuta, A.D. 1325–1354*. Vol. 2. Cambridge, 1962.

Gibbons, Herbert A. *The Foundation of the Ottoman Empire*. Oxford, 1916.

Giese, Friedrich. "Das Problem der Entstehung des osmanischen Reiches." *Zeitschrift für Semitistik und verwandte Gebiete* 2 (1924): 246–271.

Gökbilgin, M. Tayyib. "Mihal-oğulları." In *İslam Ansiklopedisi* 8 (1970): 285–292.

———. "Dawud Pasha." In *The Encyclopaedia of Islam*. Vol. 2 (1965): 184.

———. "Murad I. Tesisleri ve Bursa İmareti Vakfiyesi." *Türkiyat Mecmuası* 10 (1953): 217–234.

Goodenough, Lady. *The Chronicle of Muntaner*. Hakluyt Society, 2d ser., no. 50. London, 1921.

Groot, A. H. de. "Rum Mehmed Pasha." In *The Encyclopaedia of Islam*. Vol. 6 (1990): 1000.

———. "Karamani Mehmed Pasha." In *The Encyclopaedia of Islam*. Vol. 6 (1990): 995–996.

Güldaş, Ayhan. "Fetret devrindeki Şahzadeler mücadele—sini anlatan ilk manzum vesika." *Türk Dünyası Araştırmalar*. No. 72 (June 1991): 99–110.

Haldon, John. "Limnos, Monastic Holdings and the Byzantine State: ca. 1261–1453." In *Continuity and Change in Late Byzantine and Early Ottoman Society*. Edited by A. Bryer and H. Lowry, 161–234. Birmingham and Washington, DC, 1986.

Hammer, Joseph de. *Histoire de l'Empire Ottoman*. Translated by J. Hellert. Vol. 1. Paris, 1835.

Heywood, Colin. "Osmanlı Devletinin Kuruluş Problemi: Yeni Hipotez Hakkında Bazı Düşünceler." In *Osmanlı*. Edited by H. İnalcık. Vol. I: 137–145. Ankara, 1999.

———. "Boundless Dreams of the Levant: Paul Wittek, the George-Kreis, and the Writing of Ottoman History." *Journal of the Royal Asiatic Society*. No. 1 (1989): 30–50.

———. "Wittek and the Austrian Tradition." *Journal of the Royal Asiatic Society*, no. 1 (1988): 7–25.

Heywood, Colin, and Colin Imber, eds. *Studies in Ottoman History in Honour of Professor V. L. Ménage*. İstanbul, 1994.

Huart, Cl. "Les Origines de l'Empire Ottoman." *Journal des Savants*. New Ser., Year 15 (1917): 157–166.

———. "Review of Herbert Adam Gibbons, 'The Foundation of the Ottoman Empire.'" *Journal Asiatique* 9 (Paris, 1917): 345–350.

Hüsameddin, H. "Orhan Bey Vakfiyesi." In *Tarihi Osmanı Encümeni Mecmuası,* no. 17 (94) (İstanbul, 1926): 284–301.

Imber, Colin. Review of "Cemal Kafadar: Between Two Worlds: the construction of the Ottoman state." *Bulletin of the School of Oriental and African Studies* 60, no. 1 (1997): 211–212.

——. "Canon and Apocrypha in Early Ottoman History." In *Studies in Ottoman History in Honour of Professor V. L. Ménage.* Edited by C. Heywood and C. Imber, 117–137. İstanbul, 1994.

——. "The Legend of Osman Gazi." In *The Ottoman Emirate, 1300–1389.* Edited by E. Zachariadou, 67–76. Rethymnon, Crete, 1993.

——. "A Note On 'Christian' Preachers in the Ottoman Empire." *Osmanlı Araştırmaları* 10 (1990): 59–67.

——. *The Ottoman Empire, 1300–1481.* İstanbul, 1990.

——. "The Ottoman Dynastic Myth." *Turcica* 19 (1987): 7–27.

——. "Mahmud Pasha." In *The Encyclopaedia of Islam.* Vol. 6 (1986): 69–72.

——. "Paul Wittek's 'De la defaite d'Ankara à la prise de Constantinople." *Osmanlı Araştırmaları* 5 (1986): 65–81.

İnalcık, Halil. "How to Read Ashik Pasha Zade's History." In *Studies in Ottoman History in Honour of Professor V. L. Ménage.* Edited by C. Heywood and C. Imber, 139–156. İstanbul, 1994.

——. "The Status of the Greek Orthodox Patriarch Under the Ottomans." *Turcica* 21–23 (1991): 407–436.

——. "Mesih Pasha." *The Encyclopaedia of Islam,* Vol. 6 (1990): 1025–1026.

——. "Mehemmed II." *The Encyclopaedia of Islam,* Vol. 6 (1990): 978–980.

——. "Osmanlı İdare, Sosyal ve Ekonomik Tarihiyle İlgili Belgeler: Bursa Kadı Sicillerinden Seçmeler." *Belgeler* 10, no. 14 (1980–1981): 1–91.

——. "The Question of the Emergence of the Ottoman State." *International Journal of Turkish Studies* 2., no. 2 (1981–1982): 71–79.

——. "Osmanlı İdare, Sosyal ve Ekonomik Tarihiyle İlgili Belgeler: Bursa Kadı Sicillerinden Seçmeler." *Belgeler* 13, no. 17 (1988): 1–41.

——. *The Ottoman Empire: The Classical Age, 1300–1600.* London, 1973.

——. "The Policy of Mehmed II Toward the Greek Population of Istanbul and the Byzantine Buildings of the City." In *Dumbarton Oaks Papers.* Vols. 23/24 (1969–1970): 231–249.

——. "Ghulam." *The Encyclopaedia of Islam.* Vol. 2 (1965): 1085–1091.

——. "The Rise of Ottoman Historiography." In *Historians of the Middle East.* Edited by B. Lewis and P. Holt, 152–167. London, 1962.

————. "Ahmad Pasha Gedik." *The Encyclopaedia of Islam.* Vol. 1 (1960): 292–293.

————. "Mehmed the Conqueror (1432–1481) and His Time." *Speculum* 35 (1960): 408–427.

————. *Fatih Devri Üzerinde Tetkikler ve Vesikalar.* Ankara: Türk Tarih Kurumu, 1954.

————. *Hicri 835 Tarihli Suret-i Defter-i Sancak-i Arvanid.* Ankara, 1954.

————. "Ottoman Methods of Conquest." *Studia Islamica* 2 (Paris, 1954): 104–129.

————. "Stefan Duşan'dan Osmanlı İmperatorluğuna: XV. asırda Rumeli'de hiristiyan sipahiler ve menşeleri." In *Fatih Devri Üzerinde Tetkikler ve Vesikalar,* 137–184. Ankara, 1954.

İnalcık, H., and M. Oğuz. *Gazavat-ı Sultan Murad b. Mehemmed Han.* Ankara, 1978.

İnalcık, Halil, and Donald Quataert, eds. *An Economic and Social History of the Ottoman Empire, 1300–1914.* Cambridge, 1994.

İnalcık, Şevkiye. "Ibn Hacer'de Osmanlı'lara Dair Haberler." In *A. Ü. Dil ve Tarih-Coğrafya Fakültesi Dergisi* 6 (1948): 189–195; pp. 349–358, and pp. 517–529.

İpşirli, Mehmed. "Atik Ali Paşa." *Türkiye Diyanet Vakfı İslam Ansiklopedisi* 4 (1991): 64–65.

Jennings, R. C. "Some Thoughts on the Gazi Thesis." *Wiener Zeitschrift für die Kunde Des Morgenlandes* 76 (Vienna, 1986): 151–161.

Kafadar, Cemal. *Between Two Worlds: The Construction of the Ottoman State.* Berkeley, 1995.

Kaldy-Nagy, Gyula. "The Holy War *(jihad)* in the First Centuries of the Ottoman Empire." *Harvard Ukrainian Studies* 3–4 (1979–1980): 467–473.

Karamustafa, Ahmet T. *God's Unruly Friends: Dervish Groups in the Islamic Later Middle Period, 1200–1550.* Salt Lake City, 1994.

Kazhdan, Alexander et al. *The Oxford Dictionary of Byzantium.* 3 Vols. Oxford: Oxford University Press, 1991.

Kitsikis, Dimitri. *Türk-Yunan İmparatorluğu: Arabölge Gerçeği Işığında Osmanlı Tarihine Bakış.* İstanbul, 1996.

Kline, Galen R., ed. *The Voyage d'Outremer by Bertrandon de la Broquière.* New York and Bern, 1988.

Konyalı, İ. H. *Söğüt'de Ertuğrul Gazi Türbesi İhtifali.* İstanbul, 1959.

Kortantamer, Tunca. *Leben und Weltbild des altosmanischen Dichters Ahmedi.* Freiburg, 1973.

Koyunluoğlu, A. Memduh Turgut. *İznik ve Bursa Tarihi.* Bursa, 1935.

Köprülü, M. Fuat. *Islam in Anatolia after the Turkish Invasion*. Translated and Edited by G. Leiser. Salt Lake City, 1993.

———. *The Origins of the Ottoman Empire*. Translated and Edited by G. Leiser. Albany, 1992.

———. *Osmanlı İmparatorluğunun Kuruluşu*. Ankara, 1959.

———. *Les origines de l'empire ottoman*. Paris, 1935.

———. "Anadolu'da İslamiyet: Türk Istilasından Sonra Anadolu Tarih-i Dinisine Bir Nazar ve Bu Tarihin Menba'ları." *Darülfünun Edebiyat Fakültesi Mecmuası* 2 (1922): 281–311; 385–420, and 457–486.

Kramers, J. H. "Murad I." In *The Encyclopaedia of Islam*. New Ed. Vol. 7 (1992): 592–594.

———. "Turks." In *The Encyclopaedia of Islam*. 1st ed. Vol. 4 (1934): 959–972.

———. "Wer war Osman." *Acta Orientalia* 6 (1928): 242–254.

Kritovoulos. *History of Mehmed the Conqueror*. Translated by Charles Riggs. Princeton: Princeton University Press, 1954.

Kunter, Halim Baki. "Kitabelerimiz." *Vakıflar Dergisi* 2 (1942): 431–455 and plates.

Langer, W. L., and R. P. Blake. "The Rise of the Ottoman Turks and Its Historical Background." *American Historical Review* 37 (1932): 468–505.

Leunclavius, Johannes. "Pandectes Historiae Turcicae." Published in J. P. Migne's *Patrologiae Graecae* 149 (1866): 718–922.

Levend, Agah Sırrı. *Gazavat-nameler ve Mihaloğlu Ali Bey'in Gazavat-namesi*. Ankara, 1956.

Lindner, Rudi P. *Nomads and Ottomans in Medieval Anatolia*. Bloomington, 1983.

Lowry, Heath W. "The Fifteenth Century Ottoman Vilayet-i Keşişlik: Its Location, Population and Taxation." In *Humanist and Scholar: Essays in Honor of Andreas Tietze*. Edited by A. Bryer and H. Lowry, 15–26. Istanbul, 1993.

———. *Studies in Defterology: Ottoman Society in the Fifteenth and Sixteenth Centuries*. İstanbul, 1992.

———. "The Fate of Byzantine Monastic Properties Under the Ottomans: Examples from Mount Athos, Limnos and Trabzon." *Byzantinische Forschungen* 16 (1990): 275–311.

———. "The Island of Limnos: a Case Study on the Continuity of Byzantine Forms Under Ottoman Rule." In *Continuity and Change in Late Byzantine and Early Ottoman Society*. Edited by A. Bryer and H. Lowry, 235–259. Birmingham and Washington, DC, 1986.

————. "Fifteenth-Century Ottoman Peasant Taxation: The Case Study of Radilofo (Radolibos)." In *Continuity and Change in Late Byzantine and Early Ottoman Society.* Edited by A. Bryer and H. Lowry, 25–35. Birmingham and Washington, DC, 1986.

————. "Privilege and Property in Ottoman Maçuka during the Opening Decades of the Tourkokratia, 1461–1553." In *Continuity and Change in Late Byzantine and Early Ottoman Society.* Edited by A. Bryer and H. Lowry, 97–128. Birmingham and Washington, DC, 1986.

————. *Trabzon Şehrinin İslamlaşması ve Türkleşmesi, 1461–1583.* 2d ed., 1998. İstanbul: Bosphorus University Press, 1981.

————. "A Corpus of Extant *Kanunnames* for the Island of Limnos as Contained in the *Tapu Tahrir Defter* Collection of the *Başbakanlık* Archives." *Journal of Ottoman Studies* 1 (1980): 41–60.

Lybyer, Albert. *The Government of the Ottoman Empire in the Time of Suleiman the Magnificent.* Cambridge, 1913.

Majer, Hans-Georg. "Some Remarks on the Document of Murad I from the Monastery of St Paul on Mount Athos (1386)." In *Mount Athos in the 14th-16th Centuries.* 33–39. Athens: Institute for Byzantine Research, 1997.

Major Davy, trans. *Sharfuddin Ali Yezdi's Politics and Military Institutions of Tamerlane.* New Delhi, 1972.

Mantran, Robert. "'Ali Pasha Khadim." In *The Encyclopaedia of Islam.* Vol. 1 (1960): 396.

————. "Les Inscriptions Turques de Brousse." *Oriens* 12 (1959): 115–170.

————. "Les Inscriptions Arabes de Brousse." *Bulletin D'Etudes Orientales* 14 (1952–1954): 87–114.

Manz, Beatrice Forbes. *The Rise and Rule of Tamerlane.* Cambridge, 1989.

Mazıoğlu, Hasibe. "Hoca Sinan Paşa." *İslam Ansiklopedisi* 10 (1966): 666–670.

Melikoff, Irene. "Ewrenos." In *The Encyclopaedia of Islam.* New ed. Vol. 2 (1965): 720.

Ménage, V. L. "An Ottoman Manual of Provincial Correspondence." *Wiener Zeitschrift für die Kunde des Morgenlandes* 68 (1976): 31–45.

————. "The 'Annals of Murad II'." *Bulletin of the School of Oriental and African Studies* 39 (1976): 570–584.

————. "On the Ottoman Word Ahriyan/Ahiryan." *Archivum Ottomanicum* 1 (1969): 197–212.

————. "Some Notes on the Devshirme." *Bulletin of the School of Oriental and African Studies* 29 (1966): 64–78.

————. "Djandarli." In *The Encyclopaedia of Islam.* Vol. 1 (1965): 444–445.

————. *Neshri's History of the Ottomans: The Sources and Development of the Text*. London, 1964.

————. "The Menaqib of Yakhshi Faqih." *Bulletin of the School of Oriental and African Studies* 26 (1963): 50–54.

————. "The Beginnings of Ottoman Historiography." In *Historians of the Middle East*. Edited by B. Lewis and P. Holt, 168–170. London, 1962.

Mirmiroğlu, Vl. *Fatih Sultan Mehmet II Devrine Ait Tarihi Vesikalar*. İstanbul, 1945.

Moravcsik, Gyula. *Byzantinoturcica II: Sprachreste Der Türkvölker in den Byzantinischen Quellen*. Leiden, 1983.

Mübarek Galib. *Ankara*. Vol. 2. *Kitabeler*. İstanbul, 1928.

————. *Ankara*. Vol. 1. İstanbul, 1922.

Nedkov, Boris. *Osmano-turska diplomatika i paleografiia*. Vol. 2. Sofia, 1972.

Neşri, Mehmed. *Kitab-ı Cihan-nüma*. 2 Vols. Edited by F. R. Unat and M. A. Köymen. Ankara, 1949.

Neschri, Mevlana Mehemmed. *Die Altosmanische Chronik des Mevlan Mehemmed Neschri*. Edited by F. Taeschner. 2 Vols. Leipzig, 1951.

Nicol, Donald M., trans. and ed. *Theodore Spandounes On the Origin of the Ottoman Emperors*. Cambridge, 1997.

————. *The Last Centuries of Byzantium, 1261–1453*. 2d ed. Cambridge, 1996.

Nüzhet, Mehmed. *Ahval-i Mihal Gazi*. İstanbul, 1897.

Okiç, M. Tayyib. "Hadım ('Atik) Ali Paşa Kimdir?" In *Necati Lugal Armağanı*. 501–515. Ankara: Türk Tarih Kurumu, 1968.

Osmanzade, Ta'ib Ahmed. *Hadiqat ül-vüzera*. Freiburg, 1969.

Ostrogorsky, George. *History of the Byzantine State*. New Brunswick: Rutgers University Press, 1969.

Özcan, Abdülkadir. "Dukakinzade Ahmed Paşa." In *Türkiye Diyanet Vakfı İslam Ansiklopedisi* 9 (1994): 550–551.

Philippides, Marios, trans. *An Anonymous Greek Chronicle of the Seventeenth Century: Codex Berberinus Graecus 111*. New Rochelle, New York, 1990.

————, trans. *The Fall of the Byzantium Empire: A Chronicle by George Sphrantzes, 1401–1477*. Amherst, 1980.

Philippidis-Braat, Anna. "La Captivité de Palamas chez les Turcs." *Travaux et Mémoires* 7 (Paris, 1979): 109–222.

Pococke, Richard. *A Description of the East and Some Other Countries*. Vol. 2, part 2. London, 1745.

Quatremere, E., ed. and trans. "Al-'Umari's: Mesalek Alabsar fi Memalek Alamsar." In *Notices et Extraits des Manuscrits de la Bibliothèque du Roi* 13 (Paris, 1838): 151–384.

Raby, Julian. "Terra Lemnia and the Potteries of the Golden Horn: An Antique Revival Under Ottoman Auspices." *Byzantinische Forschungen* 21 (1995): 305–342.

Reindl, Hedda. *Manner um Bayezid: Eine prosopographische Studie über die Epoche Bayezids II (1481–1512)*. Berlin, 1983.

Reinsch, Diether Roderich, ed. *Critobuli Imbriotae Historiae*. Berlin, 1983.

Reinert, S. "Manuel II Palaeologos and His Müderris." In *The Twilight of Byzantium*. Edited by S. Curcic and D. Mouriki, 39–51. Princeton, 1991.

Riefstahl, Rudolf M., and Paul Wittek. "Turkish Architecture in Southwestern Anatolia. Part II." *Art Studies* (1931): 173–212.

Sabanović, H. "Hersek-zade." In *The Encyclopaedia of Islam*. Vol. 3 (1971): 340–342.

Sahas, Daniel. "Gregory Palamas (1296–1360) on Islam." *The Muslim World* 73 (1983): 1–21.

―――. "Captivity and Dialogue: Gregory Palamas (1296–1360) and the Muslims." *The Greek Orthodox Theological Review* 25 (1981): 409–436.

Sahillioğlu, Halil. "Slaves in the Social and Economic Life of Bursa in the Late 15th and Early 16th Centuries." *Turcica* 17 (1985): 43–112.

Schacht, J. "Aman." In *Encyclopaedia of Islam*. New ed. Vol. 1 (1960): 429–430.

Schlemmer, Ulrich, ed. *Johannes Schiltberger: Als Sklave im Osmanischen Reich und bei den Tataren, 1394–1427*. Stuttgart, 1983.

Sevinçli, Efdal. *Yusuf bin Abdullah—Bizans Söylenceleriyle Osmanlı Tarihi (Tarih-i al-i Osman)*. İstanbul, 1997.

Shinder, Joel. "Early Ottoman Administration in the Wilderness: Some Limits on Comparison." *International Journal of Middle East Studies* 9 (1978): 497–517.

Sılay, Kemal. "Ahmedi's History of the Ottoman Dynasty." *Journal of Turkish Studies* 16 (1992): 129–200.

Stavrides, Theoharis. *The Ottoman Grand Vezir Mahmud Pasha Angelovic (1453–1474)*. Ph.D. Diss. Harvard University, 1996.

Stojanovski, Aleksandar. *Vranjski kadiluk u XVI veku*. Vranje, 1985.

Stolz, Benjamin, and Suat Soucek, trans. and eds. *Konstantin Mihailovic, Memoirs of a Janissary*. Ann Arbor, 1975.

Sümer, F. "Karaman-Oghullari." In *The Encyclopaedia of Islam*. New ed. Vol. 4 (1978): 619–625.

Taeschner, F. "Nachtrage und Berichtigungen zu Beitrage zur frühosmanischen Epigraphik und Archaologie." *Der Islam* 22 (1935): 69–73.

―――. "Beitrage zur frühosmanischen Epigraphik und Archaologie." *Der Islam* 20 (1932): 109–186.

―――. *Al-'Umari's Bericht über Anatolien*. Vol. 1. Leipzig, 1919.

Tekin, Şinasi. "Türk Dünyasında 'Gaza' ve 'Cihad' Kavramları Üzerine Düşünceler-II: ['Gazi' teriminin Anadolu ile Akdeniz Bölgesinde İtibarını Yeniden Kazanması]." *Tarih ve Toplum*, no. 110 (February, 1993): 73–80.

―――. "Türk Dünyasında 'Gaza' ve 'Cihad' Kavramları Üzerine Düşünceler [Başlangıçtan Osmanlıların Fetret Devrine Kadar]." *Tarih ve Toplum*, no. 109 (January, 1993): 9–18.

―――. "XIV. Yüzyılda Yazılmış Gazilik Tarikası 'Gaziliğin Yolları' adlı Bir Eski Anadolu Türkçesi metni ve Gaza Cihad Kavramları Hakkında." *Journal of Turkish Studies* 13 (1989): 139–204.

Tekindağ, Şehabeddin. "Mahmud Paşa." *İslam Ansiklopedisi* 7: 183–188.

―――. "Mehmed Paşa." *İslam Ansiklopedisi* 7: 594–595.

―――. "Mehmed Paşa Karamani." *İslam Ansiklopedisi* 7: 588–591.

Telfer, J. Buchan, trans. *The Bondage and Travels of Johann Schiltberger, A Native of Bavaria, in Europe, Asia, and Africa, 1396–1427*. New York, 1879.

Tevhid, Ahmed. "Bursa'da En Eski Kitabe." *Tarihi Osmanı Encümeni Mecmuası* 29 (İstanbul, 1912): 318–320.

T. H. [?]. "Sinan Paşa." *İslam Ansiklopedisi* 10 (1966): 661–666.

Turan, Şerafettin. "Hersekzade Ahmed Paşa." *Türkiye Diyanet Valfı İslam Ansiklopedisi* 17 (1998): 235–237.

―――. "Hadım Sinan Paşa." *Türkiye Diyanet Vakfı İslam Ansiklopedisi* 15 (1997): 7–8.

Tursun, Beg. *The History of Mehmed the Conqueror*. Edited by H. İnalcık and R. Murphey. Minneapolis and Chicago: Bibliotheca Islamica, 1978.

Turyan, Hasan. *Bursa Evliyaları ve Tarihi Eserleri*. Bursa, 1982.

Umur, Suha. *Osmanlı Padişah Tuğraları*. İstanbul, 1980.

Uzunçarşılı, İsmail Hakkı. "Evrenos." *İslam Ansiklopedisi* 4 (1964): 413–418.

―――. "Orhan Gazi'nin, Vefat Eden Oğlu Süleyman Paşa İçin Tertip Ettirdiği Vakfiyenin Aslı." *Belleten* 27 (Ankara, 1963): 437–451.

―――. "Hızır Bey Oğlu Sinan Paşa'nin Vezir-i Azamlığına Dair Çok Kıymetli Bir Vesika." *T. T. K. Belleten* 27 (1963): 37–44.

―――. "Akıncı." *İslam Ansiklopedisi*. Vol. 1 (1950): 239–249.

―――. *Osmanlı Tarihi*. Vol. 1. Ankara, 1947.

―――. *Osmanlı Tarihi: İstanbul'un Fethinden Kanuni Sultan Süleyman'ın Ölümüne Kadar*. Vol. 2. Ankara, 1943.

———. *Osmanlı Devlet Teşkilatından Kapukulu Ocakları*. Vol. 1. Ankara, 1943.

———. "Gazi Orhan Bey Vakfiyesi." *Belleten* 5 (Ankara, 1941): 277–288.

———. "Osmanlı Tarihine Ait Yeni Bir Vesikanın Ehemmiyeti ve İzahı ve bu Münasebetle Osmanlılarda İlk Vezirlere Dair Mutalea." *Belleten* 3 (Ankara, 1939): 99–106, and *Levha* 78.

———. "Davud Paşa." *İslam Ansiklopedisi* 3: 496–498.

Uzunçarşılı, İsmail Hakkı, and Ridvan Nafız. *Sivas Şehri*. İstanbul, 1928.

Uzunçarşılı[oğlu], İsmail Hakkı. *Bizans ve Selçukiylerle Germiyan ve Osman Oğullarl zamanında Kütahya Şehri*. İstanbul, 1932.

———. *Afyon Karahisar, Sandıklı, Bolvadin, Çay, İsaklı, Manisa, Birgi, Muğla, Milas, Peçin, Denizli, İsparta, Eğirdir'deki Kitabeler ve Sahip, Saruhan, Aydın, Menteşe, İnanç, Hamit Oğulları hakkında malumat*. İstanbul, 1929.

———. *Tokad, Niksar, Zile, Turhal, Pazar, Amasya vilayet, kaza ve nahiye merkezlerindeki kitabeler*. İstanbul, 1927.

Van Dieten, Jan Louis, ed. and trans. *Nikephoros Gregoras—Rhomaische Geschichte*. Books 1–7. Stuttgart, 1973; Books 8–11. Stuttgart, 1979; Books 12–17. Stuttgart, 1988.

Vryonis, Speros, Jr. "The Experience of Christians under Seljuk and Ottoman Domination, Eleventh to Sixteenth Century." In *Conversion and Continuity (Indigenous Christian Communities in Islamic Lands Eight to Eighteenth Centuries)*. Edited by M. Gervers and R. J. Bikhazi, 185–216. Toronto, 1990.

———. "Byzantine and Turkish Societies and their Sources of Manpower." In *War, Technology and Society in the Middle East*. Edited by V. J. Parry and M. E. Yapp, 125–152. London, 1975.

———. *The Decline of Medieval Hellinism in Asia Minor and the Process of Islamization from the Eleventh through the Fifteenth Century*. Berkeley, 1971.

———. "Seljuk Gulams and the Ottoman Devshirmes." *Der Islam* 41 (Berlin, 1965): 224–252.

Wansbrough, J. "Paul Wittek and Richard Haklyut: A Tale of Two Empires." In *Osmanlı AraştIrmaları*. Vols. 7 and 8 (1988): 55–70.

Werner, Ernst. *Büyük Bir Devletin Doğuşu—Osmanlılar (1300–1482)*. Vol 1. *Osmanlı Feodalizminin Oluşum Süreci*. İstanbul; 1986 and Vol. 2. *Halk Ayaklanmaları ve Askeri Feodalizm*. İstanbul, 1988.

———. *Die Geburt Einer Grossmacht -Die Osmanen (1300–1481)*. 1966. Rev. ed. Reprint, Vienna, 1985.

Whitehead, Christine. "Khadim Sinan Pasha" and "Khodja Sinan Pasha." In *The Encyclopaedia of Islam*. Vol. 9: 630–631.

Wittek, Paul. *Menteşe Beyliği: 13–15inci Asırda Garbi Küçük Asya Tarihine ait Tetkik*. Ankara, 1944.

———. *The Rise of the Ottoman Empire*. London, 1938.

———. "De la defaite d'Ankara a la prise de Constantinople." *Revue des etudes islamiques* 12 (1938): 1–34.

———. "Deux chapitres de l'histoire des Turcs de Roum." *Byzantion* 11 (1936): 285–319.

Yınanç, Mükrimin Halil. "Bayezid I." *İslam Ansiklopedisi* 2 (İstanbul, 1962): 369–392.

Yınanç, Mükrimin Halil, ed. *Düsturname-i Enveri*. İstanbul, 1928.

———. "Gedik Ahmed Paşa." *İslam Ansiklopedisi* 1: 193–199.

Zachariadou, Elizabeth. "Co-Existence and Religion." *Archivum Ottomanicum* 15 (1997): 119–129.

———, ed. *The Ottoman Emirate, 1300–1389*. Rethymnon, Crete, 1993.

———. "Religious Dialogue Between Byzantines and Turks During the Ottoman Expansion." In *Religionsgesprache im Mittelalter*. Edited by B. Lewis and F. Niewöhner. Wiesbaden, 1992.

———. "Manuel II Palaeologus on the Strife Between Bayezid and Kadi Burhan al-Din Ahmed." *Bulletin of the School of Oriental and African Studies* 18 (London, 1980): 471–481.

———. "A Note about the Chronicle of the Turkish Sultans." [in Greek] *Hellenika* 20 (1967): 166–169.

———. *The Chronicle about the Turkish Sultans (of Codex Barberinus Graecus 111) and its Italian Prototype* [in Greek]. Thessalonica, 1960.

Index

Abdallah al-Misri, 72
Abdülhamid Han. *See* Abdülhamid II
Abdülhamid II, 40
`Abdullah, 93
Abdulvahid bin Mehmed El-Sivasi, 77
accommodationist practices. See *istimâlet*
agriculture, 107–9
Ahmed Gazi Cami, 42
Ahmed Tevhid, 38, 40
Ahmedi, 9, 39, 80, 132, 136
  on Bayezid I, 17, 21–31
  epic poem, 11, 43, 48, 70. *See also* Bursa inscription
  Iskendernâme, 15–31, 44
  and meanings of *gaza* and *gazi,* 18–20, 24, 34, 45–48, 51
  Wittek and, 11
Ahmet Beg. *See* Ahmet Bey
Ahmet Bey, *Gazi,* 42, 126
Ahmet *Paşa,* 123, 126
Akbaşli, 77
Akhi federation of craftsmen and merchants, 6
akin/akincis (raiders), 45–47, 51–54, 59, 132
`Ala'eddin, Sultan, 18, 19
Alaettin Keykubat, 41
alcohol use, 26–29, 136
`Ali Beg, *Gazi,* 59–65
`Ali Bey, 93

`Ali *Paşa,* Hadim (Eunuch), 117, 119, 121, 127, 128
Ali *Paşa,* Vizier, 27
Amirutzes, George, 123
Anatolia (Rum), 6, 10, 19, 22, 29, 71, 138, 140–42
animal husbandry, 102, 103, 107
Anna (wife of Ladislas), 123
Arnakis, George, 2, 9, 41, 96, 133
Ashura, 71–72
Aşikpaşazade, 56–58, 60, 68, 69, 74, 83, 143
askeri, 98, 99
Athonite foundations, 106
Aydin Oğlu Mehmed Beg, 42
Ayverdi, Ekrem Hakkī, 35–38, 40

Babinger, Franz, 6
Balaban, 74
Balabancik, 74, 77, 79, 90, 93
Balkans, 22, 141
Barkan, Ömer Lütfi, 58, 82
Bayezid I (Han/Sultan/Yildirim), 16, 17, 39, 40, 42, 60, 64, 96, 141
  Ahmedi on, 17, 21–31
  alcohol use and debauchery, 26–29, 136
  on Ali *Beg,* 61
  death, 25, 26
  Doukas on, 27–28
  lack of dedication to religion, 26–27, 48, 50, 136–37

Bayezid I (Han/Sultan/Yildirim)
(continued)
letter from Timur to, 78
Manuel II on, 28–29
motivated by material gain, 50
Bayezid II, Sultan, 66, 110, 112, 113,
116–18, 122, 123, 126–28
1391 imperial order, 62–63
edict to Kadis, 48–50, 52
Baykal, Kâzim, 35, 37
Bedreddin. See Sheikh Bedreddin
Revolt
Begs, Ahmedi on, 17
Berkuk, Sultan, 29
Beylik, Anatolian, 42, 131
Beylik, Germiyan, 41
Bithynia, 131
conquest of, 9
Blake, R. P., 6, 7, 133
Bodonitza, Marquess of, 141
Bokhales, Manuel, 124
Borovonics, 127
Branković, George, 119
Broquiere, Bertrandon de la, 80–81
Bursa, 71, 137
conquest and surrender of, 56, 57,
59, 70, 72, 79, 80
travelers to, during Ottoman peri-
od, 79–80
Bursa inscription, 11, 60, 70. See also
Orhan; Wittek
gazi thesis and, 35, 40, 43, 44
Byzantium, 5
defeat of, 5, 128
Byzanto-Balkan aristocracy, members
of
subsumption into Ottoman ruling
elite, 115–30

Cahen, Claude, 58
Candarli Halil Paşa, 125
Candarli İbrahim Paşa, 119, 121, 128
Catalans, 58–59
Cemaleddin El-Hafiz, 77
Chalcocondyles, Laonikos, 47
charity homes/hospices (spitaler), 80–82

Christian Church, 67
Christian peasants
conscription of youth, 117–18
life in 15th century, 95–114
Christianity, 16
Christians, 46, 52, 67, 69, 80, 131.
See also Islam, conversion to;
women
integration into Ottoman
polity/administration, 77,
86–87, 89–94
cihad (Holy War), 50. See also
gazi(s); Holy War
Coban, 77
conquest and material gain, motives of,
68–70, 135. See also specific topics
conscription, 51–54, 117–18, 128
Constantine XI Palaiologos, Emperor,
115, 116
Constantinople, Patriarch of, 67, 89,
116, 119, 142–43
cottage industry, 108
Cuinet, Vital, 108
Cydones, 28

Danismend, Ismail Hami, 57, 122
Davud Paşa, 117, 119, 121, 128
Demetriades, Vasilis, 60, 61
devsirme conscripts, 117–18, 128
dirliks, 48, 50, 51
Divitçioğlu, Sencer, 12–13
Doukas, Michael, 27–28, 46, 47,
137, 138
Dukaginzade Ahmed Paşa, 116, 122,
127, 128, 130

Eflaki, 37
El Tutan, 83
Emecen, Feridun, 12
endowment charters. See vakfiyes
Enveri, 79
Ertugrul, 18, 19, 83
Evrenes. See Evrenos Beg
Evrenos Beg, Gazi, 46, 57–60, 64–66,
90, 135, 140–42
tombstone in Yenice Vardar, 60, 61

Evrenosogullari, 64, 143
Ewrenosbeg. *See* Evrenos Beg

Fakhr al-din Uthman, 76, 77
Fatima Hatun, 77
Fatma Sultan, 127
fiefs. See *timars*
Fine, John, 101
Fodor, Pal, 11, 24, 30
"Franki," 58
Franks. *See* Catalans
"Frontier Empire," 8

Galen, 98
Gardiki, 124
gaza, 1, 2, 7, 11, 12, 21. *See also*
    Holy War
  as act of worship, 20
  Ahmedi and, 18–20, 24, 34,
    45–48, 51
  akin/akinci and, 45–47, 132
  Bayezid and, 18, 24
  meanings of, 9, 10, 20, 24, 40,
    45–54, 132, 133
  role/objective of, 20
  Wittek and concept of, 31, 33
gaza ethos, 9–11
gaza hero, notion of, 11
"*gazi* ethos," 131
gazi thesis, 1–2, 5, 7–9, 12, 13, 30,
    70. *See also* Wittek
  Bursa inscription and, 35, 40, 43,
    44
  criticisms of, 2, 7, 9, 10, 55, 92,
    131–32
  Inalcik and, 7–9
gazi(s), 11, 12, 19, 24, 34, 43. See
    also *specific topics*
  meanings of, 9, 16, 18, 40, 49–54,
    132
    Ahmedi on, 18–20, 24, 34,
      45–48
  role of, 21, 48
  Wittek and concept of, 31, 33
Gedik Ahmed *Paşa*, 116, 119, 120,
    128

ghazi, 42
"*ghazi* ethos," 7
Gibbons, Herbert A., 5–9, 57, 96, 133
Giese, Friedrich, 6
Gök Alp, 18
Gökbilgin, 87–88
Grand Vezirs, 119–22, 128–29. See
    also *specific individuals*
Gregoras, Nicephoros, 47, 57, 94
Gritti, Alvise, 142
gulams, 74, 90
Gündüz, 68
Gündüz Alp, 18

Haci Karaoglan, 82
Hadim `Ali *Paşa*. *See* `Ali *Paşa*,
    Hadim
Hadim (Eunuch) Sinan *Paşa*, 117,
    119, 122, 127
Hajar al-'Asqalani, Ibn, 79
Haji Evrenoz. *See* Evrenos Beg
Hamid, 77
Hammer, Joseph de, 57, 59
Has-Murad *Paşa*, 116
Hasan bin Mustafa, 83, 137
Hazim Sabanovic, 126
Herceg (Duke) Vlatko, 126
Hersegović, Stjepan. *See* Hersekzade
    Ahmed *Paşa*
Hersekzade Ahmed *Paşa*, 66, 69,
    117, 119, 121–23, 126–28, 130
Heywood, Colin, 11, 13
Hijaz, 79
Hoca Sinan *Paşa*, 120, 128
Holy War, 8. See also *gaza*
hospices/charity homes *(spitaler)*,
    80–82
Hundi Hatun, 126
Hurrem *Hatun*, 93
Hüsamettin Yakup, 42
Hüsrev, 41

ibn Battuta, 70–71, 131
İbrahim bin Orhan, 73
Idris, 57
İlyas, 42, 83

Imber, Colin, 11, 12, 20, 29, 40, 45, 79
Inalcik, Halil, 9, 90–93, 96, 99, 115, 118, 134
    gazi thesis and, 7–9
    "Question of the Emergence of Ottomon State," 8
    on tribal origins of Ottomans, 7–8
infidels, 18–21
Isa (Jesus) Beg, 58–61, 136, 137
İshak Han, 42
İshak *Paşa*, 117, 119–21, 125, 128
Iskendernâme (Ahmedi), 15–31, 44
Islam, 6, 10. See also *gaza; gazi(s)*
    Bayezid I's lack of dedication to, 26–27, 48, 50, 136–37
    conversion to, 6, 9, 46, 54, 67, 69, 77
        and killing of nonbelievers, 21, 48, 50, 70, 83, 92, 132, 133
        tax break induced, 105–6, 111
    converts to, 57, 59, 66, 69–70, 86.
    See also *devsirme* conscripts; *gulams*
    Murad Beg and, 22
    and Ottoman growth, 1, 2, 5, 131. See also *specific topics*
Islamic law, 92
Islamic practice, lack of adherence to, 136–37
Islamization, 10
"Islamochristian" syncretism, 137–39, 142–43
istimâlet (policy of "accommodation"), 91–92, 99, 103, 106, 109–10, 112
Iyad, 79
İzzettin Keykavus, 41

Janissary Corps, 103–4, 106, 110–11, 139
Jean, Duke, 127
Jennings, Ronald C., 2, 11, 12, 40
Jesus Christ, 21, 137
Jews, Islamicized, 67, 74
Junis (Yunus) Bey, 142

kadis (judges), 51, 52
Kafadar, Cemal, 1, 12, 41
Kaldy-Nagy, Gyula, 10
kanunname (local law code), 100, 102, 107, 108, 111, 115, 126
Karamani Mehmed *Paşa*, 119, 120, 128
Karamanids, 21–22
Kastamonu, Emir of, 71
Kiliç Arslan, 41
kitabe. See Bursa inscription
Kitsikis, Dimitri, 12
Koca Mustafa *Paşa*, 117, 119, 122, 128
Koca Sinan *Paşa*, 119
Komnenus, David, 123
Köprülü, M. Fuat, 6–9, 96
Kortantamer, Tunca, 20
Köse Mihal, 57, 66, 68, 94, 140
    descendants, 59–61, 64, 65, 93, 141, 142
    as Muslim, 8, 90
    negotiation of Bursa's surrender, 56, 79
    Orhan and, 70
    religion and, 8, 67, 77, 89–90
    titularies used for, 46
Koskos, 86–87, 89, 131
Koyunluoğlu, A. Memduh Turgut, 34, 35, 37
Kritovoulos, 124, 125
Kunter, Halim Baki, 35, 37, 38, 40

Ladislas, 123
Langer, W. L., 6, 7, 133
law code. See *kanunname*
Lazarević, Stefan, 25
Leunclavius, Johannes, 58
Limnos, 97–98, 100, 102, 104, 105, 107–12
Lindner, Rudi, 10, 12
livestock, 107–8
    taxation on, 102, 103, 107, 109, 113

Mahatib *Hatun*, 93
Mahmud bin Abu Bekr, 77

Mahmud *Paşa*, 116–17, 120, 123–28
Majd al-Din, 72
Malik, 77
"*Malik*" (Lord/King), usage of the
    title, 63–64
Malkoç, 142
Mantran, Robert, 34, 37
Manuel II Palaeologus, 28, 137
Mara/Maria, 65, 119
marriages, 141. *See also* women
Mavrozoumis, Hetaeriarch (General),
    87, 89, 131
Mehmed bin Mahmud, 77
Mehmed I, 40, 64
Mehmed II, Sultan, 56, 65, 66, 110,
    112, 124, 142, 143
    accommodating postures, 113
    attack led by, 115
    Doukas and, 46
    imperial edict, 124, 127
    imperial foundation endowed by,
        81
    law code, 115, 126
    order by, for conscription of
        Akincis, 51–54
    rise of members Byzanto-Balkan
        aristocracy under, 116–19, 124,
        126, 127, 141
Mehmed Karamanoglu, 81
Mehmed (Mohammed), 34, 52, 119,
    126, 136, 137
Mehmed Nüzhet, 63
Melik, 58
Melikoff, Irene, 57, 59–60
Ménage, 41
Menebor, Duke of, 117
Mesih *Paşa (Messit bassa)*, 66, 69,
    116, 119, 121–23, 126–28
meyhanes (saloons), 27
Michael, 124
Michael Angelovic, 123–24
Michauli, 66
Mihailović, Konstantin, 46–47, 104
Mihal, *Köse*. See *Köse* Mihal
Mihalogli `Ali Beg. See `Ali Beg
Mihaloğullari, 143

military. *See* conscription; Janissary
    Corps; *timars*
Mohammed, Prophet, 16, 18, 21,
    137
Moses. *See* Musa
mufassals, 97, 112
mühtedi (converts), 105. *See also*
    Islam, converts to
Mükrimin Halil Yinaric, 26, 116
Muntaner, 58
Murad I (Beg/Han/Hüdavendigar/
    Sultan), 21–25, 29, 34, 37, 39,
    40, 48, 63, 64, 78
    battle with Karamanids, 22
    titles, 86, 87
    witnesses signatory to 1365 vak-
        fiye, 88
Murad II, Sultan, 46, 60, 65, 119,
    139, 140
    dream (story), 140
Murad *Paşa*. *See* Has-Murad *Paşa*
Musa (Moses), 136–38
Muslims, new. *See* Islam, converts
    to

Nedkov, Boris, 51, 54
Nicol, Donald M., 55
Nicopolis, 27
Nilüfer Hatun, 64

Olivera, Princess, 29, 136
Orhan (Beg/Bey/*Gazi*), 57, 59, 60,
    63, 64, 67–70, 72–74, 77, 79,
    80, 86–87, 93, 145
    Ahmedi on, 21, 24, 25, 45. *See
        also* Ahmedi, *Iskendernâme*
    Bursa inscription and, 34–39, 42,
        43, 82–83
    decision to spread *gaza* into
        Balkans, 21
    as *gazi*, 71
    hânegâh established by, 138
    Islam and, 40, 73, 131–34
    Mekece *Vakfiye* of, 75–77
    Saroz and, 56
    sons, 73

Orhan (Beg/Bey/*Gazi*) *(continued)*
  "The *Padisahi* (Reign) of Orhan,
    Son of Osman (Ahmedi),"
    19–20
  titles, 37–39, 43, 82–85
Orhan Cami, 34
Osman (Beg/Bey/*Gazi*), 43, 59, 64,
  65, 68, 69, 74, 77, 78, 93, 135,
  140, 142. *See also* Ahmedi,
    Iskendernâme
  Ahmedi on, 21, 24, 25
  descendants of, 34, 39, 141
  Islam and, 132–34
  Köse Mihal and, 56, 118
Ostoya, Radosin, 117, 127
Ottoman foundation charters. See
  vakfiyes
Ottoman state, nature of early, 131–43
Ottomans, administrative structure
  of, 6

Pachymeres, Georges, 47, 58
Palaiologos brothers, 115, 116
Palamas, Gregory, 67, 79–80, 87
Pazarlu, 77
peasants. *See* Christian peasants
"Pirangi." *See* "Franki"
Pliny, 98
Pococke, Richard, 108
prakitika, 106, 107
"Prangi." *See* "Franki"

Quataert, Donald, 8

race(s)
  all treated as one, 8
  Ottomans as new, 5
raiders, Ottoman, 47
Ramazanzade Küçuk Nisanci, 125
Ramberti, Benedetto, 142
re' aya, 98, 99
Reindl, Hedda, 122
Riefstahl, Rudolf M., 35
Rum. *See* Anatolia
Rum Mehmed *Paşa,* 117, 119, 120,
  128

Şadeddin, 57
Şahin bin ʿAbdullah, 83
Sancak Beg, 116
Sansovino, Francesco, 140
Şaraf al-Din ʿAli Yazdi, 78
Saroz, Minister, 56, 57, 69, 77, 90, 130
Saruhan, 42
Savcī, 40
Schiltberger, Johann, 80, 81
Sekban Karaca, 83
Seljuk tradition, 74
Serbian aristocracy, 116. *See also*
  Byzanto-Balkan aristocracy
Serefeddin Mukbil, 74, 77, 82, 90, 93
Seyh Mecnun bin Hasan, 83
Shah of Karaman, 22
Shams al-Din, 71
Sharaf al-din Muqbil, 76
Sheikh Bedreddin Revolt, 138, 139
Shuja al-din Urkhan, 76
Silay, Kemal, 16
sipahis (military fief holders), 51. See
  also *timar*iots
slaves, 70, 93, 117. *See also*
  Balabancik; *gulams*
social welfare system, 80–82
Spandugnino (Spandounes),
    Theodore, 55, 65–66, 78, 81,
    119, 122, 123, 142
  on *akin/akincis,* 47
  *On the Origin of the Ottomon
    Emperors,* 55
Sphrantzes, George, 47, 124, 137
St. Sava, Duke of, 66, 117, 119, 123,
  126, 128
Stefan, 136
Stjepan, Prince. *See* Hersekzade
  Ahmed *Paşa*
Stjepan Vukčič-Kosača, 126
Stojanovski, Aleksandar, 116
Sükrullah, 21
Süleyman *Çelebi,* Prince, 16, 17, 19,
  39, 40
  Ahmedi and, 20–21, 24–26, 29–31
  death, 30
  drinking and debauchery, 26

Sulayman Tshelebi, 16
Emir Sultan Süleyman, 27, 30, 42,
    142
Süleyman bin Orhan, 73
Süleyman *Paşa*, 78, 82, 84, 85, 137
    treaty with Christian states, 141
Süleyman (Solomon), 136
Sultan bin Orhan, 73
Süreyya, Mehmed, 122, 127
swine tax, 113

Tacüddin Ibrahim bin Hidr. *See*
    Ahmedi
Taeschner, F., 35
tahrir defters (cadastral surveys),
    90–92, 97, 98, 100, 102–13, 116
Ta'ib Ahmed Osmanzade, 122
Tatars, 19
taxation, 100–3, 107, 109, 111–14
    exemptions to Christian converts,
        105–6, 111
    on livestock, 102, 103, 107, 109,
        113
Tekin, Sinasi, 11, 12, 34, 35, 39
textile industry, 108
*timar*iots (fief holders), 90, 91, 97,
    99, 104, 109, 129, 131
timars (fiefs), 48, 50, 51, 90, 91, 104,
    109, 111, 116, 141
Timur, 25, 29, 78
tin-i makhtum, 98
Trebizond, 123
tribal nature and origins of
    Ottomans, 7–8, 10, 12
Tshelebi, 16
Turahan, 140–42
Turahanogullari, 64, 143
Turkification, 10, 132
Turkish nature/origins of Ottoman
    state, 6, 9, 12
Tursun Beg, 124, 125

Umur Beg, 42, 87
Umur Beg ibn Koskos *Subaşi,* 86, 89,
    131

Uzun Hasan, 116
Uzuncarşili, İsmail Hakki, 26, 57–60,
    72, 77, 84, 85, 117

vakfiyes (Ottoman foundation char-
    ters), 75–78, 80, 82–88, 131
veled-i kuls, 104
Vezir-i 'Azam, 128
Vezir-I A'zams (Grand Vezirs),
    119–22, 128–29. See also *specific
    individuals*
Vranes (Evrenos *Bey*), 141
Vryonis, Speros, Jr., 10, 74
Vuk, 136
Vulkoğlu, 27

Werner, Ernst, 10
Wittek, Paul, 13, 50, 60, 92, 96, 131,
    132, 143, 145
    criticisms of, 10, 11
    Rise of the Ottomon Empire, 1,
        2
    sources, 11, 15
    thesis. See *gazi* thesis
    utilization of 1337 Bursa inscrip-
        tion, 33–44
    utilization of Ahmedi's
        Iskendernâme, 15–31, 44
women, non-Muslim born
    marriage to Muslim men, 94
    married to early Ottoman rulers,
        93. *See also* Byzanto-Balkan
        aristocracy
worship, 20

Yagari, Marko, 123
Yenice Vardar, 59, 61
Yıldırım Khan (Bayezid), 27
Yusuf bin Musa, 83
Yusuf-i Midilli, 111
Yusuf (Joseph), 137

Zağanos *Paşa,* 83, 119, 120, 125,
    128
Zeno, Pietro, 141

SUNY Series in the
Social and Economic History of the Middle East

Donald Quataert, editor

Thabit A. J. Abdullah, *Merchants, Mamluks, and Murder: The Political Economy of Eighteenth Century Basra*.

Ali Abdullatif Ahmida, *The Making of Modern Libya: State Formation, Colonization, and Resistance, 1830–1932*.

Rifa'at 'Ali Abou-El-Haj, *Formation of the Modern State: The Ottoman Empire, Sixteenth to Eighteenth Centuries*.

Cem Behar, *A Neighborhood in Ottoman Istanbul: Fruit Vendors and Civil Servants in the Kasap Ilyas Mahalle*.

Michael Bonner, Mine Ener, and Amy Singer, eds., *Poverty and Charity in Middle Eastern Contexts*.

Palmira Brummett, *Ottoman Seapower and Levantine Diplomacy in the Age of Discovery*.

Palmira Brummett, *Image and Imperialism in the Ottoman Revolutionary Press, 1908–1911*.

Ayse Burga, *State and Business in Modern Turkey: A Comparative Study*.

Guilian Denoeux, *Urban Unrest in the Middle East: A Comparative Study of Informal Networks in Egypt, Iran and Lebanon*.

Beshara Doumani, ed., *Family History in the Middle East: Household, Property and Gender*.

Hala Fattah, *The Politics of Regional Trade in Iraq, Arabia, and the Gulf, 1745–1900*.

Samira Haj, *The Making of Iraq, 1900–1963: Capital, Power, and Ideology*.

Caglar Keyder and Faruk Tabak, eds., *Landholding and Commercial Agriculture in the Middle East*.

Issa Khalaf, *Politics in Palestine: Arab Factionalism and Social Disintegration, 1939–1948*.

M. Fuad Koprulu, *The Origins of the Ottoman Empire*, translated and edited by Gary Leiser.

Zachary Lockman, ed., *Workers and Working Classes in the Middle East: Struggles, Histories, Historiographies*.

Heath W. Lowry, *The Nature of the Early Ottoman State*.

Donald Quataert, ed., *Manufacturing in the Ottoman Empire and Turkey, 1500–1950*.

Donald Quataert, ed., *Consumption Studies and the History of the Ottoman Empire, 1550–1922, An Introduction*.

Sarah Shields, *Mosul Before Iraq: Like Bees Making Five-Sided Cells*.